Worlds of Pain

WORLDS OF PAIN / Life in the Working-Class Family

Lillian Breslow Rubin

Basic Books, Inc., Publishers   New York

Library of Congress Cataloging in Publication Data

Rubin, Lillian B
  Worlds of pain.

  Bibliography: p.
  Includes index.
    1. Family—United States. 2. Labor and laboring classes—United States. 3. United States—Social conditions—1960–   I. Title.
  HQ536.R8   301.42'0973   76–21648

For Marci and Paul

whose love, hope, joy,
and pain I share as they struggle
to build a new family

CONTENTS

Contents

To get the whole world out of bed
And washed, and dressed, and warmed, and fed,
To work, and back to bed again,
Believe me, Saul, costs worlds of pain

John Masefield
"The Everlasting Mercy"

ACKNOWLEDGMENTS

EVERY BOOK has many unseen and unsung contributors—some participate directly in its creation, others indirectly. So it is with this one.

Foremost among the indirect contributors is the family into which I was born. There I learned about illness, death, and poverty, about the struggle to survive, and about the toll it takes on family life. There I also learned about the remarkable tenacity of the human spirit as I watched my mother's seemingly inexhaustible strength and her fierce determination to hold her small family together against devastating odds. Just by her way of being, she taught me that women are not weak and incapable, that strength, daring, and risk taking is not "for men only." For that gift, I shall always be grateful to her.

More direct is the contribution of the families whose stories are told here. These people welcomed me into their homes and shared the experiences of their lives with extraordinary generosity. In fact, they did not just contribute to the book, they *are* the book.

The research on which this book is based was supported by a grant (No. 23468) from the Behavioral Sciences Research Branch of the National Institute of Mental Health. To Joyce Lazar, chief of that branch, a special note of thanks for her unfailing encouragement and support of my work.

To Rhoda Weyr, my agent, I owe thanks for introducing me to Erwin Glikes, my editor and publisher. Erwin's early and enthusiastic support and encouragement were important in translating the idea for this book into a reality. Throughout the process, he has demonstrated his confidence by leaving me to my own devices while always being ready to answer a call for help. Thus, he has transformed the traditionally difficult relationship between editor and author into a warm and gratifying one.

Acknowledgments

In the day-to-day process of thinking, writing, and revising, I have taken a great deal from family, friends, students, and colleagues. For their critical readings of all or part of the manuscript, I am indebted to Grant Barnes, Robert Cantor, Arlene Daniels, Fred DuBow, Barbara Easton, Martin Gold, Gordon Holleb, Carole Joffe, Jeffrey Klein, Judith Klein, Edward Mooney, Stephen Pittel, Arthur Shostak, Ann Swidler, and Gladys Topkis. Their thoughtful criticisms helped make this a better book.

In addition, there are some to whom I owe a special debt. To my research assistants—Adria Blum, Nancy Feinstein, Lorie Hill, and Laurie Phillips—for sharing both the bad times and the good throughout the project. To Kim Chernin, who surely will recognize her stimulating and thought provoking contributions to the final product. To Barbara Artson and Kurt Schlesinger, whose friendships are profoundly important to both my intellectual and personal life. To Dorothy Jones, for a very long and special relationship that has enriched both my life and this book in ways too numerous to cite. And most of all, to my own family—Hank, my husband, Marci, my daughter, and Paul Knier, our most recent addition. It is with them that I've learned about shared struggle and shared growth, learned how much easier such growth is when not hemmed in by economic deprivation. Without their contributions—both intellectual and emotional—neither this book nor my present life would be possible.

Finally, acknowledgment pages in books written by men usually end with a bow in the direction of a wife who kept the children quiet, the household running smoothly, the author well-tended and well-fed, and perhaps typed and edited the manuscript. I have never seen such a statement made about a husband—generally because men don't perform such services for their wives no matter what a woman's professional stature; but perhaps also because it's unseemly. Men, after all, are expected to be occupied with the "big" tasks of life, concerned with its "big" problems. Unseemly or not, I owe my husband a debt of gratitude for keeping the household going, for keeping me fed, tended, nurtured, and loved, and for protecting me from intrusions throughout the difficult months of writing. While there was no dearth of "big" issues in his life, he managed also to read and re-read every draft of every chapter, listened with endless patience as I formulated ideas—encouraging some, criticizing others—and provided valuable editorial services throughout. I could say much about how the book benefited from his participation. Instead, I would rather say that I, as a person, am better, stronger, richer, more open, and more honest for having him in my life. For that, there is no adequate way to say thanks.

Worlds of Pain

CHAPTER

I

Introduction

WHEN THE SMOKE AND DUST of the sixties had settled, America rediscovered class, race, and ethnicity. A century after the great waves of immigration, more than seventy-five years after settlement houses and public schools undertook to "civilize" and assimilate the immigrants' children, and decades after social scientists celebrated the melting pot and wrote glowingly of our ultimate triumph—the disappearance of class distinctions and antagonisms—America choked on its differences.

Throughout the 1960s and the first half of the 1970s, the nation spewed up those differences—racial, ethnic, sex, and perhaps most important of all, class differences. In a nation where a generation of social scientists had been insisting that class didn't count —that, at least among white Anglos, upward mobility was the norm, that the *embourgeoisement* of the working class was rapidly becoming a reality, and that those who did the manual labor of our society were not only affluent, but contented—a roar of pain and rage suddenly was heard.[1] Unexpectedly, the "silent majority" had found its voice. Unexpectedly, the white working class was alive and, quite clearly, not so well—their anger and discontents chronicled in the daily headlines and nightly television news.

These are the people who had believed in the promise of America—who had believed that if they deferred today's pleasures, they would reap tomorrow's rewards. They had played by the rules of the game—rules that promised anyone could make it if they tried hard enough, worked hard enough.[2] So they tried hard, worked hard, obeyed the law, and taught their children to do the same. In return, the "lucky" ones got a collection of goods—a car, a house filled with expensive appliances, perhaps a camper, a truck, or a boat.[3] But the good life eluded them; the game was rigged. The goods—not yet paid for—often brought as many burdens as pleasures. Life was hard. The children were growing up and costing more than ever. The bills seemed to come in faster than the money. Wages were increasing, but never quite as fast as prices. There was little free time in which to enjoy the prized possessions since it took the combined income of husband and wife plus every hour of overtime they could get just to stay even.[4] In September 1975, the United States Bureau of the Census reported that, despite rising wages, the 1974 median family income dropped by nearly 5 percent when adjusted for inflation. Thus, they found themselves running—always running—to keep from falling by the wayside.

As a nation, we were caught off-guard—astonished by their complaints, frightened by their noise. "White backlashers," they were dubbed with a sneer. How could it be otherwise? Since we hadn't known they existed, how could we know who they were, what they wanted, how they lived? We knew plenty about the poor families, the dependent families, the delinquent families—those who make the headlines, who crowd the welfare rolls, who tap public resources. But we knew almost nothing of the forty million American workers—just under half the total work force—who are employed in blue-collar jobs, most of them steady workers living in stable families; most of them asking nothing and getting nothing from the government programs that give welfare to the rich and the poor—the former in enormous subsidies which take the form of tax breaks, oil depletion allowances, price supports, government-backed loans, and outright investment in research and development; the latter in the form of subsistence payments, food stamps, and medical care.

Seeking to redress the oversight, the media gave us such caricatures as Archie Bunker on television and *Joe* on film. Social scientists went back into the field to see what they had missed. But even with this recent flurry of interest, portrayals of the flesh-and-blood people who make up America's working class—portrayals that tell us something of the texture and fabric of their lives, that deal respectfully with their manners, mores, and values—are notably few.[5] Still fewer are those that focus wholly on life within the family, and that make the link between the quality of family life and the work people do—that is, their place in the class structure. Indeed, while there are hundreds of studies of marriage and the family each year, few even mention the word "class"—an indication of how invisible the class structure has been to those who conceptualize and carry out those projects. Thus, the last major study to provide a detailed examination of the family life of the white working class was completed in 1959.[6]

In the intervening seventeen years, vast changes have swept the American landscape, all having some impact on the lives of ordinary working-class Americans. The civil rights movement, the student movement, the antiwar movement, the counterculture, the women's movement—all arose and demanded some reordering of the institutions that dominate our lives. The same period brought us The Pill with its widely heralded sexual revolution, a sharply rising divorce rate, and along with it all, a deep concern about the future of the family. In fact, many experienced observers of American life have been proclaiming the death of the nuclear family and preparing its burial.

For most people, however, the issue is not *whether* the family has a future, but *what* that future will look like. For after all the questions are asked and the speculations are done, the unshakable reality remains: most Americans of all classes still live in families and will continue to do so for the foreseeable future at least. And it is there—in those families—that the stresses and strains of everyday life are played out—that children are born and brought to adulthood; that women and men love and hate; that major interpersonal and intrapersonal conflicts are generated and stilled; and that men, women, and children struggle with the demands from the changing world outside their doors.

This book is about some of those ordinary Americans—the women and men who live in white working-class families. Its central concerns are the nature of the strains, the sources of the conflicts, and the quality of the struggles which engage them. It is about their origins; about how they came to marry; about the quality of their family life; about their definitions of a good life, a good marriage, a good family; about the set of values, norms, and lifeways to which they give allegiance; about how they are responding to the forces insisting upon change; about their hopes and dreams for the future. And more. For it is also about how intimately connected all these experiences, attitudes, and behaviors are with the work people do, their place in the class structure of our society. It is written in the hope that if we understand the sources of strain in their lives—and the fact that often they derive from profound ideological and social contradictions in the American society—their lives, their culture, and their present anger will become more comprehensible.

Two main issues preoccupied me during the course of researching and writing this book. First, the "either-or" quality of the debate about the family seemed inappropriate. Will it live or die? Is it an institution of oppression or the only place of refuge and belonging in an otherwise frightening, alienated, and alienating world? From the outset, it seemed clear that questions which force such alternatives upon us distort and simplify reality and deny the subjective experience of most people who live in families. In fact, the family as an institution is *both* oppressive and protective and, depending on the issue, is experienced sometimes one way, sometimes the other—often in some mix of the two—by most people who live in families.

So it is also on the question of its life or death. The family, I am convinced, will not die nor will it live in precisely the mode we all know so well. For like all institutions in any society, its form is a product of its historical time and place and of its relationship to the other social institutions with which it connects and intersects. Just as "no man is an island," so it is with institutions. They are products of an interactional system—both shaped by and shaping the world around them. Thus, over a century ago, when an emerging industrial society required that production move from home to factory, two things came together to give birth to a new ideology and to give the family a new face. The move from home to factory meant that some new arrangements would have to be made for the care of small children. At the same time, a series of social and economic changes were sweeping the society—changes that made women expendable as part of the work force. From that confluence of forces, an ideology grew that made motherhood the paramount task for women—an ideology which, in fact, *created* the notion of childhood itself—and justified the removal of women from the productive sphere.[7]

My second central concern grew naturally out of the first. If, in fact, the family is a product of its time and place in the hierarchy of social institutions, then American families would be both similar and different—similar in that they share some common experiences, some elements of a common culture by virtue of being part of the same society; different in that class, race, and ethnic differences gives a special cast to the shared experience as well as a unique and distinctly different set of experiences. Thus, the culture of blacks in America is both American and Black—American because no one can live in a society without absorbing much of the culture and ideology of the dominant group, many of its hopes and dreams; Black because the discrimination and hostility visited upon them has created for black Americans a profoundly separate experience out of which has grown a unique set of norms, values, and ways of being and living that enable them to cope and to survive.

The same is true for class.[8] That means that instead of talking about *the* family, we would do well to think about and look at *families* as they are embedded in the hierarchy of social classes in our society. When we do, we find, at the most manifest level, some broad similarities of form—the nuclear household composed of mother, father, and children; and content—families facing similar, perhaps universal, issues relating to work, leisure, child-rearing, interpersonal relations. But beneath the surface of the similarities, we find differences—differences, for example, in what turns these issues into problems, in how families attend to those problems; differences that are rooted in class position and that are more important than the similarities in revealing the quality and meaning of people's lives. Thus, for men in working-class families, one of the major problems in work centers on jobs that require too little commitment of self; among professional middle-class men, the problem stems from jobs that require too much.

Such differences are not trivial. They define the daily experience of life. Nor are they random or accidental. They derive from differences in class situation, past and present—a situation which not only defines the ways in which families approach their problems but limits the solutions that are possible for them.

But the class issue is itself not a simple one. The manual–nonmanual, blue-collar–white-color distinction no longer clearly defines class status, and surely does not tell the whole story about lifestyle and subcultural differences. Indeed, many acute observers argue that the major division in our advanced industrial society is between the upper middle class and the combined working and lower middle class[9]—an argument with which I concur and which I, too, made in an earlier work.[10]

Why, then, did I choose to confine this book to families where the men work in blue-collar occupations? The reasons are complex. For one thing, without the empirical evidence before me, I did not wish to get lost in the theoretical debate about the composition of America's classes—about whether the working class has become middle class as liberal and conservative theorists argue, or whether the middle class has become working class as a recent strain in radical thought postulates.

But there is another, perhaps more important reason, for the choice. For although I believe that the lines between the working class and lower middle class are becoming increasingly blurred, I do not think they are yet obliterated—either objectively or subjectively. Objectively, there is still at least one important difference in the lives of hourly and salaried workers. The hourly workers are the more vulnerable to fluctuations in the economy.[11] While it may be true that the weekly pay checks of some blue-collar workers are higher than those of some white-collar workers, it is the blue-collar workers who are less likely to earn that pay check the year round.[12]

Subjectively, too, there are differences in experience. The population of the lower middle class, for example, is made up in large part of upwardly mobiles from the traditional working class.[13] Notice the words—"upwardly mobiles." Notice, too, that until I call attention to them, you, the reader, probably found nothing amiss, nothing to stop the flow of your thought. Yet, there is a value judgment implicit in those words—a judgment that lies deep in the American culture about the value of upward mobility, about the value of those who work with their hands instead of their heads; a judgment that, while rarely made explicit, is widely shared by people in all classes and in all occupations. The words we unthinkingly use to describe the process of moving through the class structure reinforce that judgment, for we move *up* or *down*, not just through. And when we speak of that movement between classes, we don't speak simply of *going* up or down; instead we *climb* into a higher class or *fall* into a lower one.

Given these shared values, even if no better off financially than the sisters, brothers, friends, and neighbors they leave behind, those who climb up have a different sense of themselves and of their relationship to the world around them. They have "made it." And whether they bear the lash of resentment of those they left behind, or the smile of approval of their newfound peers, the messages they get reinforce their self-image as not just different but better. That difference in self-concept—that sense that they have climbed not just up but out—is a profoundly important difference in subjective experience, and it alone merits making the distinction between the working class and the lower middle class.

From the outset, then, I was dominantly concerned with class *differences*—differences in the subjective and objective experience that leads to differences between working-class and middle-class families in attitudes and behaviors, in ways of being and doing. It was simple good sense, then, to compare two widely disparate groups in the hope of highlighting those differences—the stably employed white working class, as that group has been defined traditionally, and the professional middle class. If it happens that my observations apply also to large portions of the lower middle class, or even the middle middle class, so much the better for telling us something about where the major distinctions in American life actually lie.

Thus, most of the material of this book rests on an intensive study of fifty white working-class families who share the following characteristics. They are all intact families, neither husband nor wife has more than a high-school education, the husband works in what is traditionally defined as a blue-collar occupation, the wife was under forty at the time of the study, and there was at least one child of elementary-school age (under twelve) still in the home.

For purposes of comparison, and because I wanted to be sure

that what I was calling working-class behavior and attitudes were indeed that and not an artifact of my ignorance or misunderstanding, I also interviewed a smaller group of twenty-five professional middle-class families whose characteristics match the working-class group in all but their education and occupation. Both wives and husbands in this group have at least a college education, and the men are all in professional occupations.

All the people in this study participated in intensive interviews which often took as many as ten hours and required several visits. Every working-class family was interviewed in their home—in fact, welcomed me into it. Not so with the professional middle-class families where several suggested meeting in my office because, they said, the house was too crowded, children too noisy, or privacy impossible. Interesting; especially in view of the large literature that describes working-class people as insular and xenophobic, unwilling to open their doors to anyone but family members. Interesting, too, when one notes that the working-class homes are invariably smaller and more crowded than those in which the professional families live—no den, library, or "family" room where a door could be closed and quiet privacy assured. In those homes, when the interview took place in the evening, the problem of privacy was managed by either husband or wife leaving the house. Since most of the evening interviews were with the husbands, the wives usually took themselves and the children off to visit relatives, waiting there for the husband to call and signal the end of our meeting.

I made the decision to interview wives and husbands separately because I was interested in understanding the way each experiences the marriage relationship and his or her role in it. It is possible, of course, to argue that couples should be interviewed together because they would be constrained to be more truthful under each other's watchful eyes; but the experience of any family therapist suggests otherwise. It always takes some time before couples can confront each other truthfully about their feelings or about their differing perceptions of reality. In fact, to confront each other with their differences usually is so anxiety-provoking that in the initial stages of marriage or family therapy, couples tend to form an alliance against the therapist to whom they have come for help. There is every reason to assume that this pattern would be reinforced greatly if couples were interviewed jointly.

But these are negative statements about the joint interview. More important, there are positive values in interviewing wives and husbands separately. First, unlike many other sociological studies of the family, this one starts with the assumption that the perceptions of husband and wife are not necessarily congruent, and that both perspectives are necessary for understanding the reality of a marriage. Further, any woman who has participated even marginally in the women's movement and in women's groups over the last several years knows that women tend to discuss their feelings about their lives, their roles, and their marriages more freely when men are not present.

Thus, my experiences in the women's movement, my observations as a therapist who leads same-sex and mixed-sex groups, my work as a marriage and family therapist, and my experience as a sociologist studying the family all strongly support the decision to interview husbands and wives separately and privately.

The working-class families came to me in a variety of ways—through a friend who teaches nursery school in a working-class neighborhood; a chance meeting with a woman who was president of the P.T.A. in a working-class school; the minister of a church with a working-class population; and from among the women who work in a local beauty shop. But most important of all, each family was a source of referrals to others. In order to limit the bias inherent in such referrals, however, and to ensure that I was not meeting people who were all connected with each other in some way, I took no more than one referral from a family, always selecting the referred family in favor of the more distant connection. Thus, when I had the choice of a friend or an acquaintance, I interviewed the acquaintance. The success of the strategy may be judged by the fact that the families I am writing about turn out to be representative of Americans of that class as they have been measured in national samples with randomly chosen populations.

In all, the families I met live in twelve different communities around the San Francisco Bay, all lying within a radius of fifty miles from the city. Only Berkeley was systematically excluded, since the large university located there so dominates that small city as to make its population unrepresentative of the general population in the Bay Area.

But these interviews are not the only source of information for this book. Rather much of my life—past and present—prepared me for the task. I have already indicated that I am a practicing marriage and family therapist. This work, while not directly reflected in the numbers and percentages on the following pages, has enabled me to know many white working-class families intimately and is the basis for much that I understand about these people and their lives.

But that understanding, too, rests on prior experience. For while my professional training allows me to do that work, it is my personal and political background that gives it its special meaning and that facilitates deeper levels of comprehension than might otherwise be available to me. Thus, long before I became a family therapist or a social scientist, I was born into a white working-class family. I experienced all the insecurity of poverty and the pain of discovering that my teachers looked upon my widowed, immigrant mother as ignorant and upon me as a savage child. I learned young to be ashamed of my mother's foreign accent, to devalue my family, and to disesteem the culture of my home.[14]

Since I was an able student, I was graduated from high school by the time I was fifteen. But for a girl of my generation and class, college was not a perceived option. Instead, I went to work as a stenographer in a manufacturing firm and shared the family pride in a child who had taken a big step up the ladder. From a mother who worked at a sewing machine in a "dirty" factory to a daughter who worked at a typewriter in a "clean" office—yes, this was a high achievement in the world to which I was born. If a girl wanted more, she married up. Four years later, at nineteen, I did just that. I married a college boy of twenty-one who was destined to be a professional and started the long climb into middle-class professional life.

Along the way I became involved in radical politics—a commitment that kept me thinking about class issues and involved me in organizing working-class communities, both black and white. But despite political activities that seemingly kept me connected with my past, in fundamental ways I remained distant from it. My radical commitments and activities, while deeply felt, were "out there"—activities on behalf of someone other than myself, something I was doing for "them." Put that way, one wonders about the dissociation of which the human mind and psyche is capable.

Yet it should come as no surprise that I was happy to put those early experiences behind me—eager to forget the pain and shame of feeling deficient. I had made it, and I didn't want to look back —at least not into my own life and my own pain.

But no matter how far we travel, we can never leave our roots behind. I found they claimed me at unexpected times, in unexpected places—a film that triggered a flood of memories, a novel that made me weep, a classroom lecture about life in the working class that angered and puzzled me because it didn't sound like the world I knew or the life I'd lived.

Thus, when I was taught in my belated college and graduate education that America had conquered the invidious distinctions of class, I didn't believe it. All my personal and political experiences told me differently. Perhaps it was the political reawakening of the sixties; perhaps the years had put enough distance between me and the pain of childhood and adolescence that I could afford to risk experiencing it once again; perhaps it was some combination of the two, and yet more that I do not fully know or understand. Whatever the reasons, the ideas I was hearing in my classes and reading about in my books stimulated anew an interest in my origins. By the mid-sixties, I consciously began to claim them as my own, and to wonder how working-class families were *really* faring in this new era. Thus began again my connection with working-class people and their lives—a connection that has been sustained and intimate over the last decade, a connection that made both the research and writing of this book possible.

I am aware that both the methods of this study and the style of presentation are vulnerable to criticism from colleagues in the social sciences. The small sample not randomly chosen makes generalizations suspect. The anecdotal presentation raises the question of representativeness in the use of the data. The only answer to these criticisms lies in the quality of the work itself—in its ability to persuade by appealing to a level of "knowing" that exists in all of us but is not very often tapped; in its ability— to borrow a phrase from psychology—to generate an "aha experience."

We have hundreds of representative studies of one aspect or another of family life—important and useful studies. We have attitude studies and behavior studies; but few that make the link between the two. We have probability statistics on marriage, divorce, sexual behavior, and much, much more; but they tell us nothing of the experience of the flesh-and-blood women and men who make up the numbers. This is not a failure of those studies; they are not designed to do so. Still, they leave us with only a fragment of knowledge. Therefore, we need also social science that is so designed—qualitative studies that can capture the fullness of experience, the richness of living. We need work that takes us inside the family dynamics, into the socio-emotional world in which people are born, live, and die—real people with flesh, blood, bones, and skeletons. This study was designed to accomplish that.

Talking for many hours with a single respondent made possible the kind of connection and rapport that allowed me to probe into places generally hidden from public view; to see and hear things I would ordinarily not have dared to ask about; or, if asked, people would be reluctant to answer. Perhaps more important, it taught me the things I *ought* to be asking, since in such situations people want to talk about their concerns as well as yours. Sometimes theirs were the same as mine; sometimes not—but always I tried to "hear" what was important to them, and to think anew about the concepts and theory I brought with me into the research field.

On the pages that follow I shall present a portrait of the working-class families I met—a distillation of 100 interviews and perhaps 1,000 hours. It will attack some cherished beliefs in the social sciences and in the culture, and support some. But always it will be true to the spirit of the lives of the people who made this book possible.

CHAPTER

2

The Families

AS I DRIVE through the streets, each with its row of neat houses sitting primly behind a small, struggling front lawn, I'm struck with the similarities between working-class neighborhoods in the twelve different communities I have now visited. In the newer tracts, the houses sit well back from gently curving, treeless streets; the tender young plantings at their base are still too small to cover their naked cement foundations; and time has not yet softened the cruel mark the bulldozer left on the surrounding land. In the older neighborhoods, streets are straight; plantings are fuller, if less well tended; and the houses, like aging people trying to retain a semblance of youth, look tired with the effort.

An occasional tricycle, scooter, or rumpled doll give evidence that young children live and play on these streets. But at ten o'clock in the morning the streets are still, almost eerily void of life. The older children are off to school for the day; the younger ones are playing in fenced back yards; the youngest, in their cribs for the morning nap.

Their mothers are catching their first free breath of the day, perhaps perched on a stool in the kitchen, coffee cup in one hand, telephone in the other. Since five-thirty or six they have been up and about—preparing breakfast, packing lunches, feeding and changing a crying baby, scolding this child, prodding that one, brushing away a husband's hand unexpectedly on her breast as he moves toward the door. "Oh God," she thinks, "I can't say no *again* tonight; and already I'm tired."

Finally, the rush to clean up the house because this morning, for at least one of them, something different is about to happen. That lady from the university is coming to talk. She muses, "I wonder what she wants to know about me? She said she wants a few hours of my time. What could take *that* long? God, I hope the baby sleeps."

Juggling purse, tape recorder, and small briefcase, I climb out of my car into the morning sunshine. I've dressed casually but carefully for this meeting—none of my more "hip"-looking clothes, no threadbare jeans. I already know—partly because I was once a young working-class woman, partly because I've been doing research in working-class communities for years—that it's expected that I'll look like a professional woman ought to look. Anything else could be taken as a sign of disrespect, both for myself and my hostess. For those who have lived on the edge of poverty all their lives, the semblance of poverty affected by the affluent is both incomprehensible and insulting.

Across the quiet street, a camper is parked in the driveway of one house, a small boat in another. The garage is open in the house next door to the one I'm about to visit; in it a woman is stripping a table, preparing it for a new finish. A little further down the street a Sears truck, brakes squealing, stops; two men begin to unload a new washing machine. With one part of me I observe all this; with another, I become aware that, like the woman who waits inside, I feel some anxiety. "How can I make this stranger comfortable enough to talk openly to me?" I wonder. "And why is she letting me into her life at all?"

With that, I find myself facing the front door, looking around for the doorbell. Before I find it, the door opens; a young woman in her late twenties stands smiling shyly before me. I introduce myself. "Hi, I'm Lillian Rubin; you must be Mary Ann Corbett." She nods, opens the door wider, motioning me inside. "Come in," she says in the hushed voice of a mother whose baby has just been put down for a nap. Then, awkwardly, formally, "I'm glad to meet you."

As we step into the front room, she looks at the paraphernalia I carry, and asks, "Where would you like to sit? In here, or at the kitchen table?" It makes no difference to me; sometimes we stay in the living room; sometimes we go into the kitchen. This time I say, "This will be fine, if it's all right with you. I can just put my recorder on the table between those two chairs."

As I move forward to settle myself, she offers to get coffee. Mary Ann Corbett is a medium-sized, slightly round woman, with short, wavy brown hair, hazel eyes, and a self-conscious, relatively joyless smile. She is dressed neatly on this warm day—light cotton pants, a short-sleeved knit shirt, and sandals on her bare feet. As she turns and walks toward the kitchen, I have a sudden, clear image of what she will look like in twenty years. Although not yet thirty, the contours of the middle-aged woman to come are already apparent.

The room, like most I will go into, has the look of one that was tidied up for company. The furnishings are nondescript and of indeterminate age; it has a familiar look, a scene out of my girlhood. Once in a while, usually in a house in one of the newer tracts, the furnishings stand out in memory because they wear the decorator-matched and unlived-in look of the rooms on display at the local furniture store. No surprise! When a family has worked so hard, waited so long to acquire these goods, they are not treated lightly. Once in a while, the disorder is the dominant memory—yesterday's laundry spilling over the sides of a chair, unwashed dishes piling up in the sink, children's toys littering the floor, a vacuum, with its promise of cleanliness, propped against the wall. But mostly the houses look much like Mary Ann Corbett's—picked up, tucked in, well tended—a family still making do with a collection of hand-me-downs and cheap Ward's or Sears' specials bought expensively on credit when they were first married. For not only the poor, but those just up from poverty as well, always pay more. Without ready cash, they must rely on high-interest time payment purchases for all but their daily needs.[1]

In this house, as in others, a large color television set dominates the room. Indeed, as flowers turn toward the light, so everything in the room is turned expectantly toward the darkened tube. "Does *everybody* have one of these things?" I wonder. I had not yet been in a home without one; nor, as it turns out, would I be.

17

I notice another common phenomenon: there's only one small lamp in this room that doesn't even have an overhead light fixture. Some homes have no lamps at all in the living room; only a few have anything that approaches adequate reading light. I shrug, impatient with myself, trying to shake off my intellectual's bias. "So why," I ask myself, "should people who don't read spend scarce money on reading lamps?" I don't know the answer to that question. I only know it's my biggest surprise as I go from house to house, and the one I have most trouble explaining to myself comfortably.

Mary Ann re-enters the room, steaming mug in each hand. She settles herself in the chair opposite me, points to the tape recorder, and asks hesitantly, "Are you going to turn that on? I'm afraid I'll feel so funny I won't be able to talk." I reply, "If you don't mind, I'd like to try it. Most people forget it pretty quickly; but if it continues to bother you, I'll turn it off. Okay?" She shifts slightly in her chair, still uncomfortable, but nods assent. We begin the interview.

A week later, I'm back on the same street, this time to meet Jim Corbett. It's early evening—six-thirty; dinner is over, and the street is alive with activity. The sounds of children playing mix with the swish of water from a dozen houses. Here and there, women stand in twos and threes, chatting; several men are bent over the engines of their cars or trucks.

Once again, I climb out of my car and gather my equipment together. Only this time several people stop what they are doing and watch curiously. Some children come up to stand closer. "Who 'dja come to see?" asks one. "What's that?" calls out another, pointing to my recorder. We banter for the few moments it takes to collect myself. Then I head across the street. On my way, I see a man standing before a boat with a wrench in hand, puzzled. Two neighbors saunter over and offer advice.

Before I reach the front door, it is thrown open by eight-year-old Joanne. "C'mon in," she says in a rush. "We're getting ready to go to Grandma's, but my brother's a slow poke so he's not ready yet. And Mommy's mad at him. She said we were supposed to be gone before you came." Mary Ann hurries into the living room. "Hush, Joanne. Where are your manners? What kind of way is that to greet company?" And to me, "I'm sorry we're late getting out, but she's right, little Jimmy is such a slow poke, and the baby's been fussy. Jim's out in the backyard. I'll go get him, and then we'll be just about ready to leave so you two can talk privately."

Despite the pressures on her, Mary Ann's greeting is cordial, her smile genuinely friendly and welcoming. The eight hours we've spent together in the last week have created a bond between us. She has never before talked to anyone about such personal things; never before been able to express her conflicts about her life; indeed, never before even acknowledged them to herself so directly. It isn't that she doesn't have friends and family to talk to. She does. Both her mother and sister live nearby, and she sees them often. Some of her old high-school friends are now neighbors, and they retain close and warm relationships. But certain subjects—sex, for example—are too private to talk about. And others—her restless discontent, for example—are too frightening to talk about. Besides, she keeps telling herself, "What do I have to complain about? Jim's a steady worker; he doesn't drink; he doesn't hit me. That's a lot more than my mother had, and she's not complaining." Or else, "My friends, they all seem to like it okay, so there must be something the matter with me."

Such turning inward with self-blame is common among the women and men I met—a product, in part, of the individualist ethic in the American society which fixes responsibility for any failure to achieve the American dream in individual inadequacy. That same ethic—emphasizing as it does the isolated individual or, at most, the family unit—breeds a kind of isolation in American life that is common in all classes but more profoundly experienced in the working class, partly, at least, because they have fewer outside resources. It is, I suspect, the main reason why people agree to talk to me, and why they find the hours we spend together relieving. For one thing, the very fact that someone asks certain questions, raises certain issues, gives them a kind of universality and legitimacy. It means that other people must feel these feelings, too, so it's all right to talk about them—at least to this stranger who comes with the credentials of an expert. Like the rest of us, the Corbetts and their friends and neighbors feel the need for expert counsel once in a while. But if you're working class, even were it culturally acceptable to acknowledge the need, who can afford the cost? So talking to me offers the possibility for getting some advice and reassurance without even the requirement of admitting the need.

Mary Ann and Jim, the two older children trailing behind, come into the room. As the children dance around restlessly, Jim and I are introduced. He is a medium-tall, lean, sandy-haired man with long sideburns and a ruddy complexion. The lines of fatigue on his face coupled with the wrinkles around his eyes and mouth make him look older than his thirty years. His cordial words, when they come, belie his tight, anxious smile. "Mary Ann's talked a lot about you. I must say, life has been different since you've been coming around, and I'm glad to get a chance to see what you look like."

There's a small flurry as Mary Ann and the children leave, she calling out to Jim, "Call us when you're through. I won't come back until I hear from you." I object, "But it may be quite late; what about the children?" "Don't worry about that. I can put them down at Mama's; they're used to it." As they leave, Jim goes out to the kitchen to get a cold drink. I'm eager to get started. Almost half an hour has gone by since I arrived, and I know from past experience that these evenings can run very late.

I had been warned that I might be able to reach the women, but never the men. "What working-class guy will talk to a middle-class professional woman?" friends and colleagues wanted to know. Now, I knew the answer: the husbands of the women I met and talked to first. For those women became my most powerful allies in enlisting the cooperation of their men. Having found the experience pleasurable and useful, they were eager to expose their husbands to it as well, partly, no doubt, in the hope that some painful problem would be dealt with in the process. Sometimes it required a struggle—the wife pleading, cajoling, threatening. But more often, by the time I had finished visiting the wife, I had become a family "event," and the husbands were sufficiently curious and feeling sufficiently excluded that they participated willingly.

Still, I was surprised by the openness with which most of the men tried to talk about difficult and delicate subjects. So much so that I asked several about it. "Would it have been easier to talk about these personal issues with a man rather than a woman?"

The answer required little thought: "No." And it was best explained by a thirty-one-year-old heavy-equipment mechanic as he walked me to my car very late one night:

Guys don't talk about things like that to each other. Me, I'm used to talking to women. I talked to my mother when I was a kid, not my father. When I got older, I talked to girls, not to guys. And now I have my wife to talk to.

Of course, it makes sense, doesn't it? It is women, not men, who nurture, who comfort, who teach young boys. It is to women they run with their earliest pains and triumphs; it is to women they first confide their fears and fantasies. And to the degree that the American culture approves male expression of closeness or intimacy, it is between a man and a woman, not between two men.[2]

From talking to Mary Ann, I already know a great deal about Jim. Like so many men of all classes in our culture, he's a quiet, controlled man—no big mood swings for him. She's the one in the family with the ups and downs. For Jim, there are no expressions of deep sadness or despair, no unreasoning flashes of anger; but there are none of ecstasy either.

Jim is a lonely man, although he doesn't often acknowledge it. He has no close friends, no close ties with his family. There are some guys at work with whom he goes drinking once in a while, a guy with whom he goes fishing sometimes. But nobody important, nobody he can talk to, nobody he can count on for anything.

He's done a variety of different kinds of work, including a stint on the assembly line—years he recalls with distaste. For the last three years he has been employed as an ironworker in heavy construction. He likes the work because he can move around and because it keeps him outdoors. The pay is great—$9.00 an hour—and when he works regularly, the weekly pay checks are large, indeed. But he doesn't work regularly. There are lay-offs because of weather, lay-offs because of industry slow-downs, lay-offs because of accidents on the job. Two years ago, a heavy beam caught him in the foot; he didn't walk again for three months. Even so, last year he earned close to $12,000, more than ever before, but still not enough to make a dent in the debts he has accumulated over the years—loans for the house, the car, to help pay for his mother's illness, to keep them going when he was hurt. Those debts ride always on his shoulders—sometimes he carries them easily, sometimes they drag him down. At those moments, he wonders wearily, "Is this really what life's all about? How did I get to this place anyway?"

Right at the moment, as he stands before the refrigerator, he's concerned with more immediate things. Mary Ann has talked a lot about how good it made her feel to have someone to talk to. He doesn't quite understand what she means, but things have certainly been different these last few days. She's been less edgy; she hasn't hollered at the kids so much; and last night she even seemed to enjoy making love. So if talking can do that, he's willing to let her talk as much as she wants, maybe even give it a try himself. Besides, it feels kind of good to think about telling *his* side of the story of their lives. Mary Ann at least has her girl-friends and her sister to talk to; he doesn't have anybody.

With that, he straightens and heads back into the living room. He seats himself in the chair across from me and, his face smiling, his voice serious, says, "I sure hope you got those tapes locked up good." I look at him, puzzled, about to reassure him about the confidentiality of our talk. Before I can speak, he explains, "Well, I figure if they could steal those tapes from—what's his name? oh yeah—from Ellsberg's psychiatrist's office, then you better take care of your stuff. It's not that I have anything to be afraid of, but after all, I agreed to talk to you, not the whole world." I smile and assure him that the tape will be destroyed as soon as the interview is transcribed, that the interview will remain in a locked file to be seen by no eyes other than mine, and that his anonymity will be fully protected. The atmosphere in the room relaxes perceptibly. We begin the interview.

CHAPTER

3

_____

And How Did
They Grow?

_____

Life was mean and hard. My parents didn't have a lot to give us, either
in things or emotions. [*Guiltily*.] I don't blame them; they couldn't
help it. They did their best, but that's just the way it was. They were
young, and their lives weren't any fun either. They were stuck together by their poverty and their five kids.

> [*Twenty-seven-year-old beautician,*
> *second from the youngest in a family of five.*]

OVER AND OVER, that's the story—a corrosive and disabling
poverty that shattered the hopes and dreams of their young parents, and twisted the lives of those who were "stuck together" in
it. Flight is, of course, one way in which people try to get "un-
stuck"—sometimes symbolically in alcohol, sometimes literally in
divorce or desertion. Thus, of the people I met, 40 percent had at
least one alcoholic parent, usually but not always the father;[1]
almost as many were children of divorce or desertion;[2] and 10
percent spent part of their lives in institutions or foster homes
because their parents were unable, unwilling, or judged unfit to
care for them.

And how did they grow, the children of these families?

With pain:

One of the first things I remember was when the police came in the middle of the night and they dragged us out of bed. [*Struggling to hold back tears.*] God, we were scared, my sister and me; we couldn't stop crying. I don't know where my parents were. I never saw my father again; he was always drunk anyway. And my mother, I don't know where she was, maybe she was working or something. They took us to juvenile hall that night, and we didn't get to go home for nine years.

> [*Thirty-four-year-old housewife, the oldest in a family of two children.*]

... with bitterness:

I don't remember much about my father; he left when I was about six. The one thing I remember very well is that he used to beat us with a coathanger.

> [*Twenty-eight-year-old warehouseman, the middle child in a family of five.*]

... with loneliness:

When I was eight my parents got divorced, and I lived with my mother. She went out a lot. She went dancing, and she had lots of boyfriends. A lot of the time I didn't see her for two or three or four days. God, that was terrible because it was a time when I was absolutely terrified of being alone. And there I'd be—I'd come home alone; I'd take care of myself and put myself to bed. And I'd get up the next morning and wash and dress and go to school. I wandered around the streets by myself a lot in those days, partly because I was so afraid to be in the house alone, but also there was nothing to do.

> [*Thirty-year-old short-order waitress from a family where she was an only child.*]

... with anger:

I ran away from home four or five times before I turned seventeen and finally stayed away. And they didn't come looking for me none of the time. The first time after I came back, my dad just walked in and beat me up. Another time when I ran away, the dude who was running the juvenile hall sent my family a telegram, and told them that I was there, and that they should come and get me. They sent back word that they should find me a job because they didn't have no more time for me.

> [*Thirty-four-year-old sheet-metal worker*
> *from a family of six.*]

. . . with rebelliousness:

I was always in a lot of trouble. In fact, I was considered incorrigible, and I was sent to juvenile hall and made a ward of the court when I was thirteen.

> [*Twenty-nine-year-old welder,*
> *the second child in a family of five.*]

. . . with resignation:

We never did have a lot of money; it was always a rough go. We got our clothes from the Goodwill, and there wasn't a lot of food around, you can bet. They both did their best, but it just wasn't enough. But I'm not complaining. Life is what you make it, and we always made the best of it. We had fun, too. I remember we'd go out and ride around sometimes, just little things like that were very nice. You can't have everything, you know.

> [*Twenty-five-year-old housewife,*
> *the next to the youngest child in a family of four.*]

For most, the memories of childhood and the family are some tortured combination of all these feelings, and more—most notably guilt at allowing their expression and denial that any negative feelings exist at all. In fact, this guilt and denial was, for me, one of the most puzzling issues I encountered. Why, I kept asking myself, are these articulate people so distant from the sources of childhood pain and anger? Why is it necessary for them to deny so much of it? In the professional middle-class world in which I have lived for so many years, one encounters exactly the opposite response—young adults, encouraged by the psychotherapeutic milieu that pervades their culture, expose and examine the pain of childhood and the anger that accompanies it seemingly without end.

Could it be that these currents in the culture are so alien from working-class consciousness? I doubted it. For a variety of reasons —first among them, the cost, but also fears about being defined as "crazy," and the reluctance to probe the past that I observed—the women and men of the working class do not often seek out psychotherapy. But they are aware of its existence and of some of the basic premises on which it rests. In interview after interview, I heard the evidence of that psychological awareness—especially as it was expressed in their concerns about communication in interpersonal relationships and the kind of parenting they are offering to their own children.

What then? Why do we hear so much anger expressed by the middle-class child of the "committee" mother:

My mother was always busy—too busy for us. At least that's the way it felt when I was little. She was always out doing her thing—worrying about the poor people or the black people and on one damn committee to save the world or another. I used to be jealous of those people because she didn't seem to spend nearly as much time worrying about me or caring that I felt lonely or scared.

[*Thirty-one-year-old housewife, the oldest in a family of two.*]

. . . and so little anger expressed by the working-class child of the mother who left home, husband, and children for another life:

My mother never meant to leave us. She loved us. But she was young; and she wanted to have fun, too. It was really my grandmother's fault. She was my father's mother, and she lived with us. She made my mom's life miserable. My mom couldn't even paint the walls of her own bedroom the color she wanted without my grandmother interfering.

Even on the issue of a mother who works outside the home, there often are differences between the ways in which a child in a professional middle-class home experiences that:

I always hated it that my mother worked. She didn't have to. She could have stayed home and taken care of us like other mothers did.

. . . and the experience of the child in a working-class family:

My mother worked on and off all the years we were growing up. It was a hard life for her having to work and take care of all of us at the same time.

No complaints from the working-class child. What sense would it make? Mother worked because she had to—the crucial difference, it seems, in a child's understanding and experience of a working mother.[3] Children in all families frequently are "lonely or scared," or both. But the child in the working-class family understands that often there's nothing his parents can do about it. They're stuck just as he is—stuck with a life over which they have relatively little control.

In a family where all the material necessities and most of the comforts and luxuries are taken for granted, a child can feel angered and rejected by a father who "works all the time," by a mother whose energy is directed into the kind of volunteerism that engages so many women of the professional middle class, by the one who *chooses* a career. But how can poor children justify or rationalize those feelings when they know that father works two jobs to keep a roof over their heads and food on the table; that mother does dull, demeaning, and exhausting work just to help make ends meet? When the same father gets drunk or violent; when the mother "takes it," joins the father in this behavior, or, once in a great while, simply runs away, a child's condemnation doesn't come easily. However imperfectly articulated or understood, children in such families sense the adults' frustration and helplessness. Their own hurt notwithstanding, assigning blame to parents makes little sense to these children. Their anger either is turned inward and directed against self—in childhood, "if only I were somehow different or better, this life wouldn't be happening to me"; or projected outward and directed against other, less threatening objects—in adulthood, "the country would be better off if we let those welfare bums starve." But always the source of the anger is kept distant from consciousness, as this dialogue with a thirty-four-year-old truck driver, one of three children, illustrates:

Tell me something about what life was like in your family when you were growing up?

Oh, I don't know what to say. It was a happy family.

Well, can you tell me something about it—like what kind of people were your mother and father?

My father was an alcoholic, so I don't know. My mother probably should have gotten a divorce, but I think she stayed married because of the kids; and probably because she didn't have any job skills and everything like that.

It must have been difficult to grow up with an alcoholic father then, huh?

[*Reluctantly.*] Yeah. I remember my mother going down to the bar after he got paid when I was twelve, thirteen, fourteen and pleading for money to go pay the bills. But once she got down there to the bar, she'd go in and sit with him and drink beer, too. [*Quickly and defensively.*] But I don't want you to get the idea she was an alcoholic, because she wasn't. She'd just sit there and drink beer with him, that's all.

When I was a lot younger—a real little kid—I remember sitting in the car outside the bar for a long time waiting for them to come out. Sometimes I remember we would go in and ask them when they were coming home, and they'd give us a nickel or a dime to get rid of us. Then we'd go back and sit in the car. It got cold out there, and we'd be so hungry.

That sounds like it must have been a painful time for you?

Oh, I don't know. We didn't know any better; it was okay. I suppose the worst part was having to sit down there when you're a little kid and you're cold and hungry, and your mother and father are still sitting in the bar. That's the worst part. Sometimes, though, they'd let us come in and we'd sit in a corner and drink Coke, and we'd try to be quiet so nobody would see us or notice us. Those times were better. At least we could be close to them and see what was going on.

But, listen, I don't want you to get the idea that my mother was an alcoholic, too, because she wasn't. Anyhow, I don't think it's right for kids to go around blaming their parents for things they couldn't help. So I don't blame them none. They loved us and they brought us up the best they could; so you can't blame people for doing the best they can, can you?

Yes, there it is—"I don't think it's right for kids to go around blaming their parents for things they couldn't help"—a comment which, in various versions, I heard again and again.

For all children, life often feels fearful and uncontrollable. When a child's experience suggests that the adults on whom he must depend for survival have little control as well, his fears of being unprotected and overwhelmed are so great that he must either deny and repress his experience or succumb to his terror. Given those alternatives, most people rely on the mechanisms of denial and repression, for to succumb is to threaten life itself. No wonder our truck driver ends the conversation, as did so many others, with the insistent statement that "it's better to forget about things that bother you":

I don't know why I even got to thinking about these things. It don't do no good. I tell my kids all the time—it's better to forget about things that bother you; just put them out of your mind, otherwise you'll just be sitting around feeling sorry for yourself all the time. Just put those things out of your mind is what I tell them, just like I did; then they won't get to you.

But, one might wonder, isn't this an unusual family history? Isn't it true that in most families, no one drinks too much; that wives and husbands live together, raise their children together, and grow old together? The answer: yes, but barely. Among the 100 working-class men and women I met, only 54 percent of the families into which they were born were without some elements of instability—alcoholism, divorce, desertion—for some part of their lives. That means that 46 percent suffered one or more of those experiences some time during their childhood. It is that temporary quality of both the stability and instability in so many families that is noteworthy. Life changes, depending upon circumstances outside personal control. A lay-off, a serious illness in the family, an accident, a death—such events can thrust a stable family into instability for a while. Similarly, a job that pays enough to meet the bills and live with some minimum comforts can mean, for some, the shift from instability to stability.

Even in the most consistently stable families, however, the first and fundamental fact of most of their lives was that they were poor. Not one person, even those from the most solid and integrated homes, failed to mention growing up poor—some worse off than others, to be sure, but all whose dominant experience of childhood was material deprivation.

It matters little that these families may not have been poor by some arbitrary definition set by a governmental agency. What counts is the experience of the people who lived those lives. For them, the deprivation was real—real when they knew parents had trouble paying the rent, when they didn't have shoes that fit, when the telephone was shut off, when the men came to take the refrigerator away. That fact alone colors every dimension of life and, for both parents and children, contributes powerfully to a world filled with pain, anger, fear, and loneliness—a world over which neither has much control.[4] Small wonder, then, that few adults from working-class families look back over those early years with the "Oh-to-be-a-child-again" fantasy so often heard among middle-class adults. Small wonder, too, that the working-class young grow up so fast while an extended adolescence—often until the mid-twenties and later—is the developing norm in much of the professional middle class. Such a moratorium on assuming adult responsibilities is a luxury that only the affluent sector of the society can afford.

Thus, at least intermittent poverty was the common experience of the children growing up in most of these working-class families. But there are differences in how their parents adapted to that primary fact of life. Some families struggled desperately and, most of the time, successfully to remain among the "respectable" poor. Others gave up the fight and, more often than not, escaped their pain in drinking, violence, or desertion. Observing these patterns recently, one writer labeled them as the "settled-living" and "hard-living" lifestyles—a distinction that I will use as well because it rests on differences in family lifestyle and avoids some of the negative connotations of so many characterizations of working-class life.[5]

Like all such typologies, however, this one, too, should be labeled, "Approach with Caution," for at best it is only an approximation of reality. Thus, several things should be clear. First, the hard-living–settled-living styles represent two extremes rarely found in their pure states; elements of each often are found in the other. Second, just as many settled-living men and women may experience some aspects of hard-living in their own lives as they try to grasp and hold the American dream, so most hard livers of one period are settled livers in another. Third, in almost every settled-living family, there are hard-living brothers, sisters, or cousins who, while scorned, are omnipresent and painful reminders of the precariousness of the settled-living lifestyle—of the fact that at any moment external life forces might push even the most determinedly settled-living family off its course.

These terms, then, speak more to the ethos of a family rather than to a hard-and-fast reality, more to the dominant tone of life than to the day-by-day experience. The daily, weekly, even monthly experience may change at any given time. But what remains in consciousness in adulthood is the sense of how things were, the sweep of life rather than its detail.

For just over half the families I met, that "sense of how things were" suggests the settled-living lifestyle—families that were characterized by stable work histories:

My dad has been working for the same company, on the same job for the last thirty years. Times were bad sometimes. He was laid off a lot. After the union came, there were strikes. But he's still proud of the fact that they always hired him back.

. . . stable families:

I guess they must have had problems, everybody does. But my folks always seemed to get along okay, and if there was trouble, none of us kids knew about it.

. . . a sense of rootedness:

I grew up in the same neighborhood and in the same house. It was the family's pride and joy that we always had a roof over our heads, and one that we owned.

They were cautious, conservative, church-going, and if they drank, they did so with moderation. Their children were dressed neatly and attended school regularly—at least in the elementary grades. They were brought up strictly to mind their manners, and subject to a very rigid discipline:

My folks, especially my father, made us toe the line, not like kids today. When my brother got out of line, my father nearly killed him.

Actually, I guess I'm not sure how much good it did, because he kept getting into trouble.

Like it or not, the men went to work every day:

My father was always proud of the fact that he never missed a day's work and was never late. I mean, it doesn't count when he was laid off. He brought us up to respect work, too, and to be responsible and reliable.

... and the women kept house and children in shining order:

My mother was always cleaning or scrubbing or washing and ironing. It seems like I can hardly remember her doing anything else. Oh yes, she cooked, too.

In contrast to the settled livers, there were the hard-living families—just under half the people I met who recalled families that were characterized by fathers with chaotic work histories:

My father did so many things, I can't just tell you his occupation. I guess he was a painter, but he did a lot of other stuff, too. It seemed like most of the time, he was out of work.

... unstable family relations:

Something was wrong with my mother by the time I was born. She got sick—psychologically sick, I guess. She just didn't take care of us; and sometimes she'd just disappear. We—my sister and me—we ran wild until I was about nine. I didn't go to school; I couldn't read and write. My mother either wasn't there or couldn't take care of us. My father knew what was going on, but he didn't seem to care. He just got drunk all the time.

... violence:

When my father got drunk, he'd get mean and pick on whoever was around. When I was about twelve, he came home roaring drunk one night and picked me up like a sack of potatoes and threw me right across the whole room. My mother stood there and watched, and she never did a thing.

... a general rootlessness:

We moved around a lot. Sometimes we were evicted, but sometimes we just moved; I'm not sure why. I went to ten, maybe twelve, schools by the time I dropped out of high school; that was in the tenth grade.

... and alcoholism—the tragic consequences of which were experienced repeatedly by many of the children growing up in these families. At best, it meant poverty and dislocation as father moved from job to job with long periods of unemployment in between:

My dad had trouble holding a job because of his drinking. I guess he wasn't what you'd call a reliable worker. When he didn't work, things would really get tough. We were even evicted from where we lived one time.

At worst, it meant the total disruption of the family, as this story from a thirty-five-year-old woman, the middle child in a family of three, illustrates:

When I was three or so, my mother and father were separated and I was taken as a ward of the court. My father was an alcoholic; he still is a drunk. So he couldn't take us. I don't know exactly why they took us from my mother. She was pretty young at the time. Maybe she couldn't handle all the responsibility by herself. She probably wanted to have some fun, too.

I grew up partly in juvenile hall, partly in a children's home up north, and partly in a Salvation Army home for kids nobody wants. My mother and grandmother would come up to visit us once in a while— not often, just a couple of times a year. Not my father; we didn't see him again for years.

I used to tell my mother how I hated it in that home and how I wanted to go home with her, but she would tell me that until she had a good home to bring us to, they wouldn't let her take us home. So we just had to stay there.

It sounds as if those were painful years?

Yeah, it wasn't much fun. I hated everybody. I guess I made life pretty miserable for everybody around me because I thought I'd been mistreated. Being little, you get ideas like that, I guess.

I was about eleven when my mother remarried and we got to live with her again. But by then, all of us just didn't fit into the family anymore. We didn't get along with each other; my brothers and I used to fight something terrible. And we didn't get along with my stepfather. He drank a lot, too. It's funny; after all those years, and my mother marries another man who drinks. And then [*hesitating and reddening with embarrassment*], he used to make passes at me, and I couldn't stand it. I hated him, and I hated my mother because she didn't do anything about it. I don't know, maybe she didn't know; maybe she did.

Finally, we all just took off. My older brother joined the service; and I and my younger brother kept running away. Each time I'd run away, they'd catch me and put me back in juvenile hall again. So I spent all those years going back and forth between juvenile hall and home. All I could think of was getting out of that house. As soon as I turned eighteen, I just up and got married. I just had to get away from them all—my family, my parole officer, all of them; and that was the only way I could.

The hard-livers are, in some fundamental way, the nonconformists—those who cannot or will not accept their allotted social status. They are the women and men who rebel against the grinding routine of life; the dulling, numbing experience of going to the same mindless job every day; of struggling with the same problems of how to feed, clothe, and tend the children without adequate resources; of fighting an endless and losing battle with roaches, rats, sore throats, and infected ears. But rooted in the individualistic ethic of American life, the rebellion does not take the form of some constructive collective action directed at changing the social system. Rather it is a personal rebellion against what are experienced as personal constraints.

Thus, the explosive episodes of drinking and violence, the gambling away of a week's wages, the unexplained work absences (Why explain? Who would understand not showing up for that lousy job when the fish are running?), and the sudden, angry quittings. All these may make life harder in the family. But the ability to say "take your damn job and shove it" makes a man feel like a man again, at least for the moment. He can stand tall, at least until he faces the reality that his wife and children won't eat so well next week. He can defer dealing with that reality by getting drunk.

But even for the settled-living families, life was precarious—

uncertain and unpredictable. Fathers who were unemployed or underemployed—out of work or working for wages which left the family just this side of wanting—were the norm:

Tell me something about what life was like in your family when you were growing up.

A thirty-seven-year-old woman, the second child in a family of four, recalls:

It was a good family, not like a lot of others we saw. My folks cared a lot, and they were always trying. But it seems no matter how hard they tried, something went wrong, and we'd get behind. We were dirt poor most of my life. There were always money problems; sometimes there wasn't even enough food.

It seemed like every three months my father was on strike or laid off. [*Laughing.*] I guess that's an exaggeration, but he really was on strike a lot. He was a laborer in construction, and he couldn't afford to be off work like that. Maybe the guys higher up got something out of the strike—you know, the carpenters and plumbers, and those workmen— but people like my dad just lost pay. They never could make it up.

Sometimes, too, there was violence—the angry explosions of people who feel entrapped:

The family was okay. I mean, my father worked steady, and they both tried their best. But life was plenty hectic. My father worked in the mines, and there wasn't much money. There were ten of us kids, and even though for that town we lived in a big house, it certainly wasn't large enough for all of us. So there was a lot of abrasive contact all the time.

The folks had their knock-down drag-outs, and it seemed like us kids were always caught in the middle. My father would take after my mother, and then she'd come after us. There was so much violence in that house. [*Pauses thoughtfully for a moment, then adds*] I was just thinking, most of that violence happened in the winter time when we were crowded together in the house and couldn't get out. At least in the summer, we could all be outside and get away from each other a little bit.

[*Thirty-year-old ironworker.*]

Of course! Poverty and crowded living conditions go together, making a fertile breeding ground for the violent acting out of the anger, the frustration, and the pain of being defined and defining oneself a failure. For the settled livers are, at bottom, the conformists—those who have bought into the system, who believe in the ethic of hard work, who believe in the American myth that everyone can pull themselves up by their bootstraps if only they have the will and the brains. What, then, are such people to say to themselves when they don't succeed? They *know* they have the will. There's little left but to accept that they don't have the brains—a devastating self-image from which all people must seek periodic relief and surcease.

This is one of the most destructive of "the hidden injuries of class" about which Richard Sennett and Jonathan Cobb write so compellingly.[6] Most of the time, the settled livers tend to deal with this injury to personal dignity by containing their anger and pain. But in their effort to bind their wounds—to restore dignity and affirm self—they redefine success so that it is more compatible with their modest accomplishments, and they accumulate possessions as the visible symbols of their achievements and status.[7] Often, however, it's not enough; it doesn't work. Some find the respite they need in angry explosions, some in deep withdrawals. Again and again, the men and women I met recall parents, especially fathers, who were taciturn and unresponsive:

My father was a very quiet man. He almost never talked, even when you asked him a question. He'd sit there like he didn't hear you. Sometimes, an hour later (it was like he'd come out of a spell), he'd look at you and say, "Did you want something?" Most of the time, he just didn't know you were there.

> [*Thirty-one-year-old steelworker,
> the middle child in a family of three.*]

A twenty-five-year-old woman, the oldest in a family of two, recalls:

My father never seemed to talk or be a part of the family. The only thing I can remember that he enjoyed was working in his garden. He'd come home, eat, and go out in the yard almost every night of the year, even when it was raining. Otherwise, he'd just sit quiet for hours, like he wasn't there or something.

It's true that fathers in the professional middle-class homes may also be recalled as silent, as not "part of the family." But none of the adults who grew up in those homes recall the kind of brooding, withdrawn quality that so often describes the experience in a working-class home. The child of a professional father may recall that he was "always working even when he was home"; that he was "preoccupied a lot"; or that he "always seemed to have something on his mind." But that same person also is much more likely than his working-class counterpart to remember some ways in which father participated in family life, even if only to recall the dinner hour as a time for family conversation. Preoccupation, then, would seem to be the most remembered quality about fathers in professional families; withdrawal, the most vivid memory in working-class families.

This, then, is some part of the experience of life as it was lived day-by-day—sometimes chaotic and unpredictable, always difficult. If that was their present, what did the future look like to the children in these families?

When you were little, what did you think you'd like to do or be when you grew up?

A hard question for most people from poor homes—one that focuses sharply on the limitations that poverty exacts upon the future of its victims. Listen to this thirty-two-year-old appliance repairman, the middle child in a family of seven:

We were maybe one step above what you would call white trash. If we thought about it at all, we would have considered ourselves lucky to get through high school. Most of the kids in the family didn't do that.

There was no demand on any of us for any goal. You see, my father wasn't an educated man. He was taken out of school when he was nine, and him not having an education, it kept him from seeing a lot of hopes for his kids. He can hardly write his own name, even now.

37

Oh, I guess he didn't want us to be just ordinary laborers like he was, but it wasn't ever talked about. Like, going to college was never discussed. It never occurred to me to think about it. That was something other kids—rich kids—did. All I knew was that I'd have to work, and I didn't think much about what kind of work I'd be doing. There didn't seem much point in thinking about it, I guess.

In fact, there not only "wasn't much *point* in thinking about it," there was no *way* to think about it. For in order to plan for the future, people must believe it possible to control their fate—a belief that can only be held if it is nourished in experience. That seldom happens in working-class life. Instead, for most, the difficult realities of their lives often limit their very ability to envisage a future. Indeed, it is precisely that inability that most sharply distinguishes the consciousness of the working class from that of the more privileged classes.

For the child—especially a boy—born into a professional middle-class home, the sky's the limit; his dreams are relatively unfettered by constraints. In his earliest conscious moments, he becomes aware of his future and of plans being made for it—plans that are not just wishful fantasies, but plans that are backed by the resources to make them come true. All around him as he grows, he sees men who do important work at prestigious jobs. At home, at school, in the neighborhood, he is encouraged to test the limits of his ability, to reach for the stars.

For most working-class boys, the experience is just the reverse. Born into a family where daily survival is problematic, he sees only the frantic scramble to meet today's needs, to pay tomorrow's rent. Beyond that it's hard for parents to see. In such circumstances, of what can children dream?

The authors of one famous study argue, in fact, that such boys face "a series of mounting disadvantages"—that is, poverty, lack of education and vocational guidance, no role models in prestige occupations, no personal contacts to help push a career along—all come together to create an inability to plan for the future and form a vicious circle from which few ever escape.[8] It is in this process that the class structure is preserved—as if in ice—from generation to generation.

It should be clear by now that the lack of planning to which I refer is not due, as some social scientists insist, to some debilitating inability of the working class to delay gratifications; indeed, there seem to be precious few available to delay.[9] Rather in the context of their lives and daily struggles, looking either backward or forward makes little sense; planning for the future seems incongruous. Consequently, work life generally is not planned; it just happens. A thirty-six-year-old refinery worker, the oldest of four children, recalls:

I didn't think much about it. I just kind of took things as they came. I figured I knew I'd work; I worked most of my life. I started working at real jobs when I was fourteen. I worked in an upholstery place then. I used to carry those big bolts of material, and keep the workers supplied with whatever they needed, and I kept the place clean. That gave me a good idea of what work was all about. There wasn't much point in dreaming. I guess you could say in my family we didn't—maybe I should say couldn't—plan our lives; things just happened.

And from a thirty-three-year-old truck driver who grew up in a series of foster homes, we hear:

In the kind of life I lived, you didn't think about tomorrow. I didn't know where I'd be tomorrow, so how could I plan for it? In fact, I don't think I knew *how* to make plans. I wasn't even so sure about today. Tomorrow just didn't exist; it didn't have any reality.

To the degree that either men or women could answer questions about their hopes for the future, the answers were largely in the realm of fantasy[10]—for the boys: a cowboy, a pilot, a star athlete. But not one man ever recalled thinking of, let alone planning for, a professional career. With fathers, uncles, and neighbors largely in marginal jobs, there were no live models of any other kind of work. Mostly the men say they just expected to grow up, get married, and work just as their fathers had. Even the modest wish to become a policeman takes on the color of an unattainable fantasy. A twenty-eight-year-old machinist, from a family of four children with an intermittently employed father, recalls:

I dreamed I wanted to be a policeman, but I just never followed through with it.

Why was that?

I really didn't think I was smart enough, I guess. I knew you had to go through three, maybe four, years of college. And I don't know, I just kind of let it go.

Even if I *had* thought I was smart enough, there was no way I ever thought about going to college. I guess the really big dream was just to get out of high school and get a job. Things were tough at home. I wanted more than anything else to get some money in my pockets so I could do something, have some fun once in a while. Now I can't figure out why I thought working was such a big deal. But how can you know things like that when you're a kid?

Among the women, a few recall girlhood dreams of being a model or an actress, but most remember wanting only to marry and live happily ever after:[11]

I never had any goals to be anything, except I always figured I'd get married and have kids, and that would be enough for anybody.

The dream of the knight who comes to sweep her off her feet:

I used to fantasize a lot about boys, and I'd dream that one day somebody would come on his white charger and we would fly off and live happily ever after in a vine-covered cottage.

. . . or the prince who rescues Cinderella from ashes and cruelty, was alive and vital for most of these young women when they were children:

When I was about eight or so, I went to live with my oldest brother. I had to clean the house and do all the hard work there, and their own daughter didn't do nothing. Then, if we both got new shoes and she wore hers out faster than I did (and she always did), they gave her mine and I had to wear my old ones. I used to sit in that house and dream about how some day some wonderful man who looked like a prince would come and take me away, and how we'd live happily ever after.

It's not that the girls from middle-class homes dreamed such different dreams. But along with the marriage fantasy, there was for them some sense of striving for their own development. Even if that were related to enhancing marriage prospects (that is, with a college education a girl can make a "better match"), some aspiration related to self existed alongside it. And, in fact, for those middle-class women, marriage came much later since it was deferred until after college. Moreover, once these girls left home for college, they had at least some of the freedom and autonomy young people so deeply desire while, at the same time, they were engaged in an activity that brings status and respect from both family and peers.

For most young working-class girls, on the other hand, getting married was—and probably still is—the singularly acceptable way out of an oppressive family situation and into a respected social status—the only way to move from girl to woman.[12] Indeed, traditionally among girls of this class, being grown up *means* being married. Thus, despite the fact that the models of marriage they see before them don't look like their cherished myths, their alternatives often are so slim and so terrible—a job they hate, more years under the oppressive parental roof—that working-class girls tend to blind themselves to the realities and cling to the fantasies with extraordinary tenacity. For in those fantasies there remains some hope:

Things were so ugly in my family—my father drunk and in a rage, hitting one of us or beating my mother up. My mother worked most of the time. She had to because Daddy couldn't, seeing as how you could never know when he'd be drunk. She'd come home and fix supper, then we'd all sit around and wait and wait. Finally, Mom would give us kids our supper. Eventually my father came home, and if he was drunk, he'd storm around. Maybe he'd knock the pots off of the stove and make a holy mess. Or maybe he'd take out after one of us or my mother.

When I think about it now, it sounds crazy, but honestly, the worse things got at home, the more I used to dream about how I was going to marry some good, kind, wise man who would take care of me; and how we'd have beautiful children; and how we'd live in our nice house; and how we'd always love each other and be happy.

Not so crazy, when one realizes that there were no models in their lives of women who do interesting or rewarding work; indeed, few models of women who do anything but endure:

I used to get mad at my mother because she'd just stay there and take anything my father dished out. She wouldn't protect herself and she wouldn't protect us kids. My father would sometimes rant and rave like a maniac; he would get very irrational and had a lot of brute strength.

But now I think back and I understand her better, and I think maybe I shouldn't have been so mad at her then. She was just as scared as I was, I guess. He used to hit her, too, and shove her around plenty; a lot more than he shoved me around. And when he's so much bigger and stronger, and you got four kids to take care of, what's a woman supposed to do?

"When he's so much bigger and stronger . . . what's a woman supposed to do?" A good question; one it only recently has occurred to social scientists, male or female, to ask.[13] Yet even small girls in many working-class homes already know that men's greater strength is one source of male domination over women.

When the mother worked outside the home, it was at a hard, tedious, often demeaning job from which she returned home tired and angry and with yet another day's work before her as she picked up her household chores:

My mom did domestic work, and it always seemed like she never stopped working. She'd come home and clean the house, and cook dinner, and clean up the dishes, and fix our lunches for the next day. It seemed like no matter what time you woke up at night when we were little, Mom was still up doing something—ironing or something. When we got older, we kids helped some, but there was always more for her to do, it seemed.

And you know, she was never late with a meal. We ate at five-thirty every night of our lives. My father came home at five, and he got cleaned up and had a beer; then we ate. My mother always taught us that you shouldn't keep a man waiting for his supper after a hard day's work. You know, it's only recently that I began to realize that she worked hard all day, too, and nobody *ever* made supper for her. No wonder she was always in a bad mood.

Sometimes, of course, children—especially girls—were expected to take over those chores. One thirty-six-year-old cannery worker, mother of three and married for twenty years, recalls her life, her fantasies, and the paucity of alternatives:

My mom worked on and off when we were growing up. There were five of us kids, and the house we lived in was crowded and a mess all the time. My older sister and I were expected to keep things up—you know, cleaning and picking up, doing the dishes, watching the younger kids, keeping them clean, all that stuff. And let me tell you, doing the wash in those days was a lot different than now. We did it the hard way; I mean, boiling the water and scrubbing the clothes on one of those old-fashioned wash boards. You know, the kind you don't ever see anymore.

And during those years, what did you think you'd like to do or be when you grew up?

All I wanted was just to grow up and get out of there. I used to dream about how I'd grow up and get married and live in one of those big, beautiful houses like they show in the magazines—you know, magazines like *House Beautiful*. God, all the hours I spent looking at those magazines, and dreaming about how I would live in one of those houses with all that beautiful furniture, and everything just right; and how my husband would come home at night; and how I'd look beautiful waiting for him; and how the kids would be pretty and good; and how we'd all be happy together.

Life turns out a lot different in the end, doesn't it? [*Looking down at her hands folded in her lap and speaking softly, shyly.*] I guess you'll think I'm silly, but I still look at those magazines and dream about that life.

Once in a while, a woman did perceive some alternatives, but the circumstances of her life combined with her experiences at school to push her back into her "place."[14] Witness the story of a twenty-five-year-old mother of three who grew up in a family where both parents were alcoholics, and whose memories of childhood are dominated by images of fighting, drunken parents, squabbling siblings, and appalling poverty:

I started working when I was about twelve as a kind of live-in baby-sitter–housekeeper for a family with three little kids. That family was my fantasy; they gave me a kind of an idea of what a different kind of life could be like. You know, it was like they gave me an idea of something I could work for. It was like because of them I knew there was something better going on somewhere.

Given that, what did you think you'd like to do or be when you grew up?

I was a good student, and somehow I could lose myself in school. And I used to love some of my teachers; they knew so much, and everybody treated them with respect. So I used to dream about wanting to be a teacher.

I used to dream about having a family, too; I mean, I dreamed about having children. But it's funny, I never thought about getting married, just about my being a teacher. I actually was in college prep in high school, even though my counselor didn't think it was such a good idea because there was nobody to help me through college.

Then, when I was going into the twelfth grade, my father got sick and went to the hospital. My counselor told me then that she didn't think I would have the strength to go through with going to college all by myself. So she got me a scholarship. It wasn't much of a scholarship; it was to a beauty college instead of to a real college. [*Sadly.*] I don't know; I guess she was right. Anyway, she was sure she was, so I did what she told me. And then, not long after that—I was seventeen—I got married.

In most families, there was only enough money for daily necessities, sometimes not even for those. Yet, interestingly, even where financial need was compelling, it usually was the boys who *had* to work. For the girls, it was often elective; most stayed home and prepared for the life of a housewife. One twenty-eight-year-old woman, now married ten years with three children and employed throughout most of her marriage in a variety of part-time occupations, sums it up neatly:

My brother had to work after school, but I didn't. I never wanted to work, and I didn't have to. After all, boys *have to* learn how to work, but it doesn't make much difference if girls don't learn how because they're going to get married and won't have to.

And so the myth persists. Despite the fact that as long ago as 1960, 60 percent of all the women in the labor force were married, and over 30 percent of all married women living in intact families worked, most girls and their families still believed that they wouldn't "have to."[15] Just as today, even in the face of their own experiences where they work throughout most of their married years, most women define that as "temporary."

The boys, on the other hand, went to work early, partly to help the family:

Things were slim around the house; sometimes there wasn't enough food. By the time I was thirteen, I was working—doing all kinds of odd jobs. We needed the money.

. . . partly to get some pocket money for themselves:

It wasn't any fun not having any money for extras like other kids had. If you wanted something for yourself, or some money so you could have some fun, you just had to go out and get it. And that's what I did. I knew my way around, and by the time I was fourteen, I had my first real job in a lumber yard. After that I always had at least a little money so I could hang around with the guys and do things with them.

. . . and partly because it was one of the ways in which their families prepared them to meet future responsibilities:

We learned young to honor work. That's what it was about in my family—work, all work. I suppose I'm glad about that now, because I see a lot of people who don't know how to work. But on the other side, I didn't like it much then. I didn't have any freedom. I saw other kids my age going out, doing things after school; you know, having fun. [*Pauses uncomfortably.*] And well, I had to go to work.

By the time I was fourteen, I had two jobs. I worked in a bakery from two A.M. until school started. Then I came home and changed my clothes, and I went to school. Then I came home again and changed my clothes again, and I went to work in a gas station.

I'm not complaining, mind you, because now I see that it was good for me. If I didn't have that kind of training, I'd be a lot worse off than I am today. I'm making a good living now, and I know how to take care of myself and my family. My old man knew what he was doing when he made sure I'd grow up and appreciate the value of

money and work. It's just that kids don't know that when it's happening to them, because then all they want is to go out and have some fun.
[*Thirty-one-year-old mechanic,*
father of two, married nine years.]

Were there no tales of happy childhoods? The answer: very few. There are always a few good memories, some families less troubled, more loving than others; but happy childhoods: no. Often people implored, even commanded me, to believe they had happy home lives as children. I tried. I told myself that as an observer from the professional middle class, I couldn't understand what would make a working-class child happy. But that didn't make sense. I recalled my own impoverished background. Yes, there were happy moments—an ice cream cone, a small toy, an infrequent and unexpected family outing, a rare approving remark from a harassed, frightened, and overburdened mother, a few cents occasionally to spend as I would and the exquisite agony of making a choice.

But those were isolated moments, not descriptive of the warp and woof of my life. The dominant memories of childhood for me, as for the people I met, are of pain and deprivation—both material and emotional, for one follows the other almost as certainly as night follows day.

Parents who must meet each day with worry and fear are too preoccupied with the existential and material realities of life to have much left in the way of emotional support for their children. To them, it often seems the deepest possible expression of love just to do what they must to keep the family together. "You're lucky you're not in an orphanage," my widowed mother would remind me angrily—or at least so it seemed to my child's ears. And with terror I thought, "I am," even as I hated her for the threat. Today, I know it was a statement of her love—hard for a child to experience, but true nevertheless.

There's pain in such acknowledgments, and a terrible sense of disloyalty—even for me—to parents who did their best in a world where the cards were stacked against them. So we try to tell ourselves—and even more, to tell strangers—it wasn't so bad. But no matter how hard we try, it comes out "bad." The people I met tried; and I tried to help them:

Tell me some of the good things you remember about growing up in your family.

Most often the question was met with a series of halting attempts to enumerate the "good" memories. Usually, the conversation limped to an uncomfortable end:

We used to go out for a ride on Sunday sometimes. It was nice to be all together in the car.

. . . or:

I remember my father coming home sometimes and taking us all down to the railroad station to watch the trains. I liked that. I liked being with him.

But the car rides didn't happen often, and this father at least usually came home too drunk to go to the railroad station—those things had already been said with passion and force. This new information seemed insubstantial—to them as well as to me—born of a sentimental yearning to rewrite history so as to protect self and parents from exposure:

Tell me some of the good things you remember about growing up in your family.

Struggling thoughtfully with the question, one thirty-five-year-old machinist spoke more openly than most—a poignant truth that applied to most of the others as well:

It's hard to remember the good things as if they were a real part of my life because they didn't happen most of the time. I'm trying to think about whether we were happy or not, and it's hard. I can't say because I don't think we even thought about things like that in those days.

These, then, are the early experiences of the women and men who fill the pages of this book; the story of the families of the families I met. For all, even the most settled livers, life was often mean and hard—hanging in a delicate balance, easily upset. For in a society not committed to the full employment of its work force, work often was not available to the men, and parents could not adequately clothe or care for their children. Thus, even where children recall a loving, stable home, they also recall at least periods of unemployment, poverty, and deprivation.

Such periods take their toll on family life—on the self-image of the man as the "responsible" head of the household, on his self-respect, and, indeed, on the respect accorded him in the family. For if the men and women in these families accept the belief that anybody can make it if he has the brains and the will, then the man who can't must be seen as lacking—a failure. In a society where the roles in the family are rigidly fixed and stereotyped according to sex—where it's *his* job to support the family, *her* job to feed and tend it—the man who cannot perform his assigned task is stigmatized, both by himself and by those around him.

Thus, whether settled- or hard-living, most of the working-class adults I spoke with recall childhoods where, at best, "things were tight" financially. They recall parents who worked hard, yet never quite made it; homes that were overcrowded; siblings or selves who got into "trouble"; a preoccupation with the daily struggle for survival that precluded planning for a future. Whether they recall angry, discontented, drunken parents, or quiet, steady, "always-there" parents, the dominant theme is struggle and trouble. These realities not only reflect the past, but dominate the present—consciously or unconsciously underpinning the alternatives children can perceive, the choices they make, and the way they play out their roles in the new families they form as adults.

4

And So
They Were Wed

THEY WERE YOUNG when they met—sometimes just in high school, sometimes just out. They were young when they married for the first time—on the average, eighteen for the women, twenty for the men; the youngest, fifteen and sixteen respectively. And they were young when they divorced and remarried. One fourth of the women and one fifth of the men were married once before.[1] And although the present marriages average almost nine years, the mean age of the women is only twenty-eight; of the men, thirty-one:

How did you decide that this was the person you wanted to marry?

Most people hesitate, not quite sure how to respond to that question. When the answers do come, usually they are the expected ones—those that affirm the romantic ideals of American courtship and marriage. "We fell in love." "We were attracted to each other." "We were having fun." "He was the right one." As the conversation continues, however, the stories they tell about how they met and why they married are inconsistent with those first socially acceptable responses.

Some describe meetings and matings that seemed to happen by chance:

We met at the show where we all used to go on Friday nights. We started to go together right away. Four months later, I got pregnant so we got married.

[*Twenty-eight-year-old housewife, mother of four, married eleven years.*]

. . . or marriages that took place almost by accident, without choice or volition:

I don't know exactly why I married her instead of somebody else. I guess everybody always knows they're going to have to get married. I mean, everybody has to some time, don't they? What else is there to do but get married?

[*Thirty-four-year-old maintenance man, father of five, married thirteen years.*]

Some—the young divorcees—often married because they were exhausted from the struggle to support and care for their small children. One such woman, a thirty-one-year-old mother of four, married eleven years to her second husband, was divorced at nineteen. With a husband who couldn't have supported her even if he wanted to, and a family who "would have helped, but [who] had their own problems," she recalls:

I really wasn't sure I wanted to get married again. But financially, it was terrible. I got no support at all. I think even then I knew that I probably would have taken a lot more time about remarrying if I didn't have those really awful financial problems.

I was so tired of working, and I felt like I was giving my kids so little. I began to be afraid that they wouldn't even know who their mother was. It was to the point where I was picking them up, taking them home, giving them a bath, putting them to bed, putting up my hair, and going to bed myself. I was too tired for anything else—not for them and not for me. On the weekends it was just about all I could do to get things straight in the house and get ready for the next week. Rest? Who knew about that then!

It finally all caved in on me when I came to pick up my kids after work one night, and they didn't want to go home with me. [*Near tears.*] Can you believe it? They wanted to stay with the baby-sitter. I couldn't even blame them. I sure wasn't any fun to be with; and it was getting so they knew her better than me.

So Johnny was around, and he really was different than my first husband. I figured he was a responsible guy, and he cared about me and my kids. So we got married. And, you know, now I still have to work. [*Then quickly, as if wanting to take the words back.*] But it's not as bad; in fact, you can't compare it. I work only part time, and we don't have such awful money problems. Besides, I don't have to do *everything* all by myself. Johnny helps out with the kids and stuff when I need him to.

How did you decide this was the person you wanted to marry?

Often wives and husbands disagree. For just as Jessie Bernard in her book *The Future of Marriage* found two marriages—his and hers—for many couples there are also two courtships—his and hers. A twenty-nine-year-old mother of three, married eleven years, recalls:

We met at the coffee shop where some of us kids used to hang out. I guess we knew right away because we began to go steady right after. We just fell in love right away.

I thought he was a big man. I was still in high school, and it was like— you know, he wasn't just another kid in school. He got out the year before, and he was working and making lots of money (it seemed like lots then anyway), and we could go out and do cool things. Then after a couple of months, he gave me his class ring. Boy, I was surprised. It was really big, so I put a tape around it so it wouldn't fall off. Then that wasn't comfortable, so after a while, I had the ring made smaller, and I figured if he didn't say anything—I mean, if he said it was okay to do it—this must be a sure thing. And it was! And we got married.

Her thirty-year-old husband tells the story differently:

We met at this place and I kind of liked her. She was cool and kind of fun to be with. Before I knew it, we were going steady. I don't exactly know how it happened. I had this class ring from high school and she kept wanting me to give it to her. So finally one night I took it off and did it. And the next thing I knew, she took it down and had it made smaller. She made a big thing out of it, and so did her family. Don't get me wrong; I liked her good enough. But I just didn't think about getting married—not then anyhow. But then, after we were going together for almost a year, it just seemed like the thing to do. So we did.

Over and over such differences in recollections appear, each sex playing out its stereotypic role—the women more often focusing on the romantic view of the meeting and the marrying, the men on the "I-don't-know-how-she-caught-me" view. Typical of these differences is this couple, both twenty-six, married eight years. The wife:

We just knew right away that we were in love. We met at a school dance, and that was it. I knew who he was before. He was real popular; everybody liked him. I was so excited when he asked me to dance, I just melted.

The husband:

She was cute and I liked her, but I didn't have any intention of getting married. I went to this school dance and she was there. I sort of knew who she was, but I'd never talked to her before. Then that night she worked it so that her girlfriend who I knew introduced us. I felt kind of funny knowing she wanted me to dance with her, so I asked her. That started it.

Then, I don't know, we just got to seeing each other; she always seemed to be there. And like I said, she was cute and fun. By the time we graduated, everybody was just expecting us to get married. I thought about breaking it off; I even tried, but she cried so much I couldn't stand it.

Although both wives and husbands frequently start a discussion about how they came to choose their mates with a certain defensiveness and a seeming lack of awareness, the women more often than the men move rather quickly to demonstrate a sophisticated self-awareness, as this couple, parents of three children, married thirteen years, shows. The wife:

I guess the reason we got married was because he was out of a job, and he was being kicked out of his boardinghouse.

You weren't planning to marry, then?

Well, we had never really talked about marriage although maybe we both kind of knew it would happen. At the time it all happened kind of sudden. I said, "What are you going to do about this situation?" He said, "I don't know; maybe we could get married." I said, "Okay, let's do it." And we did.

But what made you say "okay"? What attracted you most about him?

I think the fact that he liked me. I guess that was really important to me. I didn't date very much, and then this guy came along, and he liked me. Also, I guess I felt needed; that's important, especially when you're just a kid. Nothing makes you feel more important. [*Pausing reflectively, then adding.*] Now that I look at him, I also see that he reminds me very much of my dad. I suppose that was part of it, too, even though back then I certainly didn't know it.

The husband:

What do you mean, how did we decide? *We* didn't really decide; *she* did mostly, if you know what I mean.

But what made you go along? What attracted you most about her?

I don't know. We were seeing each other every day, and what else was there to do but to get married. [*With a tight, angry laugh.*] She was hard to get, I guess. A lot of girls play that way, you know, because they know it gets to a guy. She sure knew how to get to me.

Undoubtedly, all these explanations speak to some part of the truth. Like women and men in all classes, however, these couples marry for a complex of reasons, many of them only dimly understood, if at all. First among those reasons may be the social-psychological milieu in which we all come to adulthood—the nuclear family which promises (even if it doesn't always deliver) intimacy, and leaves us yearning for more; a society in which almost everyone marries, and where those who don't are viewed as deviant and deficient. So we come together because we need to feel close to someone; because it's what most of us do at a certain stage of life; because it's the accepted and the expected, the thing to do if one is finally to be grown up. Still, there is a quality of urgency among the young people of the working class that is not so evident in a comparable group of middle-class, college-educated men and women—an urgency that is rooted in their class history and family backgrounds.

There are those—women and men—from hard-living families, aching with pain, needing a place in which to feel safe, a place to which they belong:

My mother left us when I was nine. It was bad enough living in the house with just my father, but then when he got married, it was just awful.

He married a real bad woman. They met in a bar. They both drink a lot—too much. And a little while after they met, she moved into our house with her two kids. I was so ashamed, I could have died—them living together in our house like that. After a year or so, they got married and things got even worse. She's got a foul mouth and she was really awful to us kids. She'd curse us and call us the most awful, terrible names. When she got drunk, she'd be even worse. She'd knock us down and kick us while she was cursing us out.

It wasn't much of a family before she came, but it was a whole lot better. My father tried the best he could. Even though he was drunk a lot of the time, he wasn't mean. And we all felt we had *somebody*. After she came, there was just nobody, nobody.

I used to dream all the time about a home of my own. I wanted so much to have a place where I'd be secure. So when I met Barney, I thought, "Here's a guy who loves me and needs me." And that felt so good so we got married.

[*Twenty-four-year-old sales clerk,
mother of two, married seven years.*]

It was not only the children of hard-living families who married young, however. Whether hard-living or settled, most lived in relatively poor neighborhoods where parents saw around them many young people whose lives were touched by the pain and delinquency that often accompanies a life of poverty.[2] In such an environment, parents tend to be terribly fearful about their children's future—fearful that they will lose control, that the children will wind up "on the streets," or worse yet, in jail. Therefore, they try to draw the reins of control very tight—keeping a close watch, imposing strict rules about manners and behavior, strict regulations about time and activities.[3]

But these same parents and children live in a society where respect is accorded to the financially successful, where the mark of ability is represented by one's annual income. Such parents, believing that they haven't "made it," feel unsure of themselves, their worth, and their wisdom—a perception that often is shared by their children.

No words are necessary to convey these feelings. Children know. They know when their teachers are contemptuous of their family background, of the values they have been taught at home. They know that there are no factory workers, no truck drivers, no construction workers who are the heroes of the television shows they watch.[4] They know that their parents are not among those who "count" in America. And perhaps most devastating of all, they know that their parents know these things as well. Why else would they urge their children on to do "better," to be "more" than they are? Why else would they carry within them so much generalized and free-floating anger—anger that lashes out irrationally at home, anger that is displaced from the world outside where its expression is potentially dangerous?

Such children, then, not only are exposed to the values of the larger society which denigrate their parents' accomplishments and way of life, but those values also are taught to them in implicit and explicit ways by their own parents. Under such circumstances, it is difficult, indeed, for working-class parents either to provide acceptable parental role models for their children or to enforce their authority.

The acceptance and transmission of definitions of self-worth that are tied to material accomplishments and acquisitions is one of the unacknowledged and most painful of the "hidden injuries"[5] that this society has visited upon the working class. When the insecurities that derive from these injuries are denied, as they most often are (for who can face the humiliation of being debased in one's own and one's children's eyes), the response is to cling ever more tightly to old and familiar ways, and to shout ever more loudly about their value.

It is of such economic and socio-cultural realities that childrearing patterns are born. And it is to those experiences that we must look to explain the origins of childrearing patterns in working-class families that, on the surface, appear rigid and repressive. In that context, the widely accepted theories that their authoritarian personalities are responsible for the observed relations between parents and children become highly questionable.[6] Instead, those theories seem to reflect the inability of their middle-class creators to understand either the context in which the behavior takes place or its subjective meaning to the actors involved.

These parenthetical comments aside, the fact remains that most working-class parents feel free to relax their vigilance only after children marry. For the young in those families, then, marriage becomes a major route to an independent adult status and the privileges that accompany it.

The fact that life is different for the college-educated, middle-class young needs little documentation; our television screens and newspaper headlines shouted the news to us through the decade of the sixties. The young people of that class find outside of marriage at least some of the independence and adult privileges that are available to the working-class young only within marriage. Thus, the children of the professional middle class consistently marry later. Among those I met, the average age at marriage was twenty-three for the women, twenty-five for the men.

In other ways, too, the children of these classes have different experiences and are expected to assume different responsibilities within the family. In the working-class home, for example, the family economy generally rests on at least some help from grown or growing sons. Thus, boys are expected to work early and contribute a substantial part of their earnings to the family. And although they may have more freedom from certain kinds of parental surveillance and restraints than their sisters, they, too, generally live at home—in houses that are too small to permit even minimal privacy—until they marry:

I had to work from the time I was thirteen and turn over most of my pay to my mother to help pay the bills. By the time I was nineteen, I had been working for all those years and I didn't have anything—*not a thing*. I used to think a lot about how when I got married, I would finally get to keep my money for myself. I guess that sounds a little crazy when I think about it now because I have to support the wife and kids. I don't know *what* I was thinking about, but I never thought about that then. But even so, my wife doesn't get it all, you can bet on that.

[*Thirty-three-year-old automobile painter, father of three, married thirteen years.*]

For the girls, the culture dictates that "nice" girls remain under the parental roof until a husband comes to take them away. For them, there is no other road to womanhood and independence:

I was only seventeen when I got married the first time. I met him just after I graduated from high school, and we were married six weeks later. I guess that was kind of fast. I don't know, maybe it was rebound. I had been going with a boy in high school for a couple of years, and we had just broken up. Actually, I guess the biggest thing was that there was no other way if I wanted to get away from that house and to be a person in myself instead of just a kid in that family. All three of us girls married when we were very young, and I guess we all did it for the same reason. All three of us got divorced, too, only for my sisters it didn't work out as lucky as for me. They've both had a lot of trouble.

[*Thirty-year-old housewife, mother of three, married nine years.*]

It is true that several couples did speak of living together before marriage, but in all but one instance, the women had been married before and had borne one or more children. One of those women said of that period of her life:

We met and things just clicked, so we started living together right away. I know that sounds terrible, but that's the way it was. Before I'd ever gotten married, I'd never have thought of doing anything like that. But after all, I'd already been married. And anyway, we only did it for a couple of months; then we got married.

Mostly, however, working-class teen-agers chafe under living conditions that are oppressive and parental authority that feels repressive. Marriage often is seen as the only escape—a route they take very early in their lives.[7]

57

But there are still other components to the urgency to marry. For while parents try desperately to circumscribe and control their children's behavior, to make them into respectful and respectable adults, the children—especially the boys—often get into youthful trouble and are themselves frightened by those experiences. Thus, there are the men who recall those years as a time when they were facing the choice between a hard-living and a settled-living life, and who saw a "good woman" as the way to the settled-living path:

I was seventeen and hanging around with a loose crowd, and all of us got into a lot of trouble—you know, with the police and all that kind of stuff. I had this girlfriend who was also seventeen. She quit school when she was about fifteen, I guess, and she already had a kid (he was about two, I guess) when I knew her. So you can see, I was just asking for it, running around with people like that.

I already had some run-ins with the police, just some juvenile, y'know, kid stuff. And then I got picked up for a heavy rap—robbery. That really scared me. While I was waiting for my trial and wondering what was going to happen to me (I used to have nightmares about going to jail), I met Ann. She was the sweetest, most honest, innocent girl I ever knew. I just knew I needed a girl like her to help me change my ways. She did, too. I beat that rap, and after that Ann would come and pick me up and take me to school every day; then she'd wait for me to take me home.

We both finished high school, and I'm proud of that because nobody else in our families did. Then we got jobs and saved our money; and then we got married. I've never been sorry either, because she still keeps me straight.

[*Twenty-seven-year-old mechanic,*
father of two, married eight years.]

Not an exceptional story when one considers that well over one third of the men and 10 percent of the women told of juvenile records—four boys and two girls being defined by the authorities as incorrigibles by age twelve or thirteen, the rest held on a variety of charges ranging from petty theft, to breaking and entering, to grand theft, to assault with a deadly weapon. These charges, which sound so serious, often grow out of such activities as breaking into a vacant house, stealing a two-by-four from a construction site, getting into a street fight, or joy-riding in a stolen car. As one young man, telling of his troubles with the police, said:

You know, they always put those terrible names on it. They always make it sound so much worse than it is.

Not always; it depends on who is getting into trouble. Several men in a comparable group of professional middle-class adults recalled similar activities, yet not one had a juvenile record. Usually, they were not even picked up. On the rare occasion when they were, they were released immediately into the custody of their parents, leading one to assume that the police tend to view such behavior differently depending upon the class composition of the neighborhood in which it is found. In working-class neighborhoods of any color, these behaviors are called crimes; in middle-class neighborhoods, they are just boyish pranks.[8]

The rate of juvenile arrests among the working-class people I met suggests a very high level of police activity in white working-class communities—activity about which we hear almost nothing. We are accustomed to the cry of police harassment from black communities whose young people also have a very high rate of arrests. But such high juvenile arrest rates in white communities catch us by surprise since they receive so little publicity. Partly, that may be because whites experience black crime as more dangerous to the society than white crime and, therefore, attend less to the latter. Partly, and not unrelated to this kind of racist consciousness among whites, it may be a matter of what the media consider news. And partly, it may indicate a less troubled relationship between the police and white working-class communities —perhaps because policemen are often white and working class in origin. The last may also be the reason why—in contrast to black youth who tend to see the police as an alien and repressive enemy who harass and victimize them without cause—the whites tend to accept police definitions of themselves and to agree that they "got what was coming." One man, aged twenty-four, recalling his juvenile troubles, says:

Boy, I always felt like a big man every time I got into trouble. I got mad when I got caught sometimes, but I always knew the cops were right and I was wrong.

Another, aged thirty-nine, says flatly:

I had plenty of run-ins with the police, but I can't say I didn't get
what was coming to me. I got what I deserved, being the
smart-alecky kid I was.

Finally, there are those—44 percent of the couples to whom I
talked—who married because the woman became pregnant, another statistic that seems extraordinarily high but that is so prevalent among working-class youth that it is experienced as
commonplace.[9] Speaking of his first marriage, a thirty-one-year-
old machinist, now in a seven-year-old second marriage, remembers:

I had gone with this girl for two years, and I suppose we expected
to get married, but not yet. She was eighteen and I was nineteen when
she got pregnant. Once that happened, there was nothing else to do
but get married. My one consolation was that I outlasted everybody
else. Everybody I knew then was getting married because the girl got
pregnant; nobody got married without that. And most of them were
getting caught a lot sooner than I did.

"Getting caught"—a phrase that was used over and over again:

I got caught right away; it really happened quick. A lot of people I
know got away with it much longer.
> [*Twenty-two-year-old housewife, mother of two children,*
> *married six years.*]

We had been fooling around for a few months, then all of a sudden,
she got caught.
> [*Thirty-year-old cook's helper,*
> *father of three, married nine years.*]

I felt so mad because I got caught when other people were doing the
same thing and getting away with it. My sister-in-law and a couple of
my girl friends were doing it, too, and they didn't get caught so they
got to have a big wedding, and to be all dressed up like a bride and all
that stuff that I wanted so bad and couldn't have because I got caught.
> [*Twenty-four-year-old clerk, mother of one, married six years.*]

"Getting caught," with its clear implication of an accident. What
does it really mean when 80 percent of these couples engaged in

sexual relations before marriage—a figure that accords with the recent literature documenting the increase over earlier generations in the rate of premarital sex. Since class and education breaks differ in these studies, none shows data that are directly comparable to mine. But the best known, Morton Hunt's *Sexual Behavior in the 1970s*, reports that among his married respondents aged twenty-five–thirty-four, 92 percent of the men and 65 percent of the women *at all educational* levels experienced premarital coitus, not necessarily with their present spouse.[10]

But the focus on the *rate* of behavior or the *change* from earlier generations, while both impressive and sensational, ignores the way in which people *experience* their behavior. And among the men and women in this study one thing is quite clear: while most people talked relatively openly about their premarital sexual experiences, most of the women, at least, were not free of guilt about them. Indeed, only one woman spontaneously commented positively about the experience of premarital sex with her husband:

I think it's a hundred percent better to have it. I mean, I don't think you should sleep with just anybody, but I think it's better. If Joe and I had gotten married and had never had anything before, it could've been a disaster. I wouldn't like to marry a man and not know anything about what he needs or how he was; and I'd rather he knew something about me, too. Otherwise, I might be afraid of failing him, or maybe he might fail me. You know, I don't mean to sleep with just everybody and anybody, but if you fall in love. . . .
[*Twenty-five-year-old mother of two,
married five years.*]

A more typical response came from a woman who still speaks with pain of that period in her life:

I was raised quite a strict Catholic, and I had many guilt feelings about having sex before we were married. Then when I got pregnant, I was so upset I almost died. It took me quite a while to get over those terrible feelings, and I still have problems.
[*Thirty-year-old mother of three,
married twelve years.*]

Another woman, aged twenty-six, married seven years, says:

My sexual adjustment after we were married was very hard. I think I felt guilty about what I had done before. I really felt terrible about it, and I just couldn't enjoy it because I felt so bad. In fact, I still have trouble with it, and I worry about what my husband is *really* thinking about me because I let him have me before we were married.

"I let him have me before we were married"—words that suggest the very traditional ways in which so many of these working-class women think about and experience their sexual activities; words that suggest their bodies are something to be given away at the socially mandated moment; words that were not heard from the college-educated middle-class women. In fact, one of the interesting class differences is that the middle-class women—72 percent of whom also engaged in premarital coitus—generally spoke with less guilt about it. Partly, that may be due to class differences in the *expressed* attitudes about such behavior. Among the working-class women—even though people around them engaged in premarital intercourse; even though they, too, were doing so—there seemed to be a wider gap than in the middle class between the ideal statements of the culture and the reality of the behavior. Thus, among the working-class women, there was a greater sense that they were doing "wrong," an act to hide in shame from the world around them.[11]

Such fears and the feelings that accompany them are mirrored in the women who resisted premarital intercourse, all of whom showed a decided sense of relief that they had not "given in," partly because it enabled them to feel superior to friends or sisters:

I wanted so bad to have a white wedding and to not have to say he had to marry me. My sisters, they had to get married, and it was *so* important to me not to have to. I didn't want ever to lose my self-respect like so many girls I knew did.

[*Twenty-seven-year-old typist, married eight years.*]

. . . and partly because experience has taught them that the women who did often were stigmatized and demeaned in the eyes of their husbands:

I'm very glad we didn't because I've heard his friends throw it back in their wives' faces now. And when I've heard that, I think, "Boy, am I glad he doesn't have that as a weapon to use on me."

[*Twenty-eight-year-old housewife,*
married ten years.]

These concerns suggest that the "good girl–bad girl" split remains alive for many of these women, and that their fears of being tagged with the "bad girl" label are rooted in social reality and reinforced in interactions with their men who "throw it back in their wives' faces." So deep is this fear, in fact, that it plays a vital part in most of the premarital pregnancies. In this era of The Pill, over three-quarters of the women who became pregnant before marriage pleaded innocent of knowledge about birth-control measures. Some may actually have known nothing. But for most, it turned out that it wasn't that they didn't know, but rather that they had believed that only "bad girls" engage in such advance planning. One woman in her early twenties, married five years, put it this way:

You know, I was really an innocent. I thought only bad girls went out and got birth-control pills. I would never have done anything like that.

Another twenty-six-year-old, married eight years, said:

I was just a dumb kid. I didn't know hardly anything at all. And I certainly wasn't the kind of girl who'd go out and get pills or something like that.

The implication here is that unmarried sex is forgivable if she is carried away on the tide of some great, uncontrollable emotion— forgivable, that is, because she succumbed to a natural force stronger than she; she just couldn't help herself. In that context, birth-control planning, implying as it does preparation for the sex act, is incompatible with her definition of self as a "good girl." The formulation goes something like this: "good girls" do but don't plan; "bad girls" do and plan.

Viewed from this perspective, few, if any, of these pregnancies could be said to be accidental. Indeed, if we shift focus from the women to the men, we see that they, too, were participants in what appears to be an unconscious drama of getting pregnant and getting married. Both men and women shared the widespread fantasy that "It couldn't happen to me." Both repeated one version or another of, "A lot of people I know got away with it, at least for a lot longer than I did"; or, "I just never thought about it happening to me." Not unexpectedly, however, when pushed about what they *did* think would happen, the women were more open than the men, more able to own their behavior, too quick to take *sole* responsibility for the pregnancy. One woman who became pregnant at seventeen explained how it happened:

I guess I was really stupid. I wasn't taking precautions; we'd just do withdrawal. I guess we'd been sleeping together for about six months when one time I just said, "Leave it in; don't take it out." And I got caught.

The use of the first-person pronoun is striking. It seems not to have occurred to her that her partner in the act might share some responsibility for protecting against an unwanted pregnancy. Small wonder, however, since social attitudes generally assume that since it is the woman who gets pregnant, it behooves her to take care—an attitude shared by the man in this family who lamented:

I felt like I got cornered, and I still get mad at her for that sometimes, even now. I never could figure out what she was thinking about, doing that. I sure wish she'd had enough sense to use some birth control.

What, one wonders, was this young man thinking about when he failed to have "enough sense" to do so? But it occurs to neither wife nor husband to ask him that question about his role in this "accidental" pregnancy.

While we can speculate about the underlying psychological causes of these pregnancies, once again, the socio-cultural context in which these young people live gives us more grounded clues. Most come from poor families, live in homes with little or no privacy, feel hemmed in by parental restraints, and yearn for the freedom, independence, and adult status that marriage seems to offer. A young woman, married at nineteen, says:

I thought finally there'd be no one telling me what to do anymore.

A young man, married at twenty:

I wanted to have something of my own finally. And I wanted to get my old man off my back, to be able to do what I wanted without having to answer to him all the time.

When asked directly to examine the reasons for their premarital pregnancies, however, the women speak more readily than the men, with more awareness of their needs and motivations. No surprise in a culture where women are trained from birth to attend to the emotional side of life, and men, the instrumental side. Exploring the "why's" of her behavior, one woman who became pregnant at eighteen mused:

I think I was ready to move out of the house, and I knew the only way I could do that was to get married. [*Looking down at her hands hesitantly.*] Do you think that had something to do with my getting pregnant? I gotta admit, inside myself I was really thrilled. I wanted to be married, and I wanted a baby. I was scared to death to tell my parents, but I was really very happy. Wow! I hardly ever thought about those things before. I sure never thought I'd dare tell anybody that.

Another, pregnant at seventeen and trying to understand that event in her life, said:

I've wondered a lot about why that happened to me. I read somewhere that you psychologists think that everything that happens to us is our fault. I mean, that we sort of do things to ourselves. Maybe that's true sometimes, not all the time, but sometimes. I sure did want to get out of that house, but my father would never stand for us girls going anyplace without being married. And I just knew I *had* to get away.

But how could you be sure that getting pregnant meant that you'd get married?

She looked puzzled, as if the question made no sense, then replied:

I don't understand. Of course if you get pregnant, you get married; everybody does. Everybody just expected us to get married when I got pregnant—my parents, his parents, our friends.

Her husband confirmed that perception:

I always figured if I messed around with anybody where it happened, I'd have to marry her. All of us guys did.

There were, of course, some pregnancies among those who did use birth control that may have been genuine accidents—cases in which the women, while never doubting that the men would marry them, vainly sought a way out. But they were defeated by a culture that offers no real options. One twenty-eight-year-old mother of three recalls that time:

When I found out I was pregnant, I didn't tell anyone but my girl-friend—not my parents, not my boyfriend, nobody. I thought I would go to some unwed mother's home and have the baby and then come back and say I was on vacation. I suppose that sounds silly now, but I wasn't able to make any other plans.

Did you ever consider abortion?

Never! I could never do that. God, I remember even now how terri-fied I was. I kept thinking it couldn't be true. I remember even thinking that I would take my mom's car and drive it off a cliff. I knew he'd marry me; I never doubted that. *But I didn't want to get married.* I wanted to *do* things, and to *have* things. I never had any clothes. In fact, it always seemed like I had less money, less everything, than anybody else. I don't mean it was my parents' fault; they gave us what they had. They just didn't have much.

I still remember how much I didn't want to get married. I wanted to get a job and have some things. I was afraid if I got married it would be the end of my chance for a better life. I wasn't wrong about that either.

But my girlfriend kept arguing with me, and finally she told my boy-friend. They both kept saying that I had to get married, and that I couldn't go away. Finally, they told my parents, and then it was all of them against me. So I got married. It never did work; we got divorced less than two years later. But by then I had two children.

What a mess!

Some of the men also spoke of their panic on hearing the news:

I just wasn't ready for that. I was too young; I was too irresponsible;
I didn't want to settle down. I looked at myself and I thought, "How
did you get here?" I just didn't know what to do. And then at the
same time, I knew there was nothing else I *could* do. No matter what
I thought, I knew I'd have to marry her.

One recalled the wedding grimly:

It's hard to think about it. I don't remember too much of that whole
period. Something you don't want to remember, you just don't
remember. I do remember that I was very nervous at the wedding. I
felt like screaming and running out, but there was just no way out.

Retrospectively, several said that they felt they had been entrapped and might do otherwise if they had it to do over again:

I'm not sure what I'd do if I had to face that again. A guy can't
help but feel he got trapped into getting married when a girl gets
pregnant like that. I don't know, maybe if I knew what I know now,
I wouldn't marry her.

But most would agree with the man who said flatly:

If a girl got pregnant, you married her. There wasn't no choice. So
I married her.

Not one person, woman or man, even considered abortion—
generally not because of religious scruples, but because the idea,
they said, was "disgusting," "impossible," "not a choice"; or because it "just never occurred" to them.[12] Not one seriously considered *not* getting married. Despite the disclaimers of some of
them, for most of the men as well as the women, marriage appears
to have been the desired outcome. The culture, we know, inhibits
men from giving voice to their needs for nurturance and to their
fantasies about marriage and family, while encouraging women to
do so. Women, therefore, find those dreams, needs, and motiva-

tions more accessible to their consciousness. But the men's behavior suggests that their unspoken, perhaps unconscious, dreams may not be so different. Thus, marriage comes young; courtships generally are short—counted in weeks or months, rarely years— even when not terminated by a pregnancy. For like young people in all classes, in all cultures, these young working-class men and women strive toward manhood and womanhood. And while what constitutes those estates differs in many ways, they are alike in one fundamental aspect. Both are tied closely to marriage and parenthood in the American culture—values that may be changing, but that still find their clearest and liveliest expression in the white working class.

CHAPTER
5

Marriage: The Dream and the Reality– The Beginning Years

When I got married, I suppose I must have loved him, but at the time, I was busy planning the wedding and I wasn't thinking about anything else. I was just thinking about this big white wedding and all the trimmings, and how I was going to be a beautiful bride, and how I would finally have my own house. I never thought about problems we might have or anything like that. I don't know even if I ever thought much about him. Oh, I wanted to make a nice home for Glen, but I wasn't thinking about how anybody did that or whether I loved him enough to live with him the rest of my life. I was too busy with my dreams and thinking about how they were finally coming true.

[Thirty-year-old typist, mother of three,
married eleven years.]

SO THE ODYSSEY STARTS—each partner not thinking much about the other, each wrapped up in his or her own dreams. For her, the realization of her womanhood—a home and family of her own. For him, the fulfillment of his manhood—a wife to care for him, sons to emulate him, and daughters to adore him. For both, an end to separateness, to loneliness.

With luck, the first few months seem to fulfill the dream. Even though she may be working, it's considered a temporary state. Her dominant emotional energy centers on the tasks of home building; his, on bringing home a pay check sufficient to the demands. Each night he comes home tired, but happy to be greeted warmly by a loving wife.

The few who are older when married—where the men already are established in trades—are spared the need to deal with economic problems at once. Similarly, those who were married before have laid aside some of their naïve expectations and are better prepared to meet the problems inherent in any new marriage. But most are married very young and with little understanding of what they're getting into. For them, the dream fades quickly before the harsh and tedious realities of everyday life.

The men, most barely out of their teens, are often intermittently employed at unstable, low-paying jobs. The few who have settled on a trade are only just beginning to find their way into it; the jobs they hold usually are unsteady, not protected by seniority. For them, being married means drastic changes in lifestyle and self-concept:

Was there some period of adjustment after you were married?

Was there? Wow! Before I got married, I only had to do for myself; after, there was somebody else along all the time. I mean, before, there was my family but that was different. They weren't there *all the time*; and even though I had to help out at home, they weren't absolutely depending on me.

Then, I suddenly found I had to worry about where we'd live and whether we had enough money, and all those things like that. Before, I could always get a job and make enough money to take care of me and give something to the house. Then, after we got married, I suddenly had all those responsibilities. Before, it didn't make a difference if I didn't feel like going to work sometimes. Then, all of a sudden, it made one hell of a difference because the rent might not get paid or, if it got paid, there might not be enough food money.

But since your family was poor, you already knew something about things like that, didn't you?

70

Yeah, but it was different. That was my father's responsibility. I even sometimes was mad at him when I was a kid because he didn't do better by us. And, I don't know, maybe I just always figured I'd be more of a man than he was. I mean, I guess I always knew that's what getting married meant, that I'd have to take on all those responsibilities. But it's different when it really happens to you.

> [*Thirty-year-old refinery operative,*
> *father of three, married ten years.*]

While different in content, for the women, being married means an equally wrenching confrontation between fantasy and reality. Most, still in their teens, and either already pregnant or quick to become so, almost immediately find themselves struggling with the task of managing a household and feeding a family on an inadequate income:

Was there some period of adjustment after you were married?

Yeah, I don't know how we survived that period. The first thing that hit us was all those financial problems. *We were dirt poor.* Here I'd gotten married with all those dreams and then I got stuck right away trying to manage on $1.50 an hour—and a lot of days he didn't work very many hours.

It felt like there was nothing to life but scrimping and saving; only there wasn't any saving, just scrimping.

But since your family was poor, you already knew something about things like that, didn't you?

Yeah, sure I did. I know it doesn't make sense. I mean, when I look back now, I know it doesn't make sense. But then, I just wanted so much for it to be different for us that I believed it would be even though I knew Dick wasn't making much money.

That's part of the trouble—people get married without really paying attention to what they're getting into. Then, it's also different when it's not you who's doing the scrimping. I mean, when it was my mom who had to figure it all out, it was different. As a kid, I just knew I couldn't have a lot of things I wanted, but it wasn't until after I got married that I really understood what my mom went through.

> [*Twenty-seven-year-old pantry woman,*
> *mother of two, married ten years.*]

"We were dirt poor." That's the refrain that sets the stage for the transition from youth to adulthood, the refrain that tells the story of the conditions under which the adjustment to marriage is made and the dreams compromised. The beautiful home of the magazine pictures is not to be theirs. Instead, even for those lucky enough to have had the "big white wedding" and the bridal showers that usually accompany it, the gifts received provide only a minimal start and ten years later, most homes still are not furnished in "dream style":

As you can see, that dream I had about getting married and having a storybook life didn't exactly work out.

What did that storybook life include?

The first thing was my own little family, in my own house, and everything pretty and shiny and new, like in magazine pictures.

Life sure doesn't match the dreams, does it? Here I am living in this old, dumpy house and the furniture is a grubby mess. I still have those pictures of the storybook life in my head, but I have a lot more sense now than when I was young. Now I know we're lucky just to be able to keep up with the bills.

"When I was young"—the phrase spoken by a twenty-seven-year-old sales clerk, mother of three, married ten years. "When I was young"—a phrase used repeatedly by working-class women and men well under thirty; a phrase that surprised my middle-class professional ears, accustomed as they are to hearing students, patients, children of friends, my own children—all of like age—struggling with problems of identity, reluctant to step into adulthood, still defining themselves in terms of youth and the youth culture. Such an extended psycho-social moratorium and concomitant crisis of identity is, it would seem, a luxury of the affluent middle class—a luxury that belongs to an economy and a culture that can afford to permit its young the privileges of adulthood without its responsibilities.[1]

For the working-class young, those privileges—including separate domiciles and sexual relations outside marriage that are legitimated and accepted in the community—come only with marriage. For them, this is yet another of the hidden injuries of class. For them, there is no time for concern about the issues of their own growth and development that so preoccupy the college-educated middle-class youth in this era; no time to wonder who they are, what they will do, how they can differentiate themselves from parents, how they can stand as separate, autonomous selves. Instead, early marriage and parenthood combine to catapult them, ready or not, into adult responsibilities.

The first of those responsibilities is economic, and it is in that sphere of life that the realities hit hardest and fastest. Twenty percent of the families in this study report having had to rely on welfare, at least for brief periods, during the early years of their marriage:

When I was six months pregnant, I wasn't well, so I had to stop work early. Then, all of a sudden, Johnny got fired from his job. I don't think I was ever so scared in my life. After a while, things got so bad (I couldn't work, and he wasn't working) that we signed up for welfare. I'll never forget how ashamed I was.

> [*Twenty-seven-year-old beautician,*
> *mother of two, married eight years.*]

The rest were only slightly luckier; for although most stayed off the welfare rolls, almost all knew the bitter taste of hard times. For some, things got so bad that they were forced to move back into the family home from which they had so recently fled:

Right after our first kid was born, I got laid off, and it looked like it would be a long time before I'd be working again. The company I worked for was cutting back, and I didn't have seniority or anything like that. And I didn't have much in the way of skills to get another job with.

My unemployment ran out pretty quick, and Sue Ann couldn't work because of the baby, and she wasn't feeling too good anyhow after the baby came. So we moved in with my folks. We lived there for about a year. What a mess. My mom and Sue Ann just didn't get along.

> [*Thirty-year-old welder, father of four,*
> *married eleven years.*]

Others managed to make it with less profound disruption of their nascent families:

Ray has never been really job secure, and it was much worse when we were first married. He just sort of kept going from one job to another with months in between sometimes when he wasn't working at all.

I never could figure out whether it was just bad luck like he said, or whether he just wasn't a very good worker in those days. Anyhow, there wasn't much money around.

I don't know why I said that like that. The truth is we were just plain poor, dirt poor, and the only thing that got us through was that we used to eat at my parents' almost every day. They couldn't do much for us; they never had much either. But they always had enough food to share even if maybe they all had to eat a little less.

Also, even though I couldn't go out to work, I used to take in ironing and watch some kids. Between it all, we would just manage to get through most of the time. But I'm not complaining; we were luckier than a lot of people we knew because we didn't have to go down to the welfare like they did.

> *[Thirty-four-year-old bakery clerk,*
> *mother of five, married seventeen years.]*

Exacerbating the financial problems of most of these young couples was the fact that the children were born just months after the wedding. The modal time between marriage and the birth of the first child was seven months, the average, nine months—leaving little time for the young couple to stabilize their financial position before assuming the burdens of parenthood. Unlike the professional middle-class families I met where, on the average, the first child was born three years after they were married and where most wives worked during that time, the working-class families were forced almost at once to give up the wife's earnings. The professional families thus are doubly advantaged. Their jobs pay more and offer career patterns that are more stable than those in the blue-collar world. And by deferring childbearing, young wives are able to work while the men are becoming established.

Other investigators, observing the same phenomena, have theorized that it is precisely those differences that account for professional success—that is, that putting off marriage and childbearing is a symbol of the middle-class ability to defer immediate gratifications in the interest of future rewards. Conversely, the early marriage and childbearing of the working class allegedly is symptomatic of their inability to defer gratifications and the cause of their low status in the society.[2] If one examines the facts through a less self-righteous and self-congratulatory prism, however, we can see instead that it is those at the lower ends of our socio-economic order who are forced to delay gratifications, while those at the upper levels usually manage to have their cake and eat it. For example, among the college-educated middle class, premarital sexual behavior is not only more widely held to be legitimate but the opportunities for engaging in such behavior are more readily and comfortably available. In the last decade, even dormitories—those last bastions of parietal regulations—largely have given up the attempt to control the sexual activities of their student residents. For those young people, a bed and privacy are easily found; sex can be undertaken in leisure—a sharp contrast from the stories told by most working-class youth who still must resort to the back seat of a car or a dark corner in a park.

Similarly, for highly educated middle-class women to delay childbearing may simply be to defer one pleasurable activity in favor of another since they often do some kind of interesting and rewarding work that pays substantially more than the low-level clerical, sales, or factory work available to most high-school–educated working-class women. Most of the middle-class women I talked to, for example, worked at interesting jobs that they liked— social worker, freelance editor, writer, teacher, accountant, office manager, personnel manager, calligrapher. Those who either did not enjoy working or who had jobs they found dull and unrewarding often had their first child in considerably less than the three years cited as the average—a decision that can be made in professional families without the enormous economic costs exacted in the working class.

The economic realities that so quickly confronted the young working-class couples of this study ricocheted through the marriage, dominating every aspect of experience, coloring every facet of their early adjustment. The women, finding their dreams disappointed, felt somehow that their men had betrayed the promise implicit in their union. They were both angry and frightened. Those who came from hard-living families with unstable, sometimes alcoholic, fathers often were fearful that they were about to relive that experience, only this time as wife and mother rather than daughter:

When Chuck got laid off right after we were married, all I could think
of was "Here I go again." It was like I couldn't make myself believe
than he wouldn't just go off and go on a drunken binge because
that's what my father always did, and my mother used to tell us we
should understand him and that he did it because his life was so hard.
So now here was my husband, and *his* life was hard, so I figured that's
what he'd do, too.

God, I was so scared; I didn't know what to do. I felt sorry for him
and I felt angry at him. It was like the two feelings were always there
inside me, fighting with each other, until I got a terrible headache.
Or else, I'd get so upset, I'd throw up and not be able to eat because my
stomach hurt so much.

Every time he'd have a beer, everything would get worse because then
I was *sure* he was just going to be another drunk. That's still a problem
with us. I can't stand to see him take a drink because it scares me so
much.

[*Twenty-three-year-old housewife,
mother of two, married six years.*]

Such fears were not limited to women from hard-living families,
however, since even those from the most settled-living families
have been close enough to the hard-living style—aunts, uncles,
cousins, siblings—to be fearful that in their new lives they would
be cast into that painful place and angry at men who might permit that to happen to them:

I could hardly ever forgive him for getting fired from his job. We
never stopped arguing about that. I felt so frightened, I almost couldn't
stand it. I was scared we'd just get into deeper trouble and before we
knew it, we'd become like some other people in the family.

When I married Ed, my mother was worried about that. You know,
I have an older sister who married a guy who's a real bum. Then, when
Ed got fired, my mother said, "You see, he'll turn out like your sister's
husband, and you'll turn out like her—living on the wrong side of
the tracks with a bunch of kids you can't feed."

It was a real hard time. I couldn't understand how anybody could
get fired from a job. I mean, I'm *never* going to get fired from a job.
And my father never got fired from his job. He's been working on the
same job for thirty-two years, and nobody could ever say he wasn't

a real good worker. He's always been a real stable man, and he'd never do anything to jeopardize his job.

My husband is not stable that way. He calls in sick a lot. My father never did that. Even now, after we've had things so hard and they're finally beginning to settle down a little, he still does things like that, and I'm always worrying about what will become of all of us if he keeps up those ways.

*[Twenty-six-year-old beautician,
mother of two, married seven years.]*

The men, disappointed in themselves and equally frightened as they looked toward an uncertain future, responded defensively and uncomprehendingly to their wives' angry concerns. A thirty-year-old postal clerk, father of three, married nine years, recalls:

I couldn't figure out what the hell she wanted from me. I was trying, and I didn't like how things were coming out any better than she did.

Did you tell her that?

Tell her? Who could tell her anything? She was too busy running off at the mouth—you know, nagging—to listen to anything. I just got mad and I'd take off—go out with the guys and have a few beers or something. When I'd get back, things would be even worse.

Sometimes I'd feel like hitting her just to shut her up. I never could figure out why the hell she did that. Did she think I didn't care about not making enough money to take care of my family?

For the men, whose wish for marriage was more ambivalently expressed than the women's, these fears and the struggles they generated made the process of settling down more difficult. Thus, some men began to look longingly at their single friends, idealizing and romanticizing that life[3]:

I spent a lot of time wondering how I got myself into this spot in the first place. I'd look at my old buddies, and they were still having a good time, nobody telling them what to do and how to spend their money, working when they felt like it. I'd look at those guys who weren't married yet and wish I was still there.

It's funny, the more I did that, the worse things got between us. I guess she kind of knew what I was thinking and that would make her mad.

77

Then I'd get even madder because I couldn't even *think* what I wanted anymore without her starting up a fight.

> [*Twenty-seven-year-old truck driver,*
> *father of two, married seven years.*]

Some looked enviously, if ambivalently, at their hard-living friends:

You know, I had this friend, he's got no money, no nothing. Whenever he got his hands on something, he'd blow it. Even though he was married, he still played around quite a bit. He'd run around every night, stay out until four or five in the morning some nights. Then when he'd come home, his wife was there waiting for him, never saying a word. And when we were first married, I used to look at him and think, "Boy, that's cool. I'd really like some of that. I'd really like a wife who would never say a word like that. Look how stuck I am; Peggy'd never put up with that stuff."

But then I'd get scared at even having thoughts like that. In another part of my head, I knew I didn't want to fall into that trap; that kind of life ain't no good. He's got no life, no money. And now he hasn't even got a wife no more. All those years of saying nothing, then one day he came home and she was gone—just gone without a word.

> [*Thirty-one-year-old warehouseman,*
> *father of four, married eleven years.*]

A few started to spend time again with the old crowd, stopping off for a beer on the way home from work, dropping in at the favorite hang-out after dinner—behavior their wives resented and which escalated the conflict between the couple. A thirty-year-old housewife, mother of two, married twelve years, remembers:

Things were very bad right after we got married. I think he used to feel like I didn't do anything but scream at him all the time. And I suppose that was true.

We were very young and really immature, and we weren't ready for marriage and the problems you have to face right away. We both felt tied down, but he was worse about it than me. He had all his high school buddies in the neighborhood, and when he'd get bored, he'd just go out and hang out with them.

I used to get jealous because I thought he wanted more than just me, and I thought I should be plenty for him. So I'd get mad and scream at him on top of my lungs, and he'd just withdraw. The more I screamed, the more he'd withdraw, until finally I'd go kind of crazy. Then he'd leave and not come back until two or three in the morning sometimes. That made me even madder, especially because I couldn't go anyplace. At first I had this big belly what with being pregnant. Then when the baby was born, who would take care of her if I went out, too? So I felt like I was stuck in the house when he was out having a good time.

Her husband, a thirty-one-year-old painter, agrees with his wife's version of those early years, and adds:

I didn't know how to handle her when we were first married. I couldn't understand what she was screaming about all the time. I guess I used to think she was too possessive and too jealous, like she wanted to own me.

Now I realize that it comes from her background. You know, I mean, she just didn't trust me then. She'd been around a father who was a drunk and her two brothers are drunks and goof-offs. They both cheat on their wives and run around a lot. I guess she used to think all guys are like that, and she used to worry that I'd get into bad company and wind up like them.

She still gets mad if I go out with the guys too often. But it's not the same now. I guess she trusts me more. I've been working at the same job for seven years now, and the money comes in regular. And you know, it makes a difference with the kids being a little older, and we can do things together again sometimes.

Indeed, children born just months after the wedding added emotional as well as economic burdens to the adjustment process. Suddenly, two young people, barely more than children themselves, found their lives irrevocably altered. Within a few months —too few to permit the integration of the behaviors required by new roles in new life stages, too few to wear comfortably even one new identity—they moved through a series of roles: from girl and boy, to wife and husband, to mother and father.

They often responded with bewilderment, filled with an uneasy and uncomprehending sense of loss for a past which, however difficult, at least was known:

I was so depressed and I felt so sad all the time. I felt like I'd fallen into a hole and that I could never climb out of it again. All I wanted was to be a little girl again, real little, so that somebody would take care of me.

. . . an angry and restless discontent with an uncomfortable present:

I don't know why but I was just angry all the time. Everything she did would make me angry—crazy angry.

. . . and an enormous well of fear about an unknown future:

All of a sudden, you couldn't tell what would happen tomorrow. I was scared out of my wits half the time; and when I wasn't scared, I was worried out of my mind.

As with all of us, however, such a welter of feelings are rarely recognized, let alone understood. At best, we are aware only that we're experiencing turmoil without knowing what it's about. One young mother expressed it well:

All I knew was that I was churning up inside all the time.

Most immediately, both wives and husbands knew that the fun and good times that had brought them together were gone—replaced by a crying, demanding infant, and the fearsome responsibilities of parenthood. No longer were they free to run around with the old crowd, to prowl the favored haunts, to go to a movie, bowling, or partying whenever the mood struck. Both wives and husbands were shaken as it quickly became clear that the freedom they had sought in marriage was a mirage, that they had exchanged one set of constraints for another perhaps more powerful one. They felt stuck—thrust abruptly into adulthood, unexpectedly facing the fear that their youth was behind them. A twenty-eight-year-old clerk in a cleaning store, mother of three, married eleven years, sums up those feelings:

Marriage: The Dream and the Reality—The Beginning Years

One day I woke up and there I was, married and with a baby. And I thought, "I can't stand it! I can't stand to have my life over when I'm so young."

Her thirty-one-year-old husband recalls:

I had just turned twenty and, all of a sudden, I had a wife and kid. You couldn't just go out anymore when you felt like it. If you wanted to go anyplace, you had to take the kid, and that meant carrying the milk and stuff wherever you went. By the time you got him all together and ready to go, it wasn't worth going.

We used to run around a lot before he was born, and then we couldn't anymore. I guess it wasn't all his fault; we didn't have money to go places and do things anyway. But I still used to get mad at him, and at her, too—my wife, I mean—because I felt like it was on account of them I was stuck.

The wife:

I felt like I had no freedom, just no freedom. I had to depend on him for everything. Even poor as we were when I was growing up, I never had to ask my mother for money. She knew I needed lunch money and she gave it to me. She knew when I needed a pair of shoes; I didn't have to tell her. Now, all of a sudden, I had to ask him for everything, and he couldn't understand why that bothered me. I felt like I was a charity ward case or something.

Then he'd get mad because he didn't always have the money for the things I needed, and he'd get mad because he felt bad about that. But how was I supposed to know that then? I was only a kid myself, and I was stuck with a bawling baby, and not enough money, and having to depend on a husband who didn't even go to work all the time.

The husband:

I'd get so mad at her, at my whole life, that I'd cut out on work a lot, and that would make things worse because then we had more money problems. Even when I worked steady, my paycheck wasn't big enough; then when I missed days, we were really in trouble.

But, you know, a guy's got to have some freedom. He's got to feel like he doesn't *have* to go to that same lousy place every day of his life, just like a slave.

I used to think I was already in the same place as my father, and here I was only twenty. I felt like I was old, and I couldn't stand it. I just *had* to do something to get away from that feeling. When I cut out on work, it was sort of like I could be a kid again, just hanging around, doing what I wanted to, like cutting school and just hanging out on the street.

The struggle to adapt simultaneously to so many new situations was complicated by young husbands who were jealous of their wives' suddenly divided time and attention. Before they had a chance to adapt to a twosome in marriage, they became a three-some, with the third member of the household a noisy, demand-ing, helpless infant. The young wife, anxious about her capacity to be a good mother, became absorbed in the child. Between house-hold and baby-tending chores, both days and nights were full, leaving little time and energy for companionship or lovemaking. The young husband, until then accustomed to being the center of her life, felt excluded and deprived. Each time he made a move toward her that was rebuffed, the situation worsened. He became more hurt and jealous; she became more angry and defensive. The conflict escalated—both husband and wife acting out their frus-tration in painful and hurtful ways.[4] Typical of such interactions is the story told by this couple, both twenty-nine, married ten years. The husband:

Our first kid was born less than a year after we were married. By the time he came, it seemed like she'd either been pregnant or with the baby the whole time we were married.

When we were first married, I'd come home from work and she'd be kind of dressed up and fixed up, you know, looking pretty for me. Then she kept getting bigger and bigger, and she'd be tired and com-plaining all the time. I could hardly wait for her to finish being preg-nant. And when that was over, she was too busy and too tired to pay me any mind.

I used to get mad and holler a lot. Or else I'd stay out late at night and get her worried about what I was doing. We had nothing but fights in those days because all she wanted to do was to take care of the baby, and she never had any time for me. It sounds dumb when I talk about it now—a man being jealous of a little kid, but I guess I was.

Marriage: The Dream and the Reality—The Beginning Years

The wife:

It felt like I was going crazy. There I was with a new baby and he was all the time nagging at me for something or other. Instead of helping me out so that I wouldn't be so tired, he'd just holler, or else he'd run out and stay out all night. Then he'd come home and expect me to be friendly and loving. Why should I? What was he doing for me? I didn't like being stuck with all those dirty diapers any more than he did, but *somebody* had to do it and he sure wasn't.

We used to have the most terrible fights after my son was born; it was just awful. I couldn't understand how he could be jealous of a little, tiny baby, but he was. It made me so mad, I just didn't know what to do. But I sure didn't feel much like loving him.

The adjustment problems that attend the arrival of the first child—including the jealousy of the young husband—are, of course, not class-specific. Nancy Chodorow argues persuasively that the conflict and resentment men experience at the birth of a child stem from the structure of family relations—particularly from the fact that the mother, as the primary nurturer, is the first love relationship for the child. This relationship is vital to the child not only because it is experienced as exclusive and all-embracing, but because survival depends on it. As they negotiate the Oedipal phase, boys are forced to repress that early infant attachment to their mother and, consequently, spend the rest of their lives seeking to re-establish that first exclusive relationship with another woman. The period in marriage before the first child is born seems to recapture that early experience, to meet those infantile needs. But the birth of a child interrupts and interferes with the exclusivity of the relationship with his wife, and the husband becomes jealous and resentful.[5]

These psychoanalytic speculations notwithstanding, the issues that arise in young families tend to have more long-range consequences among working-class families than among professional ones. For one thing, the pain of the experience is heightened among those who are so young and so unprepared to assume the trials and traumata of the parental role. For another, where childhoods are severely deprived, marriage often is looked upon as a place to be cared for, perhaps the only place where one can find a haven. When a child arrives to disrupt that dream, especially for the men, the pain can be intense and the consequences to the marriage long-lasting.

Thus, among the six men in this study who grew up in institutions or foster homes, the wounds of that early period are still raw. A thirty-five-year-old driver of heavy construction equipment, married at eighteen because he had spent most of his childhood in institutions, still recalls that time with pain:

I got married because I wanted the security of marriage and a home. In fact, I needed it very much. I had been a lonely child, living a lonely life, most of the time in institutions. Once in a while, I lived in a foster home for short periods but that wasn't much better. I was completely on my own from sixteen onwards and, by the time I was eighteen, I was ready to be married and have somebody take care of me.

Unfortunately, Ellen was pregnant when we got married and five months after, our first kid was born. That was when things really sort of collapsed around me. I was filled with resentment of him because then I didn't have someone who just cared about me anymore. There I was, just a kid myself, and I finally had someone to take care of me. Then suddenly, I had to take care of a kid, and she was too busy with him to take care of me. The whole thing didn't make sense.

I never have gotten along with that oldest son of mine. I guess I never really got over being jealous of him, and she never really got over feeling like she had to protect him from me.

His wife, married at seventeen, a mother before her eighteenth birthday, recalls that time with a complex of feelings that alternate between anger, incomprehension, compassion, and an inability to forgive:

Our biggest problem is that he's very jealous and always has been. Can you imagine a man being jealous of his own kids?

Oh, I guess I really understand a little. He never had a family of his own, and we were just kids ourselves when we were married—too young to be married, I guess, and much too young to have kids. But even so, I never could understand why he behaved so badly. Did he think babies grew up and took care of themselves? Wouldn't you think that he'd have wanted for us to be good parents when he didn't have any? Instead, he would just fume all the time. He'd go out and get drunk and come home raising the roof and wake up the baby with all his noise. Then he'd be furious with me because I couldn't pay attention to him with the baby screaming.

I still have trouble forgiving him for that. He made our lives so hard, so much harder than they had to be. It's hard to understand why someone would do that.

While time eventually mitigated the worst of this jealousy, the issue remains a live one in many working-class families. For in contrast to the lifeways of the professional middle class where the wife/husband roles tend to remain central even during the early childrearing years, in most working-class families, parental roles become ascendant, relegating spouse roles to a subordinate position.[6]

It is not that parents of one class have more or less concern than those of another for their children's future. Rather, there are differences in the ways in which they attend to the central concerns of living, differences in the solutions to common problems—childrearing, parental roles, and the approved interactions between children and parents, to name but a few—that are rooted in their different class positions. At the most manifest level, there is more money in the professional families with which to buy childcare services and to continue to engage in valued adult leisure pursuits. This simple difference in the facts of their lives permits a more adult-directed lifestyle with more emphasis on the adults as a couple rather than simply as parents. When a family can afford financially to pay for competent help with the children, the parents can afford emotionally to attend to their adult needs as a couple.

At the deeper level, the issues are more complex. Parents in professional middle-class families have a sense of their own success, of their ability to control their world, to provide for their children's future, whatever that might be. For them, the problem is not how to support the children through tomorrow, not *whether* they can go to college or professional school, but *which* of the prestigious alternatives available to them ought to be encouraged. For working-class parents, however, the future is seen as uncertain, problematic. For them, the question is most often *whether*, not *which*—and that "whether" more often asks *if* children will finish high school; *if* they will grow up without getting "into trouble"; *if*, even with maximum vigilance, they—the parents—can retain some control over their children's future.

Their own histories remind them about how easily children can get into trouble, how easily they stray from parental values and injunctions. Thus, like their parents, they believe that children need to be carefully and constantly watched. It matters little that they resented such parental authority, even that they often subverted it. Instead, retrospectively they tend to argue that it was good for them; that without it they might have gotten into still more trouble; that it was a sign of parental love and concern; and that had their parents been less strict, they might not now be living a settled, stable life. A twenty-eight-year-old plumber's helper, father of three, married nine years, speaks cogently to the issue:

You've got to watch out over kids all the time if you expect them to grow up decent. I know from when I was a kid how easy it is to get into trouble, and I don't want my kids into none of that kind of stuff. That's why Karen makes sure she knows where they are and who they're playing with all the time.

All you need is one rotten apple, one bad kid on the block, and there's no telling what a kid'll do, especially a boy when he gets to be a teen-ager. You got to start off teaching them right from wrong when they're just little kids.

Complicating the matter still further, the men and women of these families are not at ease with most of the public or private institutions that share responsibility for socializing young children. They can't do much about the public schools with their mandatory attendance requirements and their "too liberal" teachers, although in recent years they have been trying.[7] But they *can* keep their children at home with them as long as possible. Thus, where nursery school attendance is a commonplace among the children of middle-class families, it is rare among those of the working class—not primarily for financial reasons, nor because working-class parents value education less, but because they look with question and concern at the values that are propagated there:[8]

I think little kids belong at home with their mothers not in some nursery school that's run by a bunch of people who think they're experts and know all about what's good for kids and how they're supposed to act. I saw some of those kids in a nursery school once. They act like a bunch of wild Indians, and they're dressed terrible, and they're filthy all the time.

> [*Twenty-seven-year-old housewife,*
> *mother of two, married seven years.*]

So strong are these feelings that even in those families where mothers work part- or full-time, institutional childcare facilities are shunned in favor of arrangements with grandmothers or neighbors—arrangements that keep children close to home and in the care of people who share parental values.[9] Typical are these comments from one young couple. The twenty-five-year-old wife, mother of two, married seven years, who works part-time as a file clerk, says:

I don't want my kids brought up by strangers. This way it's just right. My mother-in-law comes here and stays with them and it's family. We don't have to worry about what kind of stuff some stranger is teaching them. We know they're learning right from wrong. I'd be afraid to leave them in a school or someplace like that. I'd worry that they might get too far away from the family.

Her husband, a twenty-seven-year-old refinery worker, agrees:

I wouldn't let Ann work if we couldn't have my mother taking care of the kids. Even though it helps out for her to work, I wouldn't permit it if it meant somebody I didn't know was going to raise my kids and tell them how to act and what to think. With my mother, I know it's all okay; she teaches them the way she taught me.

Thus, both husbands and wives agree on the primacy of their parental responsibilities. But the costs to a marriage of ordering priorities thus can be heavy. For the demands of parenting often conflict with the needs of the wives and husbands who are the parents—needs for privacy, for shared adult time and leisure, for companionship, for nurturance from a husband, a wife. The deprivation of those needs is a constant strain in working-class families—a strain from which there is little relief either in the material conditions of their life or in their culture. Their economic situation doesn't permit them to buy free time in the form of baby-sitters or "adults only" vacations. Their culture requires that children be watched closely—partly because parents are afraid of what the children might do; but partly also because they are afraid of what the institutions to which they might send them— institutions which are staffed by middle-class professionals and controlled by middle-class values—might do to the children.

Finally, these early years bring with them the inevitable in-law problems. Despite the prevalence of mother-in-law jokes that focus on the wife's mother, it is not the men but the women who complain most regularly and vociferously about mothers-in-law, especially in the beginning years of the marriage. Fully half the working-class women spoke of problems with mothers-in-law as second only to the financial ones; a few even put the in-law problems first. The primary struggle was over "who comes first"—wife or mother:

That first year was terrible. He called her every single day when he came home from work. As soon as he'd walk through the door, he'd go to the telephone to talk to his mother. And then, a few times he went to see her before he ever even came home. That really did it. I said, "Listen buster, this has to stop. I'm not going to take that anymore. Either I'm going to come first or you can go live with your mother."

> [*Twenty-four-year-old typist,
> mother of two, married five years.*]

He was so used to helping out around his mother's house that he just kept right on doing it after we were married. Can you imagine that? He'd go there and help her out with the yard work. Here our yard would need trimming, and he'd be over there helping his mother.

> [*Thirty-eight-year-old housewife,
> mother of four, married twenty years.*]

He used to stop off there on his way home from work and that used to make me furious. On top of that, they eat supper earlier than we do, so a lot of times, he'd eat with them. Then he'd come home and I'd have a nice meal fixed, and he'd say he wasn't hungry. Boy, did that make me mad. We were always having these big fights over his mother at first.

> [*Thirty-two-year-old housewife,
> mother of three, married thirteen years.*]

Others complain that their mothers-in-law never treated them well because they didn't think "any girl was good enough" for their sons:

I got along all right with his father, but the relationship with his mother never was too cool. She never was very fond of me and, at the beginning, it was always a big hassle. I think she thought he was a big prize catch or something because he had a steady job. She thought I married him for just what I could get out of him—at least that's what she told him before we were married. Even he knew she would never think any girl was good enough for him.

[*Twenty-six-year-old waitress,*
mother of three, married nine years.]

This is not to suggest that conflicts around in-laws do not exist in other strata of society. But no professional middle-class wife or husband talked of these problems with the heat and intensity that I heard among the working-class women. Partly, that may be because few of the middle-class couples had families who lived close by at the time of the marriage which often took place when husbands were still in professional schools far from their hometowns. This gave these young couples a chance to negotiate the initial adjustment hurdles without interference from either family. Equally important, however, even when they live in the same city now, most of these professional couples do not have the kinds of relationships with parents that keep them actively intertwined in their lives. No grandparent in a professional family, for example, baby-sits with young children while their mother works—a common arrangement among working-class families; one which makes it difficult for the young couple to insist upon their autonomy and independence, to maintain their privacy.

Adding to the in-law problems, many of the women were aggrieved because their mothers-in-law had spoiled their sons—waiting on them, tending their every need, always sacrificing self for the men and boys in the family—thus making the lives of their wives more difficult. For men like these expected similar "services" from their wives—services most modern young women of any class are not so willing to perform:

His mother was like a maid in the house, and he wanted me to do the same kinds of things and be like her. I know it's my job to keep the

house up, but wouldn't you think he could hang up his own clothes?
Or maybe once in a while—just once in a while—help clear the table?

[*Twenty-eight-year-old housewife,*
mother of three, married ten years.]

Again, obviously, it is not only working-class mothers who spoil their sons. Still, no middle-class wife offered this complaint—a fact that, at least in part, may be because the professional men all had lived away from home for several years before they married. Without a mother or wife to do things for them, these men had to learn to care for themselves—at least minimally—in the years between leaving the parental home and getting married. In contrast, the working-class men generally moved from parental home to marriage, often simply transferring old habits and living patterns, along with their wardrobe, to a new address.

Indeed, overriding all these reasons why more working-class than professional middle-class women had complaints about mothers-in-law may be the simple fact that most working-class men lived with their families and contributed to the support of the household before they were married. Their departure from the family, therefore, probably is felt both as an emotional and an economic loss. Mothers, already experiencing some panic over the loss of maternal functions which have provided the core of their identity for so long, suffer yet another erosion of that function—a problem women in professional middle-class families deal with when children leave for college rather than when they marry. And the family economy, relying on income from all its working members, suffers the loss of his dollar contribution:

His parents didn't accept me at all. Tim was a devoted son and his
mother needed that; she couldn't bear to give him up to anyone. Then,
he also helped out a lot when he was living there. They needed the
money and he turned his pay check over to his mother. They made me
feel like I was taking a meal ticket from them when we got married.

[*Thirty-year-old file clerk,*
mother of four, married twelve years.]

And so it went—traditional marital adjustment problems compounded by youth and economic insecurity, both past and present. All together, these issues made for very difficult beginnings in most marriages. For the men, their self-esteem was on the line every time they brought home a pay check that was inadequate to meet the bills or, worse yet, failed to bring one home at all. Such feelings cannot be written off to some inappropriate conception of the meaning of manhood since they were confirmed in their daily lives and in their relationships with their wives.

For the women, whose self-esteem and status are so intimately tied to their husbands' accomplishments, the issue became one of "husband-esteem." Those whose husbands were unemployed, intermittently employed, or underemployed were quick to let them know of their disappointment:

I couldn't understand how he couldn't get a job. I knew I could get a job any time I really wanted one, but I had to stay home with the baby. It seemed like he was just dumb or something that he couldn't find a good, steady job. And you know, no woman likes to think she's smarter than her husband. But I've got to admit, I did, and he didn't like it one bit. Neither did I.

> [*Twenty-nine-year-old cashier,*
> *mother of two, married nine years.*]

When we had to go down to the welfare, I hated him for letting us get into that position. I felt like scum having to go down there and ask for a handout. No matter how poor we were, my father always took care of us better than that. Larry just wasn't a responsible man. I don't know even now if I can ever forgive him for that. What kind of man lets his family go on welfare?

> [*Thirty-three-year-old adjustment clerk,*
> *mother of three, married fifteen years.*]

Whether overtly or covertly, these feelings were communicated to the men and, quite naturally, heightened the marital conflict. The men began to act out their anger and frustration—sometimes by drinking and staying out late, sometimes by violence, and almost always by assuming a very authoritarian stance within the family. How else could they assert their manliness? How else could they establish their position as head of the household? The women resisted—some because they honestly didn't believe they ought to submit:

He kept saying I was too independent and that I had to learn to listen to him. He used to say he wanted me to be more feminine, to act more like a *real* woman. What that meant was that he wanted to order me around and have me listen all the time. I told him I wasn't his mother and he wasn't his father.

[*Twenty-six-year-old housewife, mother of three, married seven years.*]

... and some as a statement of their disrespect:

A man who can't take care of his family hasn't got the right to come in and order people around. A man's got to deserve it to have people listen to him when he talks. As long as he wasn't supporting us very good, he didn't deserve it.

[*Thirty-five-year-old assembler, mother of four, married eighteen years.*]

These, then, were the beginning years—the years when illusions were shed along with childhood; the years when the first disappointments were felt, the first adjustments were made; the years of struggle for stability economically and emotionally—both so closely tied together; the years during which many marriages founder and sink. Some of these couples had already had that experience once; they were determined not to let it happen again. Whatever the reasons, all weathered these first storms, all survived—some in more, some in less stable relationships, but all still engaged in the struggle to build a marriage and a family.

CHAPTER

6

Marriage: The Dream and the Reality— The Middle Years

I guess I can't complain. He's a steady worker; he doesn't drink; he doesn't hit me. That's a lot more than my mother had, and she didn't sit around complaining and feeling sorry for herself, so I sure haven't got the right.

[*Thirty-three-year-old housewife, mother of three, married thirteen years.*]

"HE'S A STEADY WORKER; he doesn't drink; he doesn't hit me"—these are the three attributes working-class women tick off most readily when asked what they value most in their husbands. Not a surprising response when one recalls their familiarity with unemployment, alcoholism, and violence, whether in their own families or in those around them.[1] That this response is class-related is evident from the fact that not one woman in the professional middle-class families mentioned any of these qualities when answering the same question. Although there was no response that was consistently heard from the middle-class wives, they tended to focus on such issues as intimacy, sharing, and communication and, while expressed in subtle ways, on the comforts, status, and prestige that their husbands' occupation affords. Janet Harris, writing about middle-class women at forty, also comments that she never heard a woman list her husband's ability to provide or the fact that he is "good to the children" as valued primary traits. "The security and financial support that a husband provides are taken for granted," she argues; "it is the emotional sustainment which is the barometer of a marriage."[2]

Does this mean, then, that working-class women are unconcerned about the emotional side of the marriage relationship? Emphatically, it does not. It says first that when the material aspects of life are problematic, they become dominant as issues requiring solutions; and second, that even when men are earning a reasonably good living, it is *never* "taken for granted" when financial insecurity and marginality are woven into the fabric of life. These crucial differences in the definition of a good life, a good husband, a good marriage—and the reasons for them—often are obscured in studies of marriage and the family because students of the subject rarely even mention class, let alone analyze class differences.[3]

Still, it is a mixed message that these working-class women send; for while many remind themselves regularly that they have no right to complain, their feelings of discontent with the emotional aspects of the marriage are not so easily denied. Indeed, once the immediate problems and preoccupations of the early years subside, once the young husband is "housebroken," an interesting switch occurs. Before the marriage and in the first years, it is the wife who seems more eager to be married; the husband, more reluctant. Marriage brings her more immediate gains since being unmarried is a highly stigmatized status for a woman, especially in the working-class world. Both husband and wife subscribe to the "I-chased-her-until-she-caught-me" myth about courtship in America; both believe that somehow, using some mysterious feminine wiles, she contrived to ensnare him. It is no surprise, then, that it is he who has more trouble in settling down at the beginning—feeling hemmed in, oppressed by the contours and confines of marriage, by its responsibilities.

With time, he begins to work more steadily, to earn more money. The responsibilities seem to weigh a little lighter. With time, he finds ways to live with some constraints, to circumvent others. For him, marriage becomes a comfortable haven—a place of retreat from the pressures and annoyances of the day, a place where his needs and comforts are attended to by his wife, the only place perhaps where he can exercise his authority. He begins to feel that he's made a good bargain. It's true, it costs plenty. He has to commit to a lifetime of hard work—sometimes at a job he hates, sometimes not. But the benefits are high too; and there's no other way he can get them:

I like being married now. I don't even feel tied down anymore. I'm out all day and, if I want to have a drink with the boys after work, I just call her up and tell her I'll be home later. When I get home, there's a meal—she's a real good cook—and I can just relax and take it easy. The kids—they're the apples of my eyes—they're taken care of; she brings them up right, keeps them clean, teaches them respect. I can't ask for any more. It's a good life.

> [*Thirty-eight-year old plumber, father of three, married seventeen years.*]

For his wife, time works the other way. She finds herself facing increasing constraints or, at least, experiencing them as more oppressive.[4] For her, there are few ways to circumvent them—no regular work hours:

When I was a kid and used to wish I was a boy, I never knew why I thought that. Now I know. It's because a man can go to work for eight hours and come home, and a woman's work is just never done. And it doesn't make any difference if she works or not.

... no stopping off for a relaxing moment after work:

He gets to stop off and have a drink when he feels like it. But me, I have to rush home from work and get things going in the house.

... no regular time off in which to develop her own interests and activities:

I know I shouldn't complain. Bringing home a check and food for the family and keeping a roof over our heads is a lot of responsibility. But it's his *only* responsibility. I work too, and I still have to worry about everything else while he comes home and just relaxes. He has time to do other things he wants to do after work, like getting out there and fooling around fixing his truck, or other projects he likes to do. Me, I don't have time for anything.

. . . no night out she can count on:

He gets out once a week, at least. I don't always know what he does. He goes to a ball game or something like that; or he just goes out with some of the guys. Me, if I'm ever dumb enough to take a night off to do something, I pay for it when I come home. He can't—or maybe he won't—control the kids, so the house looks like a cyclone, and he's so mad at the kids and me, you can't live with him for days.

. . . and perhaps more important, no way, short of years of nagging or divorce, to defy her husband's authority and dicta about what she may or may not do with her life:

I begin to worry what's going to happen to me after the kids are grown up. I don't want to be like my mother, just sort of hanging around being a professional mother and grandmother. So I thought I could go to school—you know, take a few courses or something, maybe even be a teacher eventually. But he says I can't and no matter how much I beg, he won't let me.

"He won't let me"—a phrase heard often among working-class women. "He won't let me"—a phrase spoken unself-consciously, with a sense of resignation, as if that's the way of the world. Indeed, that is the way for most of these women.

It is not only in the working class that this is true, however. Rather, it is only there that a *language* exists which speaks of husbands "permitting" wives. Not once did a professional middle-class man speak about refusing his wife permission to do something—whether to go to work, to school, or to have an abortion. Not once was a wife in a professional family heard to say, "He won't let me." Such talk would conflict with the philosophy of egalitarianism in the family that finds its fullest articulation among men and women of this class. But the tension between ideology and reality is high and, as William Goode writes in *World Revolution and Family Patterns*, ". . . the more educated men are more likely to concede more rights ideologically than they in fact grant." The mere fact that the discussion takes place around what men will "grant" is itself a telling statement. For in relations between equals, one need not grant rights to another; they are assumed as a matter of course.

To understand the reality of middle-class life around this issue, the shell of language with which the more highly educated protect themselves must be pierced. When it is, the behavior with which men effectively deny women permission stands revealed. Thus, referring to an unplanned pregnancy and his wife's wish for an abortion, one professional man said:

It's her choice; she has to raise the kids. I told her I'll go along with whatever she decides. [*After a moment's hesitation.*] But, you know, if she goes through with it, I'll never agree to have another child. If we destroy this one, we don't deserve to have another.

Have you told her that?

[*Defensively.*]Of course! She has to know how I feel.

How did she respond?

She cried and got angry. She said I wasn't giving her much of a choice. But it seems to me she ought to know what the consequences of her actions will be when she makes the decision, and those are the consequences. Anyhow, it's all over now; she's decided to have the baby.

Such are the "choices" that confronted this woman as she struggled to make the decision.

The difference, then, is not that middle-class marriages actually are so much more egalitarian, but that the *ideology* of equality is more strongly *asserted* there. This fact alone is, of course, not without consequences, paradoxical though they may be. On the one hand, it undoubtedly is a central reason why middle-class women are in the vanguard of the struggle for change in the family structure. On the other hand, an ideology so strongly asserted tends to obscure the reality, leaving middle-class women even more mystified than their working-class sisters about how power is distributed in their marriages. Thus, the middle-class wife who wants an abortion but decides against it because of her husband's threats, doesn't say, "He won't let me." Instead, she rationalizes:

It was a hard choice, but it was mine. Paul would have accepted anything I decided, but it just didn't seem right or fair for me to make that kind of decision alone when it affects both of us.

For the working-class woman, the power and authority of her husband are more openly acknowledged—at least around issues such as these. She knows when he won't let her; it's direct and explicit—too much so for her to rationalize it away.

Such differences in ideology are themselves a concomitant of class and the existential realities which people confront in their daily lives. First, there are important differences in what is expected of wives—in how they relate to their husbands' work, for example—and important consequences that flow from those expectations. Wives in professional middle-class families actually are expected to participate in their husbands' professional lives by cultivating an appropriate social circle, by being entertaining and charming hostesses and companions.[5] Most large corporations, after all, do not hire a middle or top executive without meeting and evaluating the candidate's wife. By definition, the tasks of such a wife are broader than those of the working-class wife. The wife of the executive or professional man must be active in the community, alert to world events, prepared to "shine"—only not *too* brightly— at a moment's notice. Husbands who require wives to perform such services must allow them to move more freely outside the home if they are to carry out their tasks properly.

The working-class man has no need of a wife with such accomplishments since his work life is almost wholly segregated from his family life. His wife has no positive, active role in helping him to get or keep a job, let alone in his advancement. No one outside the family cares how she keeps the house, raises the children, what books she reads, what opinions she holds on the state of the nation, the world, or the neighborhood. Her husband, therefore, is under no pressure to encourage either her freedom of movement or her self-development; and she has no external supports to legitimate whatever longings she may feel. Among the wives of the professional middle class, those longings and the activities they generate are supported by the requirements of the role. A charming hostess must at least be conversant with the world of ideas; an interesting companion must know something about the latest books. But for the working-class woman to develop such interests would require a rare order of giftedness, a willingness to risk separation from the world of family and intimates, and a tenacity of purpose and clarity of direction that few of us can claim.

In other ways, too, the realities of class make themselves felt both inside and outside the home. The professional man almost invariably is more highly educated than his wife—a fact that gives him an edge of superiority in their relationship; not so with his working-class counterpart. The professional man has the prospect of a secure and orderly work life—his feet on a prestigious and high-salaried career ladder; not so with his working-class counterpart. The professional man is a respected member of the community outside his home—his advice sought, his words valued; not so with his working-class counterpart.

Thus, the professional middle-class man is more secure, has more status and prestige than the working-class man—factors which enable him to assume a less *overtly* authoritarian role within the family. There are, after all, other places, other situations where his authority and power are tested and accorded legitimacy. At the same time, the demands of his work role for a satellite wife require that he risk the consequences of the more egalitarian family ideology. In contrast, for the working-class man, there are few such rewards in the world outside the home; the family usually is the only place where he can exercise power, demand obedience to his authority. Since his work role makes no demands for wifely participation, he is under fewer and less immediate external pressures to accept the egalitarian ideology.

Yet, despite the fact that, under these conditions, egalitarianism in the family—whether ideal or real—offers little benefit to working-class men, these men are not wholly without some understanding of the difficulties of their wives' position in the family. Listen to this twenty-eight-year-old assistant pressman, father of two, married ten years:

Whose life would you say is easier—a man's or a woman's?

Actually, I would say the man's life is easier because even though I do go to work every day and it's hard, when the day's over, that's it for me. But for her, when the kids are sick, she has to take care of them. And after supper, she's still doing things around the house.

I kind of rely on her for a lot of stuff, too. You know, like, "Where's my socks?" and all that sort of stuff. I only have one thing to think about. She has all these things. I mean, I have worries too, about how much money I'm going to make, and how we're going to do this thing or that, but that's not every day. She's got to worry every day about whether she's got enough money for groceries and for the kids' shoes and all the stuff she takes care of. And on top of that, she's got to worry about if I'm going to come home in a bad mood.

Indeed, there are more than twice as many husbands and wives who think that a man's life is simpler than a woman's than those who think the converse. And the answers—whether from women or men—are remarkably similar in content, although very different in tone.

The men tend to express these thoughts with a cool calmness—mildly regretful that life is so for their wives but with the assumption that it is ordained:

That's just the way life is. It's her job to keep the house and children and my job to earn the money. My wife couldn't do my job, and I couldn't be as good a cook and housekeeper as she is. So we just ought to do what we do best.

The women more often express themselves with heated frustration—angry that life is thus and wondering how they can change it:

It seems like I do everything. It's just taken for granted that I'm supposed to get it all done—as if it were natural.

I like sports, too. I wonder what would happen if I sat down in front of the TV and watched all the time like he does.

Especially when they also work outside the home, the women feel keenly the weight of all the burdens. For regardless of class, there is plenty of evidence that the amount of time husbands spend in family roles is unrelated to whether their wives work or not.[6] The major difference among the people I met is that the employed wives of professional middle-class men are more likely to hire someone to help with at least the heavy household chores. Not so among working-class women for whom household help is almost nonexistent.

Whose life would you say is easier—a man's or a woman's?

A thirty-year-old beautician, mother of two, married twelve years says:

Definitely, I'd say the man's life is simpler. He goes to work at a certain time, he comes home at a certain time, and it's over. We get up and it's there, and we go to bed and it's there. It's always there.

Another working mother of three, married seven years, replies:

The man's life is a lot easier; there's no doubt about it. He gets up in the morning; he gets dressed; he goes to work; he comes home in the evening; and he does whatever he wants after that.

As for me, I get up in the morning; I get dressed; I fix everybody's breakfast; I clean up the kitchen; I get the children ready for school and the baby ready to go to his baby-sitter; I take him to the baby-sitter. Then I first go to work. I work all day; I pick up the baby; I come home. The two older kids come home from my neighbor who takes care of them after school. Everybody wants me for something but I can't pay them any mind because I first have to fix dinner. Then I do the dishes; I clean up; I get the kids ready for bed. After the kids are finally asleep, I get to worry about the money because I pay all the bills and keep the checking account.

Doesn't your husband do anything at all?

Sometimes he helps get the kids to bed, but he won't touch a dish—not even to help clear the table. Mostly he's doing some project he likes or he's watching TV.

Her husband says:

It's not as bad as she says. I do a lot more around here than she gives me credit for. I won't do the dishes; that's her job, not mine. I didn't get married so I could do the dishes. But I help her out with some other things if she asks.

"If she asks"—that's precisely the issue in contest so much of the time, the issue about which women so often cry out:

Why do I have to ask? It's his house, too. They're his kids, too. Don't you think most women would like to have a husband help out once in a while without having to ask? It makes me feel like I'm begging him to do me a favor or else that I'm nagging him to death since he'll *never* do anything without my asking.

Interestingly, however, almost no one argues about the language of "him helping her." All agree that it's *her* job; the only difference between a couple is whether he *ought* to help her with it.[7]

Such are the contours of modern marriage. With all the talk about the changing structure of family roles, a close look reveals that when it comes to the division of labor in the family, it's still quite traditional. Over and over, that's the story: He does man's work; she does woman's work:

I make the money for her to bake the bread. Only women today don't bake bread anymore.

He "helps her out" when he feels like it:

If he wants to do something, then he does it. Yesterday, he helped clean up the yard, but that's because he wanted to do it. If he doesn't feel like it, he won't do anything, no matter what I say.

Household chores, when shared at all, are divided as they have been historically: he does the outside work; she does the inside. That means: he cleans the garage twice a year; she cleans the house every day. The one inside task he does most consistently is to take out the garbage but that, too, often doesn't get done without a struggle:[8]

I'll leave it in front of the door so he has to trip over it to get out. Even then, he'll walk around it sometimes, and I have to ask him to do it.

102

More often than not, work in the yard is shared, with the wife doing the lion's share. But even where the sharing is real, it is usually she who must take the responsibility for organizing and planning, she who reminds him of what needs to be done and when.

The big change, then, may lie in the fact that more women than ever before are now in the labor force, giving them the doubtful privilege of doing two days work in one—one on the job and the other after they get home at night. This is true not just in working-class families but in the professional middle class as well. Again, the ideology and rhetoric are different, but the reality is much the same. Thus, in the vast majority of those homes as well, there is more talk than action when it comes to the allocation and distribution of household and childrearing tasks.[9] With only a few exceptions, when a man does anything around the house that falls within the domain traditionally defined as the woman's, it is spoken of also as "helping her" and is almost always at the wife's instigation. The difference is in the women's attitudes toward the situation. For whether they work outside the home or not, more middle-class wives are angry about the burdens they carry in the family and more are able to express that anger with less fear and ambivalence than their working-class counterparts.

Among the working-class women, those who do not have outside jobs are least likely to complain about the division of labor in the family:

I think a woman should do all the housework. If I was working at a job, then I would expect him to do more.

That reasonable expectation, however, is quickly tempered with:

I wouldn't ever ask him to do something unless he wanted to do it, though.

Even those who spend many hours each week on jobs outside the home often try to assuage their anger with injunctions to themselves not to complain, and with reminders about how lucky they are compared to others. Indeed, hardly are the words out of their mouths than they try to modify or take back their complaints.

Typical are these comments of a twenty-nine-year-old woman who, remembering her alcoholic father and mindful of her sister's violence-prone husband, says:

Help around the house? Walter? I'm satisfied if he doesn't throw his clothes around when he comes home or, when he changes, if he puts his old clothes in the hamper instead of just dropping them.

But I really haven't got a right to gripe. I don't have a lot of problems that a lot of women I know do. I feel very lucky. My husband doesn't drink; he never does anything mean to me; he's nice to anyone that comes over; he doesn't gamble. So I really can't complain too much.

Another, aged thirty-two, qualifies her remarks:

I don't want you to think I'm complaining now. He's a good man, a lot better than most. Any woman who's got a man who hardly ever gets violent and who doesn't drink much hasn't got a lot to complain about.

But when I'm working, I sure wish I could have more help. With five kids and all, it's hard to work and do everything yourself. The kids help, but there's a lot they can't do.

When I'm not working, I think it's perfectly natural and right that I should do everything. Even now, I still feel it's my job; but it would be nice if he could help a little when I'm gone at work so much.

If they're not qualifying their complaints, they're denying them, and suffering all the anguish, pain, and depression that come when conflicts are repressed:

I don't know what's the matter with me. For the last few years it feels like there's two "me"s in there [*pointing to her head*]. One pulls me one way and the other pulls me the other way. It's like they're trying to pull me apart, and I keep trying and trying not to let it happen. I get so tired.

And I feel so guilty because I know I ought to be happy, and I can't figure out why I'm not. I have nothing to complain about, yet there's that "me" in there that keeps pulling at me and making me miserable and depressed all the time.

[*Twenty-four-year-old clerk,
mother of two, married seven years.*]

It is not just the household chores that so many women find so burdensome, however. Rather it is the very shape and structure of their lives, the sense that in every way they bear the responsibility for the family—its present and future:

Whose life would you say is easier—a man's or a woman's?

The question opens the floodgates of pain and frustration, especially for the women:

He just goes to work and brings some money home, but I have all the responsibilities. I tell him what the bills are. I know when there's not enough money to pay them all. I know when something's wrong in the family. I know when his brother and sister-in-law are splitting up. I know when his mother's unhappy. I know when there's a problem with the kids. Why, I'm even the one who knows when there's a problem in our marriage. I have to tell him about all those things and most of the time he just listens to a few words and tunes it out. I'm the one who knows about it; and I'm the one who gets stuck worrying what to do about it.

> [*Twenty-nine-year-old sandwich maker,*
> *mother of three, married ten years.*]

It is true that some men think their lives are harder than women's, and some women agree with them. Always, the reason is the same: she doesn't have to go to work every day. Yet, even those men who assert that view most adamantly, recoil with distaste when asked if they could conceive of changing places with their wives:

I couldn't stand being home every day, taking care of the house, or sick kids, or stuff like that. But that's because I'm a man. Men aren't supposed to do things like that, but it's what women are supposed to be doing. It's natural for them, so they don't mind it.

Few women would agree that they "don't mind it." They may believe it's their job, that it's what they *ought* to want to do. They may be frightened at the thought of having to support a family; they may even prefer the tasks of housewifery to a job once held that was dull and constricting. But no woman reacts with repugnance to the idea of changing places with her husband. Indeed, even those who say they would like it least refer only to his role as breadwinner, finding other aspects of their husbands' lives appealing:

I guess I wouldn't like to change places with him because I couldn't support the family like he does. Anyhow, it's not much fun knowing you have all the responsibility on your head. On the other hand, that's all men have to do. I don't mean it's easy, but it's *all* they do. We—women I mean—have a lot more to do and to worry about all the time. I guess what it boils down to is that the man does the harder physical work, but the woman does the harder emotional work. I mean, he has to get up every morning and go to work; I don't. It's true, I work three days a week; but it's different. The family doesn't depend on my working; it does on his. But when it comes down to the emotional work in the family, that's mine, all mine. In the long run, I guess that's harder because it never ends; the worries are always there—whether it's about the kids, or our families, or how we're getting along, even about money. He makes most of it, but it's never enough. And I have to worry how to pay the bills.

I get mad sometimes and wish I could change places with him. It would be such a relief to worry only about one thing. It feels like I drag around such a heavy load.

In well over three-quarters of the families, that "heavy load" includes the responsibility for paying the bills in a household where often there's either not enough income to match outgo, or where they're just balanced. The median income in these families is $12,300—a figure that sounds high until one looks at the Bureau of Labor Statistics figures which estimate that, in late 1974, a typical urban family of four in the San Francisco Bay Area needed $9,973 just to get by and $15,127 to maintain a moderate standard of living. Over 70 percent of these working-class families fall well below the amount designated for a moderate living standard. Of the remaining 30 percent, most barely reach that level, and all except two require two incomes and lots of overtime to get there. For most, then, there is little discretion in how earnings are allocated and spent:

Who manages the money in the family?

There's nothing to manage; it's all very predetermined. He puts his pay check in the bank, and I figure out what bills *have* to be paid this week, and write the checks.

So then, you decide how the money will be spent?

There's nothing to decide. I told you! It's already decided before we get the pay check. I have a budget, and there's nothing extra. If we ever *have* to buy something extra, we put it on Bank Americard, and then it's just another bill.

Decisions, then, are limited to which bills to pay now, which can be deferred—in effect, to assessing the best strategy for juggling the creditors:

I pay all the bills and manage the money—if you can call it managing. All it means is that I get stuck with all the scut work. When there's a problem with dun notices, or what have you, I'm the one who faces it. If there's anything that has to be explained or worked around so that things like the electric don't get turned off, I'm the one who gets stuck with it. Like, just the other day, P. G. & E. was going to shut off the electric, and I was the one who had to face them and figure out a way so they wouldn't do it.

> [*Thirty-four-year-old sales clerk,*
> *mother of three, married fourteen years.*]

Observers of American family life often point to the fact that so many women handle the family finances as evidence that they wield a great deal of power and influence in the family. A look *behind* that bare fact, however, suggests some other conclusions.[10] Among the professional middle-class families, for example, where median income is $22,000—a level that allows for substantial discretionary spending—the figures flip over almost perfectly; the *men* manage the money in three-quarters of the families. Moreover, among those working-class families where some discretion in spending exists, almost always the husband handles the money, or the wife pays the bills while he makes the decisions. A thirty-three-year-old housewife, mother of three, married fifteen years, says:

I handle the money, but he makes the decisions. Like, he decided about whether we were going to buy this house or not, or whether we should buy a car, and how much we should spend for it. Some things I decide, like when the kids need shoes. But he watches out for what we're spending money on, and I pretty well know what it's okay for me to do and what's not okay.

Her husband, a thirty-six-year-old plumbing foreman, agrees:

Yeah, I make the major decisions as far as financial things, as far as any important things are concerned, I guess. I don't think she minds, though. She agrees with me that I'm used to making decisions and she's not, and that I know more about making decisions and have more experience in that type of thing.

Conversely, in the few professional families where the women manage the money, almost invariably they are families just beginning the climb upward—incomes are still quite low, and the choices around spending are very limited.

It seems reasonable to conclude, then, that men manage the money when there is enough of it so that the task involves some real decision-making. Only then is the job worth their while. A thirty-five-year-old automobile bodyman says:

She used to handle the money. It was a pretty cut-and-dried affair then, and I didn't need to spend my time on it. But now there's more of it, and there are decisions that have to be made about what we need to buy and when we should buy it. So I do it now.

His wife comments acidly:

Now that we're better off, he takes care of the money. When there wasn't enough, he was glad for me to do it because then he didn't have to worry about what bills to pay. As soon as we got a little more money, he started to butt in all the time. So it was okay with me when he decided to take it over. When I was doing it, I was just handling the chores. I didn't have any control over the money or the decisions about how it was spent. So what was I giving up?

While it's true that no one likes to do the difficult or tedious tasks of life, and that men have the option of turning some, such as these, over to their wives, this is not the *only* reason why they do so. At least as compelling, perhaps, is the fact that it permits them to avoid confronting the painful reality that they are not bringing home enough money to buy all the necessities they need and the comforts they would like. If he hands over his pay check and it doesn't stretch quite far enough, he can behave as if the problem lies not with his inadequate income but with her short-comings as a manager. Listen to this couple, parents of three children, married eight years. The wife:

It takes quite a bit of managing to run the house with so little money, and with taxes and prices going up all the time, and his wages not going up. Every time we fix up the house a little bit, they call it an improve-ment and increase the property tax. But it's really just that we're trying to keep the place together so it shouldn't fall down on our heads.

It's really a problem because I never know how much the new taxes are going to be. I save a little every week to put away for taxes and then, all of a sudden the new tax bill comes and it's higher than I ex-pected. So we have to go into debt to pay the taxes again. And he gets mad because he says if I managed better, it wouldn't happen.

The husband:

She spends too much. I don't know why she can't manage better. We always seem to be behind; she just can't save anything. As soon as she's got a couple of bucks in her hands, she finds something to spend it on. It makes me mad as hell sometimes when I work so hard and there's not enough money for me to spend on something I want.

You know, I'm dying to get away on vacation, to see some of the country. But there's never any money. Can you believe it, I've been to Vietnam but I've never seen the Grand Canyon. Hell, I've never even been to Lake Tahoe.

One husband, at least momentarily aware of the bind he puts his wife in, comments:

I know it's not fair to her sometimes. I let her take care of the money, and then she has to listen to me asking her why we don't have enough, as if it's her fault.

Under such circumstances, managing the money in the family becomes yet another onerous chore to which the woman must attend. Adding to her burdens is the wife's knowledge that this is a difficult issue for her husband, and that almost anything she says on the subject is likely to turn out badly:

It's hard to talk about it because if I complain about money or that things are hard, he thinks it's a reflection on him. So I really try not to do that.

There couldn't be a harder-working person, so it's not his fault. It's just the way it is, and I try not to make him feel bad because there's not enough money sometimes. But even if I don't talk about it, he knows it. And sometimes he just needs to blame me even though we both know it's not my fault any more than it's his fault.

It is not only around decisions that involve spending money that men remain dominant, but in almost every other sphere of domestic life as well. Indeed, the studies of family power which tote up the number of decisions each spouse makes without reference to their relative importance, then conclude that wives and husbands are equally powerful, are absurd.[11] But the myth of egalitarianism runs so deep that even the marriage partners can be deluded by it:

How are the decisions made in the family?

Most people say "fifty-fifty." Yet, when one pushes the question a little further the illusion is quickly dispelled.

Who has veto power over a decision?

Almost all agree: the husband. One man's comments are typical:

It's kind of a joint effort up to a point. We'll talk it over and, if we agree, we do it. But if I say a flat "Forget it," that's it.

What happens if she says no to something you want?

Then she has to convince me. But she very seldom says no if I want it. Maybe that's because she knows she'd have a hard time convincing me.

In general, "fifty-fifty" turns out to mean that when both agree, they act. If he wants something she doesn't want, he can usually get it. If it's the other way around, she has to convince him or find ways to "get around him." When they decide together, he makes policy, she executes it:

How are decisions made in the family?

They're mutual, you know, fifty-fifty. She asks me whether we can buy some furniture, let's say. If I say okay, she goes out and looks around. When she picks out something she likes, she asks me to go look at it. If I approve of it, she buys it. If not, she looks some more.

Some decisions are exclusively his—cars, for example:

When it comes to cars, I make the decisions. But that's because she doesn't know anything about it.

. . . and insurance:

I said I wanted to have more insurance because I worry about what will happen. He said, "No, we don't need any more." Also, I thought we should have earthquake insurance, and he said No, and that it was dumb for me to worry about things like that.

Regardless of who actually writes the checks and pays the bills, only he can spend any substantial amount of money without asking permission:

She wouldn't dare go out and spend $100 without asking me.

Would you dare?

If I decided we could afford it, sure I would.

Even on such decisions that are traditionally thought to be women's—the house, for example—his needs usually come first:

I wanted to live someplace further from the Bay, someplace where it's sunnier. I'm always cold here, and I just feel a lot better in a warmer place. But he wanted to live someplace that wasn't too far to go to work, so we bought this place.

If his needs are not the primary consideration, then most likely his desires will be:

She wanted to get a house right away, but I wanted to get some other things before we bought the house. I knew we'd get the house someday, but I wasn't so sure about the other things. I thought we ought to have a nice car, and I wanted a boat before we got the house. So we got them, and then we got the house. Patty still doesn't like this house; she wanted a nicer one. She doesn't like the neighborhood either, but I don't see anything wrong with it. I'd like to get her a house she likes better someday, but this is plenty good enough for us for now.

And he *always* decides how much money they can spend on the house which, of course, effectively determines what kind of house they will buy and the neighborhood they will live in:

I wanted a better house, so I was willing to spend more money. He said, "No, we spend this much and no more." And that's the way it was. I suppose it's not unfair because he has to work to pay the bills.

So stuck are we in our traditional ways of viewing relationships in the family that most of us nod assent to this seemingly reasonable statement. "That's right," we think, "it's fair; he *does* have to work to pay the bills," forgetting, as she does, that this woman also works both inside and outside the house, and that it is she who struggles with the problems of balancing the budget and the checkbook.

Thus, decision-making, too, still largely breaks down along traditional lines. Women are more apt to have a relatively free hand in decisions relating to internal household issues and bringing up the children, although the latter often is a source of conflict. Wives complain that husbands don't pay enough attention to children, that they're stuck with all the tasks of training and discipline. Husbands complain that wives can't control the children, that they're not strict enough.

Generally, then, it's safe to say that women decide what to have for dinner tonight, when the kids need new shoes, when they need to see a doctor. Men make the other—bigger—decisions: what kind of car the family will own, when to buy a house and where it will be, even whether their wives will work or not. Today's more companionate marriages mean that there may be more discussion, that a wife has a chance to "say her piece," that the battle to reconcile the differences will have more heat and smoke. But in the final analysis, when a difference remains, almost always, it is the man who decides; almost always, it is he who holds the final veto power.

On the surface, working-class women generally seem to accept and grant legitimacy to their husbands' authority, largely because they understand his need for it. If not at home, where is a man who works on an assembly line, in a warehouse, or a refinery to experience himself as a person whose words have weight, who is "worth" listening to? But just below the surface, there lies a well of ambivalence; for the cost of her compliance is high. In muting her own needs to be responsive to his, she is left dissatisfied—a dissatisfaction that makes her so uncomfortable she often has difficulty articulating it even to herself. What right have I to complain? she is likely to ask herself. After all, I'm so much better off than my mother, she keeps reminding herself. But ask her what her dreams are for her children, and the dissatisfaction comes tumbling out:

What would you like for your children when they grow up?

Almost every woman in the study was unequivocal in her hope that her daughter would not marry so young:

I'd like her to be independent and not to have to rush into marriage.

I'd like my girls to think about getting a job and getting out and seeing a little of the world after high school before they settle down to family life.

I sure hope she doesn't get married until she's at least twenty-two or -three.

I don't want the girls to have the regrets I've had, so I hope they take their time and do whatever they want to do before they get married and can't do anything more. Don't misunderstand! I'm glad I'm married, and I want them to be married; only not so young.

Could anything more clearly reveal the feelings these women have about their own lives?

CHAPTER

7

Changing Expectations:
New Sources
of Strain

I give her a nice home, a nice car, all those fancy appliances. I don't cheat on her. We got three nice kids—nobody could ask for better kids. And with all that, she's not happy. I worry about it, but I can't figure out what's the matter, so how can I know what to do? I just don't know what she wants.

> [*Twenty-nine-year-old truck driver, married nine years.*]

"I JUST DON'T KNOW what she wants"—that's the plaintive and uncomprehending cry of most working-class men, the cry that bedevils most marriages. Sadly, she often also doesn't know what she wants. She knows only that the dream is not being fulfilled—that she's married but feels lonely:

It sounds silly, I know, but here I am in a house with three kids and my husband, and lots of times I feel like I might just as well be living alone.

... that life feels curiously empty:

You wake up one day and you say to yourself, "My God, is this all there is? Is it really possible that this is what life is all about?"

... that she's often filled with an incomprehensible anger:

I feel like I go crazy-angry sometimes. It makes me say and do things to Randy or the kids that I hate myself for. I keep wondering what makes me do those things when one part of me knows I don't really mean it.

... and that guilt and anxiety are her steady companions:

I don't know what's the matter with me that I don't appreciate what I've got. I feel guilty all the time, and I worry about it a lot. Other women, they seem to be happy with being married and having a house and kids. What's the matter with me?

"What's the matter" with her is that, even apart from the financial burdens incurred in buying all those goods, they add little to the emotional satisfactions of life. The advertisers promises of instant happiness prove to be a lie—good for the gross national product but not for the human soul.

Sure, it's great to show those goodies off to friends and neighbors. After all those years of poverty, it makes you feel good finally to have something and to let people see it. Besides, they make life easier, more comfortable. Now there's time for things other than household drudgery. But what things? Companionship? Intimacy? Sharing? What are those things? And how does one find them?

She has a vague idea. Television shows, the women's magazines —they all talk about something called communication. Marriage partners have to communicate, they say; they have to talk, to tell each other how they feel. So she talks. And he tries to listen. But somehow, it doesn't work. He listens, but he cannot hear. Sometimes sooner, sometimes later, he withdraws in silence, feeling attacked:

When she comes after me like that, yapping like that, she might as well be hitting me with a bat.

... vulnerable:

It makes me feel like I'm doing something wrong, like I'm not a very good husband or something.

... and helpless:

No matter what I say, it's no good. If I try to tell her she's excited over nothing, that only makes it worse. I try to keep my cool and be logical, but nothing works.

This is the dilemma of modern marriage—experienced at all class levels, but with particular acuteness among the working-class families I met. For once marriage is conceived of as more than an economic arrangement—that is, as one in which the emotional needs of the individual are attended to and met—the role segregation and the consequent widely divergent socialization patterns for women and men become clearly dysfunctional.[1] And it is among the working class that such segregation has been most profound, where there has been least incentive to change.

Thus, they talk *at* each other, *past* each other, or *through* each other—rarely *with* or *to* each other. He blames her: "She's too emotional." She blames him: "He's always so rational." In truth, neither is blameworthy. The problem lies in the fact that they do not have a language with which to communicate, with which to understand each other. They are products of a process that trains them to relate to only one side of themselves—she, to the passive, tender, intuitive, verbal, emotional side; he, to the active, tough, logical, nonverbal, unemotional one.[2] From infancy, each has been programmed to be split off from the other side; by adulthood, it is distant from consciousness, indeed.[3]

They are products of a disjunction between thought and feeling, between emotionality and rationality that lies deep in Western culture. Even though she complains, both honestly believe what the culture has taught them. To be rational is the more desired state; it is good, sane, strong, adult. To be emotional is the less desired state; it is bad, weak, childlike. She:

I know I'm too emotional and I can't really be trusted to be sensible a lot of the time. I need him; he's the one in the family you can always count on to think about things right, not mixed up, like me.

He:

She's like a kid sometimes, so emotional. I'm always having to reason with her, to explain things to her. If it weren't for me, nothing would happen very rational around here.

This equation of emotional with nonrational, this inability to apprehend the logic of emotions lies at the root of much of the discontent between the sexes, and helps to make marriage the most difficult of all relationships.

Her lifetime training prepares her to handle the affective, expressive side in human affairs; his, to handle the nonaffective, instrumental side. Tears, he has been taught, are for sissies; feelings, for women. A *real* man is the strong, silent type of the folklore—a guy who needs nothing from anyone, who ignores feelings and pain, who can take it on the chin without a whimper. For a lifetime, much of his energy has gone into molding himself in that image—into denying his feelings, refusing to admit they exist. Without warning or preparation, he finds himself facing a wife who pleads, "Tell me your feelings." He responds with bewilderment. "What is there to tell?"[4]

When they try to talk, she relies on the only tools she has, the mode with which she is most familiar; she becomes progressively more emotional and expressive. He falls back on the only tools he has; he gets progressively more rational—determinedly reasonable. She cries for him to attend to her feelings, her pain. He tells her it's silly to feel that way; she's just being emotional. That clenched-teeth reasonableness invalidates her feelings, leaving her sometimes frightened:

I get scared that maybe I'm crazy. He's always so logical and reasonable that I begin to feel, "What's the matter with me that I'm so emotional?"

. . . sometimes angry:

When he just sits there telling me I'm too emotional, I get so mad, I go up the wall. Sometimes I get so mad I wish I could hit him. I did once, but he hit me back, and he can hurt me more than I can hurt him.

. . . almost always tearful and despairing:

I wind up crying and feeling terrible. I get so sad because we can't really talk to each other a lot of times. He looks at me like I'm crazy, like he just doesn't understand a word I'm saying.

Repeatedly, the experience is the same, the outcome of the interaction, predictable. Yet, each has such a limited repertoire that they are consigned to playing out the same theme over and over again—he, the rational man; she, the hysterical woman.

But these almost wholly sociological notions—notions which speak to socialization patterns—tell only one part of the story of human development. The other part is told in the language of psychology—a language that is given its fullest and most complex expression in psychoanalytic theory. From that theory, Nancy Chodorow has presented us with a brilliant and provocative reformulation of Oedipal theory which successfully crosses the sociological with the psychological as it accounts for the dynamics of both the inner and outer world as they affect sex-role development.[5]

Her argument starts from the premise that the differences in male and female personality are rooted in the structure of the family—in particular, in the fact that women are the primary childrearers. As a result, the mother becomes the first object with which an infant—male or female—identifies, the first attachment formed. Coincident with the forming of these identifications and attachments, other developmental tasks emerge in the period between infancy and childhood—a primary one being the development of an appropriate gender identity. For a girl, that task is a relatively straightforward one—a continuous and gradual process of internalization of a feminine identity with mother as model. For a boy, however, role learning is discontinuous involving, as it must, the rejection of his early identification with his mother as he seeks an appropriate masculine identity.

Since a girl need not reject that early identification in order to negotiate the Oedipal phase successfully, feminine personality is based on less repression of inner objects, less fixed and firm ego-splitting, and greater continuity of external relationships. With no need to repress or deny their earliest attachment, girls can define and experience themselves as part of and continuous with others. Consequently, women tend to have more complex inner lives, more ability to engage in a variety of interpersonal relationships, and more concern with ongoing relational issues.

On the other hand, boys must repress these same attachments as they shift their identification from mother to father. That means that they must distinguish and differentiate themselves in a way that girls need not. In doing so, they come to define and experience themselves as more separate from others and with more rigid ego boundaries; and adult masculine personality comes to be defined more in terms of denial of connection and relations.

Such ideas present profound implications for the marriage relationship. For if it is true that their earliest experiences in the family mean that men must deny relations and connection while women must be preoccupied with them, we are faced anew with the realization—this time from the psychoanalytic perspective—that the existing structure of family relations, especially in its delegation of the parenting function solely or dominantly to the mother, makes the attainment of compatible relations between women and men extraordinarily difficult.

It hardly need be said that such relationships between men and women are not given to the working-class alone. Without doubt, the description I have been rendering represents the most common interactional pattern in American marriage. These are the behavioral consequences of the dominant sex-role socialization patterns in the culture and of the existing structure of family relations within which boys and girls internalize an appropriate identity—patterns which generate the role stereotypes that women and men bring to marriage and which effectively circumscribe their emotional negotiations.

Still, it is also true that the norms of middle-class marriage for much longer have called for more companionate relationships—for more sharing, for more exploration of feelings, and for more exchange of them. Thus, middle-class women and men have more practice and experience in trying to overcome the stereotypes. And, perhaps more important, they have more models around them for how to do so. This is not to suggest that they have done it so well, as a casual glance at the divorce rate will show; only that the demands on the marriage partners for different behaviors have been around for much longer, that there is a language that gives those demands legitimacy, and that there has been more experimentation in modifying the stereotypes.

Among working-class couples, the demand for communication, for sharing, is newer. Earlier descriptions of working-class family life present a portrait of wives and husbands whose lives were distinctly separate, both inside and outside the home—the wife attending to her household role, the husband to his provider role. He came home at night tired and taciturn; she kept herself and the children out of his way. For generations, it was enough that each did their job adequately—he, to bring home the bacon; she, to cook it. Intimacy, companionship, sharing—these were not part of the dream.[6]

But dreams change—sometimes before the people who must live them are ready. Suddenly, new dreams are stirring. *Intimacy, companionship, sharing*—these are now the words working-class women speak to their men, words that turn *both* their worlds upside down. For while it is the women who are the discontented, who are pushing for change, they, no less than their men, are confused about what they are asking:

I'm not sure what I want. I keep talking to him about communication, and he says, "Okay, so we're talking; now what do you want?" And I don't know what to say then, but I know it's not what I mean.

... and frightened and unsure about the consequences:

I sometimes get worried because I think maybe I want too much. He's a good husband; he works hard; he takes care of me and the kids. He could go out and find another woman who would be very happy to have a man like that, and who wouldn't be all the time complaining at him because he doesn't feel things and get close.

The men are even worse off. Since it's not *their* dream, they are less likely still to have any notion of what is being asked of them. They only know that, without notice, the rules of the game have been changed; what worked for their fathers, no longer works for them. They only know that there are a whole new set of expectations—in the kitchen, in the parlor, in the bedroom—that leave them feeling bewildered and threatened.[7] She says:

I keep telling him that the reason people get divorced isn't *only* financial but because they can't communicate. But I can't make him understand.

He says:

I swear, I don't know what she wants. She keeps saying we have to talk, and then when we do, it always turns out I'm saying the wrong thing.

I get scared sometimes. I always thought I had to think things to myself; you know, not tell her about it. Now she says that's not good. But it's hard. You know, I think it comes down to that I like things the way they are, and I'm afraid I'll say or do something that'll really shake things up. So I get worried about it, and I don't say anything.

For both women and men, the fears and uncertainties are compounded by the fact that there are no models in their lives for the newly required and desired behaviors. Television shows them people whose lives seem unreal—outside the realm of personal experience or knowledge. The daytime soap operas, watched almost exclusively by women, *do* picture men who may be more open and more available for intimacy. But the men on the soaps don't work at ordinary jobs, doing ordinary things, for eight, ten, twelve hours a day. They're engaged either in some heroic, life-saving, glamour job to which working-class viewers can't relate or, worse yet, work seems to be one long coffee break during which they talk about their problems. Nighttime fare, when the men are home, is different, but no less unreal, featuring the stoic private eye, the brave cop, the tight-lipped cowboy.

The argument about the impact of the mass media on blue-collar workers is complex, contradictory, and largely unsatisfactory. Some observers insist that the mass media represent the most powerful current by which blue-collar workers are swept into conformity with middle-class values and aspirations;[8] others that blue-collar men especially resist exposure to middle-class manners and mores as they are presented on television—minimizing that exposure by exercising great discrimination in program choices;[9] still others that the idealized and romanticized figures on television are so unreal to the average blue-collar viewer that they have little impact on their lives and little effect on their behavior.[10]

Perhaps all three of these seemingly irreconcilable perspectives are true. The issue may not be *whether* television or other mass media affect people's lives and perceptions. Of course they do. The question we must ask more precisely is: In what ways are Americans of any class touched and affected by their exposure to television? For the professional middle class, it may well be an affirming experience; for the working class, a disconfirming one since there are no programs that deal with their problems, their prospects, and their values in sympathetic and respectful ways.[11]

If their own lives in the present provide no models and the media offer little that seems relevant, what about the past? Unfortunately for young working-class couples, family backgrounds provide few examples of openness, companionship, or communication between husbands and wives:

I don't think we ever had a good concept of what marriage was about. His family was the opposite of mine. They didn't drink like mine did, and they were more stable. Yet he feels they didn't give him a good concept either. There wasn't any drinking and fighting and carrying on, but there wasn't any caring either.

Even those few who recall their parents' marriages as good ones don't remember them talking much to one another and have no sense at all that they might have shared their inner lives:

Would you describe a typical evening in the family when you were growing up?

A twenty-five-year-old manicurist, mother of two, married seven years, replies:

Let me think. I don't really know what happened; nothing much, I guess. My father came home at four-thirty, and we ate right away. Nobody talked much at the table; it was kind of a quiet affair.

What about your parents' relationship? Do you remember how they behaved with each other; whether they talked to each other?

Gee, I don't know. It's hard to think about them as being *with* each other. I don't think they talked a lot; at least, I never saw them talking.

I can't imagine them sitting down to talk over problems or something like that, if that's what you mean.

Yes, that *is* what I mean. But that was the last generation; what about this one?

Would you describe a typical evening in your own family now?

For some, less than half, it's better—a level of companionship, caring, and sharing that, while not all they dream of, is surely better than they knew in their past. Fathers attend more to children; husbands at least try to "hear" their wives; couples struggle around some of the emotional issues I have identified in these pages. For most, however, nothing much has changed since the last generation. Despite the yearning for more, relations between husband and wife are benumbed, filled with silence; life seems empty and meaningless; laughter, humor, fun is not a part of the daily ration. Listen to this couple married seven years. The wife:

Frank comes home from work; now it's about five because he's been working overtime every night. We eat right away, right after he comes home. Then, I don't know. The kids play a while before bed, watch TV, you know, stuff like that. Then, I don't know; we don't do anything except maybe watch more TV or something like that. I don't know what else—nothing, I guess. We just sit, that's all.

That's it? Nothing else?

Yeah, that's right, that's all. [*A short silence, then angrily.*] Oh yeah, I forgot. Sometimes he's got one of his projects he works on. Like now, he's putting that new door in the kitchen. It's still nothing. When he finishes doing it, we just sit.

Her husband describes the same scene:

I come home at five and we eat supper right away. Then, I sit down with coffee and a beer and watch TV. After that, if I'm working on a project, I do that for a little while. If not, I just watch.

Life is very predictable. Nothing much happens; we don't do much. Everyone sits in the same place all the time and does the same thing every night. It's satisfying to me, but maybe it's not for her, I don't know. Maybe she wants to go to a show or something once in a while, I don't know. She doesn't tell me.

Don't you ask her?

No. I suppose I should, but it's really hard to think about getting out. We'd need someone to stay with the kids and all that. Besides, I'm tired. I've been out all day, seeing different people and stuff. I don't feel like going out after supper again.

Is there some time that you two have for yourselves, to talk things over and find out how you feel about things?

The wife:

There's plenty of time; we just don't do it. He doesn't ever think there's anything to talk about. I'm the one who has to nag him to talk always, and then I get disgusted.

He'd be content just living, you know, just nothing but living for the rest of his life. It don't make no difference to him where he lives or how people around him are feeling. I don't know how anybody can be like that.

A lot of times I get frustrated. I just wish I could talk to him about things and he could understand. If he had more feelings himself, maybe he'd understand more. Don't you think so?

Her husband agrees that he has problems handling both his feelings and hers:

I'm pretty tight-lipped about most things most of the time, especially personal things. I don't express what I think or feel. She keeps trying to get me to, but, you know, it's hard. Sometimes I'm not even sure what she wants me to be telling her. And when she gets all upset and emotional, I don't know what to say or what to do.

Sometimes she gets to nagging me about what I'm thinking or feeling, and I tell her, "Nothing," and she gets mad. But I swear, it's true; I'm not thinking about anything.

Difficult for her to believe, perhaps, but it *is* true. After a life-time of repressing his feelings, he often *is* a blank, unaware that he's thinking or feeling anything. Moreover, when emotions have been stored for that long, they tend to be feared as especially threatening or explosive. He continues:

Maybe it sounds a little crazy, but I'm afraid once I let go, I might get past the point where I know what I'm doing. If I let myself go, I'm afraid I could be dangerous. She keeps telling me that if you keep things pent up inside you like that, something's going to bust one day.

I think a lot of the problem is that our personalities are just very different. I'm the quiet type. If I have something I have to think about, I have to get by myself and do it. Elly, she just wants to talk about it, always talking about her feelings.

Yakketty-yakkers, that's what girls are. Well, I don't know; guys talk, too. But, you know, there's a difference, isn't there? Guys talk about things and girls talk about feelings.

Indeed that *is* the difference, precisely the difference I have been pointing to—"Guys talk about things and girls talk about feelings" —a difference that plagues marriage partners as they struggle to find ways to live with each other.

Again, the question presents itself: Is this just a phenomenon of working-class life? Clearly, it is not, for the social and psychological processes that account for the discrepant and often incompatible development of women and men apply across class and throughout the culture. Still, there are important class differences in the way these broad socio-cultural mandates are interpreted and translated into behavior—differences that are rooted in class situation and experience. Thus, there are differences in the early childhood and family experiences of children who grow up in working-class homes and those who live in professional middle-class homes, differences in the range of experiences through their adolescence and young adulthood, and differences in the kinds of problems and preoccupations they face in their adult lives—on the job and in the family.

Whether boys or girls, children in the homes of the professional middle class have more training in exploring the socio-emotional realm and more avenues for such exploration. It's true that for the girls, this usually is the *focus* of their lives, while for the boys, it is not. Nevertheless, compared to childrearing patterns in working-class families, professional middle-class families make fewer and less rigid sex-role distinctions in early childhood.[12] As small children, therefore, boys in such middle-class homes more often get the message that it's all right to cry, to be nurturant as well as nurtured, to be reflective and introspective, even at times to be passive—in essence, in some small measure, to relate to their expressive side.

Not once in a professional middle-class home did I see a young boy shake his father's hand in a well-taught "manly" gesture as he bid him good night. Not once did I hear a middle-class parent scornfully—or even sympathetically—call a crying boy a sissy or in any way reprimand him for his tears. Yet, these were not uncommon observations in the working-class homes I visited. Indeed, I was impressed with the fact that, even as young as six or seven, the working-class boys seemed more emotionally controlled —more like miniature men—than those in the middle-class families.

These differences in childrearing practices are expressed as well in the different demands the parents of each class make upon the schools—differences that reflect the fact that working-class boys are expected to be even less emotional, more controlled than their middle-class counterparts.[13] For the working-class parent, school is a place where teachers are expected to be tough disciplinarians; where children are expected to behave respectfully and to be punished if they do not; and where one mark of that respect is that they are sent to school neatly dressed in their "good" clothes and expected to stay that way through the day. None of these values is highly prized in the professional middle class. For them, schools are expected to be relatively loose, free, and fun; to encourage initiative, innovativeness, creativity, and spontaneity; and to provide a place where children—boys as well as girls—will learn social and interpersonal skills. The children of these middle-class families are sent to nursery school early—often as young as two and a half—not just because their mothers want the free time, but because the social-skill training provided there is considered a crucial part of their education.

These differences come as no surprise if we understand both the past experience and the future expectations of both sets of parents. Most highly educated parents have little fear that their children won't learn to read, write, and do their sums. Why should they? They learned them, and learned them well. Their children have every advantage that they had and plenty more: books, games, toys—all designed to excite curiosity and to stimulate imagination—and parents who are skillful in aiding in their use.

Working-class parents, however, have no such easy assurances about their children's educational prospects. Few can look back on their own school years without discomfort—discomfort born of painful reminders of all they didn't learn, of the many times they felt deficient and inadequate. Further, when they look at the schools their children attend now, they see the same pattern repeating itself. For, in truth, the socio-economic status of the children in a school is the best indicator of school-wide achievement test scores—that is, the lower the socio-economic status, the lower the scores.[14]

Observing this phenomenon, many analysts and educators argue that these low achievement records in poor and working-class schools are a consequence of the family background—the lack of culture and educational motivation in the home—an explanation that tends to blame the victim for the failure of our social institutions. Elsewhere, I have entered the debate about *who* is to blame for these failures on the side of the victims.[15] Here, the major point is simply that, regardless of where we think responsibility lies, working-class parents quite rightly fear that their children may not learn to read very well; that they may not be able to do even the simple arithmetic required to be an intelligent consumer. Feeling inadequate and lacking confidence that they can pass on their slim skills to their children, such parents demand that the schools enforce discipline in the belief that only then will their children learn all that they themselves did not.

This, however, is only one part of the explanation of why the sons of the professional middle class are brought up in a less rigidly stereotypic mode than are the sons of the working class— the part that is rooted in past experience. But past experience combines with present reality to create future expectations, because parents, after all, do not raise their children in a vacuum— without some idea of what the future holds for them, some sense of what they will need to survive the adult world for which they are destined. In fact, it is out of just such understandings that parental attitudes and values about childraising are born.[16] Thus, professional middle-class parents, assuming that their children are destined to do work like theirs—work that calls for innovation, initiative, flexibility, creativity, sensitivity to others, and a well-developed set of interpersonal skills—call for an educational system that fosters those qualities. Working-class parents also assume that their children will work at jobs roughly similar to their own. But in contrast to the requirements of professional or executive work, in most working-class jobs, creativity, innovation, initiative, flexibility are considered by superiors a hindrance. ("You're not getting paid to think!" is an oft-heard remonstrance.) Those who must work at such jobs may need nothing so much as a kind of iron-willed discipline to get them to work every day and to keep them going back year after year. No surprise, then, that such parents look suspiciously at spontaneity whether at home or at school. No surprise, either, that early childhood training tends to focus on respect, orderliness, cleanliness—in a word, discipline—especially for the boys who will hold these jobs, and that schools are called upon to reinforce these qualities.

Finally, men in the professional middle class presently live in an environment that gives some legitimacy to their stirrings and strivings toward connection with their emotional and expressive side. The extraordinary proliferation of the "growth-movement" therapies, which thrive on their appeal to both men and women of the upper middle class, is an important manifestation of that development. Another is the nascent men's movement—a response to the women's movement—with its men's groups, its male authors who write to a male audience encouraging their search for expressiveness. While it may be true that numerically all these developments account for only a small fraction of American men, it is also true that whatever the number, they are almost wholly drawn from the professional middle class.

For working-class men, these movements might as well not exist. Most don't know of them. The few who do, look at their adherents as if they were "kooks," "queers," or otherwise deficient, claiming to see no relevance in them to their own lives. Yet if one listens carefully to what lies beneath the surface of their words, the same stirrings for more connection with other parts of themselves, for more intimate relations with their wives are heard from working-class men as well. Often inchoate and inarticulately expressed, sometimes barely acknowledged, these yearnings, nevertheless, exist. But the struggle for their realization is a much more lonely and isolated one—removed not only from the public movements of our time but from the lives of those immediately around them—a private struggle in which there is no one to talk to, no examples to learn from. They look around them and see neighbors, friends, brothers, and sisters who are no better—sometimes far worse off—than they:

We're the only ones in the two families who have any kind of a marriage. One of my brothers ran out on his wife, the other one got divorced. Her sister and her husband are separated because he kept beating her up; her brother is still married, but he's a drunk. It makes it hard. If you never saw it in your family when you were growing up, then all the kids in both families mess up like that, it's hard to know what a good marriage is like. I guess you could say there hasn't been much of a model of one around us.

Without models, it is indeed hard—hard to know what to expect, hard to know how to act. You can't ask friends because they don't seem to have the same problems, not even the same feelings. One twenty-nine-year old husband lamented:

I sometimes think I'm selfish. She's the support—the moral support—in the family. But when she needs support, I just don't give it to her. Maybe it's not just selfishness, it's that I don't know what she wants and I don't know how.

The worst thing is, I've got nobody to talk to about how a guy can be different. The guys at work, all they ever talk about is their cars or their trucks. Oh, they talk about women, but it's only to brag about how they're making it with this chick or that one. And my brother, it's no use talking to him; he don't know where anything's at. He runs around every night, comes home drunk, beats up his wife.

I know Joanie's not so happy, and I worry about what to do about it. But the guys I know, they don't worry about things like that.

Don't they? He doesn't really know because he dare not ask.

How do you know they don't worry about such things? Have you asked them?

He looks up, puzzled, as if wondering how anybody could even think of such a thing, and answers quickly:

Ask them? No! Why would I do that? They'd think I was nuts or something. People don't talk about those things; you just *know* where those guys are; you don't have to ask them.

In fact, many of those men are suffering the same conflicts and concerns—wondering, as he does, what happened to the old familiar world; fearful, as he is, that their masculine image will be impaired if they talk about the things that trouble them. But if they can't talk to brothers, friends, work mates, where do they turn?

Maybe you could talk to Joan about what you could do to make things better in your marriage?

Dejectedly, he replies:

What good would that do? She's only a girl. How would she know how a guy is supposed to act?

The women generally also suffer alone. Despite all the publicity generated by the women's movement about the dissatisfactions women experience in marriage, most working-class women continue to believe that their feelings are uniquely theirs. Few have any contact with the movement or the people in it; few feel any support for their struggle from that quarter:

They put you down if you want to be married and raise kids, like there's something the matter with you.

Nor do they want it. For the movement is still a fearsome thing among working-class wives, and their responses to it are largely ambivalent, largely dominated by the negative stereotypes of the media. "Bra-burners," "man-haters"—these labels still are often heard.

Most believe in equal pay for equal work, but even that generally is not unequivocal:

Yes, I believe women should be paid the same as men if they're doing the same job. I mean, most of the time, I believe it. But if a man has a family to support and she doesn't, then it's different.

Few believe that women should compete equally in the job market with men:

If a man with a wife and kids needs a job, no woman ought to be able to take it away from him.

Neither response a surprise, given their history of economic deprivation and concern. Neither response to be heard among the wives of professional men. Also no surprise given their lifetime of greater financial security and the fact that they "take for granted" that their husbands will provide adequately for the family.

Beyond these two issues, one after the other the working-class women responded impatiently and with almost identical words to questions about what they know about the movement:

I don't know anything about it, and I don't care to know either.

You sound angry at the women's movement.

That's right, I am. I don't like women who want to be men. Those libbers, they want men and women to be just alike, and I don't want that to happen. I think men should be men and women should be women. They're crazy not to appreciate what men do for women. I like my husband to open the car door for me and to light my cigarettes. It makes me feel like a lady.

As if reciting a litany, several women spoke the same words over and over—"I like a man to open the car door and light my cigarettes." Perplexed at the repetition, at the assertion of value of these two particular behaviors, I finally asked:

When was the last time your husband opened a car door for you or lit your cigarette?

Startled, the open face of the woman who sat before me became suffused with color; she threw her head back and laughed. Finally recovering, she said:

131

I've gotta admit, I don't know why I said that. I don't even smoke.

Of course, she doesn't know why. To know would mean she'd have to face her fears and anxieties more squarely, to recognize that in some important ways the movement speaks to the issues that plague and pain her in her marriage. If, instead, she can reach for the stereotypes, she need not deal with the reality that these issues have become a part of her own life and aspirations, that their questions are also hers, that her own discontent is an example of what so many women out there are talking about.

For her, a major problem is that it remains "out there." Unlike the experience of the women in professional families, it is not *her* sisters, *her* friends, *her* neighbors who talk of these things, but women she doesn't know, has never met; women who aren't her "kind." So she hides her pain and internalizes her guilt.

Do you talk to your friends about some of the things we've been discussing—I mean about your conflicts about your life and your marriage, and about some of the things you dream about and wish for?

No, we don't talk about those kinds of things. It's kind of embarrassing, too personal, you know. Besides, the people I know don't feel like I do, so it's no point in talking to them about those things.

How do you know how they feel if you don't talk about it?

You just know, that's all. I know. It's why I worry sometimes that maybe there's something the matter with me that I'm not satisfied with what I've got. I get depressed, and then I wonder if I'm normal. I *know* none of my friends feels like that, like maybe they need a psychiatrist or something.

It's all right to complain about money, about a husband who drinks or stays out late, even about one who doesn't help around the house. But to tell someone you're unhappy because your husband doesn't talk to you—who would understand that?

You don't talk about things like that to friends like I've got. They'd think I was another one of those crazy women's libbers.

Yes, there is concern among these working-class women and men about the quality of life, about its meaning. Yes, there is a deep wish for life to be more than a constant struggle with necessity. The drinking, the violence, the withdrawn silences—these are responses of despair, giving evidence that hope is hard to hold on to. How can it be otherwise when so often life seems like such an ungiving, uncharitable affair—a struggle without end? In the early years, it's unemployment, poverty, crying babies, violent fights. That phase passes, but a whole new set of problems emerge —problems that often seem harder to handle because they have less shape, less definition; harder, too, because they are less understandable, farther outside the realm of anything before experienced. But if there is one remarkable characteristic about life among the working class, it is the ability to engage the struggle and to survive it—a quality highly valued in a world where life has been and often remains so difficult and problematic. With a certain grim satisfaction, a twenty-six-year-old housewife, mother of two, summed it up:

I guess in order to live, you have to have a very great ability to endure. And I have that—an ability to endure and survive.

8

The Marriage Bed

I suppose the problems and conflicts you've had have played themselves out in your sexual adjustment?

A CHORUS of yes's greets the question. Not one couple is without stories about adjustment problems in this difficult and delicate area of marital life—problems not just in the past, but in the present as well. Some of the problem areas—such as differences in frequency of sexual desire between men and women—are old ones. Some—such as the men's complaints about their wives' reluctance to engage in variant and esoteric sexual behaviors—are newer. All suggest that there is, in fact, a revolution in sexual behavior in American society—a revolution that runs deep and wide, a revolution in which sexual behaviors that formerly were the province of the college-educated upper classes now are practiced widely at all class and educational levels.

The evidence is strong that more people are engaging in more varieties of sexual behavior than ever before—more premarital, post-marital, extra-marital sex of all kinds. In 1948, for example, Kinsey found that only 15 percent of high-school-educated married men ever engaged in cunnilingus, compared to 45 percent of college-educated men. But the world changes quickly. Just twenty-five years later, a national survey shows that the proportion of high-school-educated men engaging in cunnilingus jumped to 56 percent.[1] And among the people I met, the figure stands at 70 percent.

But to dwell on these impressive statistics which tell us what people *do*, without attention to how they *feel* about what they do is to miss a profoundly important dimension of human experience —that is, the *meaning* that people attribute to their behavior. Nowhere is the disjunction between behavior and attitude seen more sharply than in the area of sexual behavior. For when, in the course of a single lifetime, the forbidden becomes commonplace, when the border between the conceivable and the inconceivable suddenly disappears, people may *do* new things, but they don't necessarily *like* them.

For decades, novelists, filmmakers, and social scientists all have portrayed working-class men as little more than boorish, insensitive studs—men whose sexual performance was, at best, hasty and perfunctory; at worst, brutal—concerned only with meeting their own urgent needs. Consideration for a woman's needs, variety in sexual behaviors, experimentation—these, it is generally said, are to be found largely among men of the upper classes; working-class men allegedly know nothing of such amenities.[2]

If such men ever lived in large numbers, they surely do no longer. Morton Hunt's *Playboy* study, which does not control for class but does give data that are controlled for education, provides evidence that men at all educational levels have become more concerned with and more sensitive to women's sexual needs—with the greatest increase reported among high-school-educated men. Comparing his sample with the 1948 Kinsey data on the subject of foreplay, for example, he notes that Kinsey reported that foreplay was "very brief or even perfunctory" among high-school-educated husbands, while college-educated husbands reported about ten minutes. Twenty-five years later, Hunt found that the median for non-college and college-educated husbands was the same—fifteen minutes. Similar changes were found in the variety of sexual behaviors, the variety of positions used, and the duration of coitus —with especially sharp increases reported among high-school-educated men.

Not surprisingly, it is the men more often than the women who find the changing sexual norms easier to integrate—generally responding more positively to a cultural context that offers the potential for loosening sexual constraints. For historically, it is men, not women, whose sexuality has been thought to be unruly and ungovernable—destined to be restrained by a good (read: asexual) woman. Thus, it is the men who now more often speak of their wish for sex to be freer and with more mutual enjoyment:

I think sex should be that you enjoy each other's bodies. Judy doesn't care for touching and feeling each other though.

. . . who push their wives to be sexually experimental, to try new things and different ways:

She thinks there's just one right position and one right way—in the dark with her eyes closed tight. Anything that varies from that makes her upset.

. . . who sometimes are more concerned than their wives for her orgasm:

It's just not enjoyable if she doesn't have a climax, too. She says she doesn't mind, but I do.

For the women, these attitudes of their men—their newly expressed wish for sexual innovation, their concern for their wives' gratification—are not an unmixed blessing. In any situation, there is a gap between the ideal statements of a culture and the reality in which people live out their lives—a time lag between the emergence of new cultural forms and their internalization by the individuals who must act upon them. In sexual matters, that gap is felt most keenly by women. Socialized from infancy to experience their sexuality as a negative force to be inhibited and repressed, women can't just switch "on" as the changing culture or their husbands dictate. Nice girls don't! Men *use* bad girls but marry good girls! Submit, but don't enjoy—at least not obviously so! These are the injunctions that have dominated their lives—injunctions that are laid aside with difficulty, if at all.

The media tell us that the double standard of sexual morality is dead. But with good reason, women don't believe it. They know from experience that it is alive and well, that it exists side by side with the new ideology that heralds their sexual liberation. They know all about who are the "bad girls" in school, in the neighborhood; who are the "good girls." Everybody knows! Nor is this knowledge given only among the working class. The definitions of "good girl" and "bad girl" may vary somewhat according to class, but the fundamental ideas those words encompass are not yet gone either from our culture or our consciousness at any class level.

We need only to look at our own responses to two questions to understand how vital the double standard remains. When we are asked, "What kind of woman is she?," we are likely to think about her sexual behavior; is she "easy" or not. But the question, "What kind of man is he?" evokes thoughts about what kind of work he does; is he strong, weak, kind, cruel? His sexual behavior is his private business, no concern of ours.

Whether these issues are especially real for working-class women, or whether women of that class are simply more open in talking about them than their middle-class counterparts, is difficult to say. Most of these middle-class women came to their first sexual experiences at college where, during the early-to-middle 1960s, they suddenly entered a world where sexual freedom was the byword. These were the years when it was said, "Sex is no different than a handshake"; when it was insisted that if women would only "do what comes naturally," they'd have no problems with sexual enjoyment; when the young women who did have such problems experienced themselves as personally inadequate; when it was "uncool" for a girl to ask questions about these issues —even, God forbid, to say no. Thus for well over a decade, these college-educated women have lived in an atmosphere that was at once sexually permissive and coercive—permissive, in that it encouraged them to unfetter and experience their sexuality; coercive, in that it gave them little room to experience also the constraints upon that sexuality that their culture and personal history until then had imposed upon them. That combination, then, would make them at once less guilty about their sexuality *and* less ready to speak of the inhibitions that remain.

All that notwithstanding, one thing is clear. Among the people I spoke with, working-class and middle-class couples engage in essentially the same kinds of sexual behaviors in roughly the same proportions. But working-class wives express considerably more discomfort about what they do in the marriage bed than their middle-class sisters.

Take, for example, the conflict that engages many couples around the issue of oral-genital stimulation. Seventy percent of the working-class and 76 percent of the middle-class couples engage in such sexual activity. A word of caution is necessary here, however, because these gross figures can be misleading. For about one-third of each group, engaging in oral-genital stimulation means that they tried it once, or that it happens a few times a year at most. Another 30 percent of the middle-class couples and 40 percent of the working-class couples said they have oral sex only occasionally, meaning something over three times but less than ten times a year. Thus, only about one-fourth of the working-class couples and one-third of the middle-class couples who engage in oral sex use this sexual mode routinely as a standard part of their repertoire of sexual techniques. Still, fewer of the working-class women say they enjoy it unreservedly or without guilt. Listen to this couple, married twelve years. The husband:

I've always been of the opinion that what two people do in the bedroom is fine; whatever they want to do is okay. But Jane, she doesn't agree. I personally like a lot of foreplay, caressing each other and whatever. For her, no. I think oral sex is the ultimate in making love; but she says it's revolting. [*With a deep sigh of yearning.*] I wish I could make her understand.

The wife:

I sure wish I could make him stop pushing me into that (ugh, I even hate to talk about it), into that oral stuff. I let him do it, but I hate it. He says I'm old-fashioned about sex and maybe I am. But I was brought up that there's just one way you're supposed to do it. I still believe that way, even though he keeps trying to convince me of his way. How can I change when I wasn't brought up that way? [*With a pained sigh.*] I wish I could make him understand.

Notice her plaintive plea for understanding—"I wasn't brought up that way." In reality, when it comes to sex, she, like most of us, wasn't brought up *any* way. Girls generally learn only that it's "wrong" before marriage. But what that "it" is often is hazy and unclear until after the first sexual experience. As for the varieties of sexual behavior, these are rarely, if ever, mentioned to growing children, let alone discussed in terms of which are right or wrong, good or bad, permissible or impermissible.

Still, the cry for understanding from both men and women is real. Each wishes to make the other "understand," to transform the other into oneself for a brief moment so that the inner experience can be apprehended by the other. Yet, given the widely divergent socialization practices around male and female sexuality, the wish is but another impossible fantasy. The result: he asks; she gives. And neither is satisfied with the resolution. Despairing of finding a solution with which both are comfortable, one husband comments:

Either I'm forcing my way on her or she's forcing her way on me. Either way, you can't win. If she gives in, it isn't because she's enjoying it, but because I pushed her. I suppose you could say I get what I want, but it doesn't feel that way.

It's true, on the question of oral sex, most of the time, she "gives in"—hesitantly, shyly, uncomfortably, even with revulsion. Sometimes women act from a sense of caring and consideration:

We don't do it much because it really makes me uncomfortable, you know [*making a face*], a little sick. But sometimes, I say okay because I know it means a lot to him and I really want to do it for him.

Sometimes from a sense of duty:

Even though I hate it, if he needs it, then I feel I ought to do it. After all, I'm his wife.

Sometimes out of fear of losing their men:

He can find someone to give it to him, so I figure I better do it.

Sometimes out of resignation and a sense of powerlessness:

I tell him I don't want to do it, but it doesn't do any good. If it's what he wants, that's what we do.

And sometimes it is offered as a bribe or payment for good behavior—not surprising in a culture that teaches a woman that her body is a negotiable instrument:

He gets different treats at different times, depending on what he deserves. Sometimes I let him do that oral stuff you're talking about to me. Sometimes when he's *very* good, I do it to him.

While most of the working-class women greet both cunnilingus and fellatio with little enthusiasm or pleasure, cunnilingus is practiced with slightly greater frequency and with slightly less resistance than fellatio. Partly, that's because many women are talked into cunnilingus by their husbands' "If-I'm-willing-why-do-you-care?" argument:

I don't like him to do it, but I can't figure out what to say when he says that *I* shouldn't care if *he* doesn't.

. . . and partly, and perhaps more important, because cunnilingus is something that is done *to* a woman—an act not requiring her active engagement as fellatio does; and one, therefore, not quite so incongruent with her socialization to passivity. In all areas of life, she has been raised to wait upon the initiative of another, to monitor both behavior and response carefully so as not to appear too forward or aggressive. Nowhere are these lessons more thoroughly ingrained than in her sexual behavior; nowhere has she learned better to be a reflector rather than a generator of action. Thus, fellatio, perhaps more than any other sex act, is a difficult one for a woman.

Even those women who do not express distinctly negative feelings about oral sex are often in conflict about it—unsure whether it is really all right for them to engage in, let alone enjoy, such esoteric sexual behavior, worrying about whether these are things "nice girls" do. One twenty-eight-year-old mother of three, married ten years, explained:

I always feel like it's not quite right, no matter what Pete says. I guess it's not the way I was brought up, and it's hard to get over that. He keeps telling me it's okay if it's between us, that anything we do is okay. But I'm not sure about that. How do I know in the end he won't think I'm cheap.

Sometimes I enjoy it, I guess. But most of the time I'm too worried thinking about whether I ought to be doing it, and worrying what he's *really* thinking to get much pleasure.

"How do I know he won't think I'm cheap?"—a question asked over and over again, an issue that dominates these woman and their attitudes toward their own sexuality. Some husbands reassure them:

She says she worries I'll think she's a cheap tramp, and she doesn't really believe me when I keep telling her it's not true.

Such reassurances remain suspect, however, partly because it's so hard for women to move past the fears of their own sexuality with which they have been stamped; and partly because at least some men are not without their own ambivalence about it, as is evident in this comment from one young husband:

No, Alice isn't that kind of girl. Jesus, you shouldn't ask questions like that. [*A long, difficult silence.*] She wasn't brought up to go for all that [*pause*] fancy stuff. You know, all those different ways and [*shifting uncomfortably in his chair, lighting a cigarette, and looking down at the floor*] that oral stuff. But that's okay with me. There's plenty of women out there to do that kind of stuff with. You can meet them in any bar any time you want to. You don't have to marry those kind.

As long as that distinction remains, as long as men distinguish between the girls they marry and the girls they use, many women will remain unconvinced by their reassurances and wary about engaging in sexual behaviors that seem to threaten their "good girl" status.

Those assurances are doubly hard to hear and to believe when women also know that their husbands are proud of their naïveté in sexual matters—a pride which many men take little trouble to hide:

It took a long time for me to convince her that it didn't have to be by the books. She was like an innocent babe. I taught her everything she knows.

Even men whose wives were married before will say with pleasure:

It's funny how naïve she was when we got married. She was married before, you know, but still she was kind of innocent. I taught her just about everything she knows.

For the women, the message seems clear: He wants to believe in her innocence, to believe in the special quality of their sexual relationship, to believe that these things she does only for him. She is to be pupil to his teacher. So she echoes his words—"He taught me everything I know." Repeatedly that phrase or a close equivalent is used as women discuss their sexual behavior and their feelings about it. And always it is said with a sure sense that it's what her husband wants and needs to believe, as these incongruent comments from a woman now in her second marriage show:

One thing I know he likes is that he taught me mostly all I know about sex, so that makes him feel good. It also means that I haven't any habits that have to be readjusted to his way or anything like that.

That seems a strange thing to say when you were married for some years before.

Startled, she looked at me, then down at her hands uncomfortably.

Yeah, I guess you'd think so. Well, you know, he likes to feel that way so why shouldn't he, and why shouldn't I let him?

Given that knowledge, even if it were possible to do so on command, most women would not dare risk unleashing their sexual inhibitions. From where a woman stands, the implicit injunction in her husband's pride in her innocence is that her sexuality be restrained. And restrain it she does—a feat for which she is all too well trained. The price for that training in restraint is high for both of them, however. He often complains because she doesn't take the initiative:

She never initiates anything. She'll make no advances at all, not even subtleties.

She often replies:

I just can't. I guess I'm inhibited, I don't know. All I know is it's very hard for me to start things up or to tell him something I want. Maybe that comes from back when women weren't supposed to enjoy sex. Now that's supposed to be changed, but I don't know.

On the other hand, not infrequently when women put aside that restraint and take the initiative, they may find themselves accused of not being feminine enough:

It isn't that I mind her letting me know when she wants it, but she isn't very subtle about it. I mean, she could let me know in a nice, feminine way. Being feminine and, you know, kind of subtle, that's not her strong point.

Sensitive to the possibility of being thought of as "unfeminine" or "aggressive," most women shy away from any behavior that might bring those words down upon their heads. For it is painful for any woman of any class to hear herself described in these ways:

I don't like to think he might think I was being aggressive, so I don't usually make any suggestions. Most of the time it's okay because he can usually tell when I'm in the mood. But if he can't, I just wait.

These, then, are some of the dilemmas and conflicts people face around the newly required and desired sexual behaviors. Among working-class women, isolation and insulation compound their problems. It is one thing to read about all these strange and exotic sexual behaviors in books and magazines, another to know others like yourself who actually do these things:

He keeps trying to get me to read those books, but what difference would it make? I don't know who those people are. There's a lot of people do lots of things; it doesn't mean I have to do them.

If the books aren't convincing, and it's not culturally acceptable to discuss the intimate details of one's sex life with neighbors, friends, co-workers, or even family, most women are stuck with their childhood and adolescent fears, fantasies, and prohibitions. Small wonder that over and over again during my visit the atmosphere in the room changed from tense anxiety to exquisite relief when subjects such as oral sex were treated casually, with either the implicit or explicit understanding that it is both common and acceptable sexual practice:

Jim keeps telling me and telling me it's okay, that it's not dirty. But I always worry about it, not really knowing if that's true or not. I read a couple of books once, but it's different. I never talked to anyone but Jim about it before. [*Smiling, as if a weight had been lifted from her shoulders.*] You're so cool about it; talking to you makes it seem not so bad.

In contrast, discussion of these issues with the middle-class women was considerably more relaxed. Regardless of their own feelings about engaging in oral sex, it was clear that most middle-class women recognize that it is a widely practiced and acceptable behavior. In fact, more often than not, they tended to feel guilty and uncomfortable about their own inhibitions, not because they weren't able to please their husbands but because they believed their constraint reflected some inadequacy in their personal sexual adjustment. It was also from middle-class women that I more often heard complaints when their husbands were unwilling to experiment with oral-genital sex. Of the working-class couples who never engage in oral sex, only one woman complained about her husband's unwillingness to do so. Of the middle-class couples in a similar situation, four women offered that complaint.

But it is also true that, generally, the husbands of these middle-class women send fewer ambiguous and ambivalent messages about their wives' sexuality, tend less to think in good girl–bad girl terms, more often expect and accept that their wives had other sexual experiences before they met. Further, these middle-class women more often are in contact with others like themselves in an environment where discussion of sexual issues is encouraged —a course in human sexuality, a women's group, for example.

Still, the recitation of these differences in experience ought not to be read to suggest that middle-class women are now sexually free and uninhibited. The most that can be said on that score is that more of them live in an atmosphere that more seriously encourages that goal, hence more—especially those under thirty—may be closer to its attainment. Meanwhile at all class levels, most women probably feel comfortable enough with their own sexual responses to be willing participants in sexual intercourse. But when it comes to oral sex—especially among the working class—generally they submit just as their mothers before them submitted to more traditional sexual behaviors.

Sexual conflicts in marriage are not always constellated around such exotic issues, however; nor, as I have said, are any of them the exclusive problem of a particular class. Thus, although what follows rests on material taken from my discussions with working-class couples, much of it applies to the professional middle-class as well. True, the middle-class couples more often are able to discuss some of their issues more openly with each other. But despite the current, almost mystical, belief in communication-as-problem-solving—talk doesn't always help. True, middle-class couples much more often seek professional help with these problems. But sexual conflicts in a marriage are among the most intractable—the recent development and proliferation of sex therapies notwithstanding. Those therapies can be useful in dealing with some specific sexual dysfunction—prematurely ejaculating men or nonorgasmic women. But the kinds of sexual conflicts to be discussed here are so deeply rooted in the socio-cultural mandates of our world that they remain extraordinarily resistant regardless of how able the psychotherapeutic help we can buy. Thus, while there are subtle differences between the two classes in the language and tone with which the problems are dealt, in the amount of discussion about them, and in their ability and willingness to seek professional help, in this instance, those differences are not as important as the similarities that remain.

In fact, the earliest sexual problems rear their heads with the couple's first fight. Regardless of what has gone before, at bedtime, he's ready for sex; she remains cold and aloof. Listen to this couple in their mid-to-late-twenties, married nine years. The wife:

I don't understand him. He's ready to go any time. It's always been a big problem with us right from the beginning. If we've hardly seen each other for two or three days and hardly talked to each other, I can't just jump into bed. If we have a fight, I can't just turn it off. He has a hard time understanding that. I feel like that's all he wants sometimes. I have to know I'm needed and wanted for more than just jumping into bed.

The husband:

She complains that all I want from her is sex, and I try to make her understand that it's an expression of love. I'll want to make up with her by making love, but she's cold as the inside of the refrig. Sure I get mad when that happens. Why shouldn't I? Here I'm trying to make up and make love, and she's holding out for something—I don't know what.

The wife:

He keeps saying he wants to make love, but it just doesn't feel like love to me. Sometimes I feel bad that I feel that way, but I just can't help it.

The husband:

I don't understand. She says it doesn't feel like love. What does that mean, anyway? What does she think love is?

The wife:

I want him to talk to me, to tell me what he's thinking about. If we have a fight, I want to talk about it so we could maybe understand it. I don't want to jump in bed and just pretend it didn't happen.

The husband:

Talk! Talk! What's there to talk about. I want to make love to her and she says she wants to talk. How's talking going to convince her I'm loving her.

In sex, as in other matters, the barriers to communication are high; and the language people use serves to further confuse and mystify. He says, "I want to make love." She says, "It doesn't feel like love." Neither quite knows what the other is talking about; both feel vaguely guilty and uncomfortable—aware only that somehow they're passing each other, not connecting. He believes he already has given her the most profound declaration of love of which a man is capable. He married her; he gives her a home; he works hard each day to support her and the children:

What does she want? Proof? She's got it, hasn't she? Would I be knocking myself out to get things for her—like to keep up this house— if I didn't love her. Why does a man do things like that if not because he loves his wife and kids? I swear, I can't figure what she wants.

This is one time when *she* knows what she wants:

I want him to let me know in other ways, too, not just sex. It's not enough that he supports us and takes care of us. I appreciate that, but I want him to share things with me. I need for him to tell me his feelings. He keeps saying no, but to me, there's a difference between making love and sex. Just once, I'd like him to love me without it ending up in sex. But when I tell him that, he thinks I'm crazy.

For him, perhaps, it *does* seem crazy. Split off, as he is, from the rest of the expressive-emotional side of himself, sex may be the one place where he can allow himself the expression of deep feelings, the one place where he can experience the depth of that affective side. His wife, on the other hand, closely connected with her feeling side in all areas *but* the sexual, finds it difficult to be comfortable with her feelings in the very area in which he has the greatest—sometimes the only—ease. She keeps asking for something she can understand and is comfortable with—a demonstration of his feelings in non-sexual ways. He keeps giving her the one thing he can understand and is comfortable with—his feelings wrapped up in a blanket of sex. Thus do husbands and wives find themselves in an impossibly difficult bind—another bind not of their own making, but one that stems from the cultural context in which girls and boys grow to adulthood.

I am suggesting, then, that a man's ever-present sexual readiness is not simply an expression of urgent sexual need but also a complex compensatory response to a socialization process that *constricts the development of the emotional side of his personality in all but sexual expression.* Conversely, a woman's insistent plea for an emotional statement of a nonsexual nature is a response to a process that *encourages the development of the affective side of her personality in all but sexual expression.*[3]

Such differences between women and men about the *meaning* of sex make for differences between wives and husbands in frequency of desire as well—differences which lead to a wide discrepancy in their perceptions about the frequency of the sexual encounter.[4] Except for a few cases where the women are inclined to be more sexually active than the men, he wants sex more often than she. To him, therefore, it seems as if they have sex less often than they actually do; to her, it seems more often. But the classical caricature of a wife fending off her husband's advances with a sick headache seems not to apply among working-class women. Once in a while, a woman says:

I tell him straight I'm not in the mood, and he understands.

Mostly, however, women say:

I don't use excuses like headaches and things like that. If my husband wants me, I'm his wife, and I do what he wants. It's my responsibility to give it to him when he needs it.

Whether she refuses outright or acquiesces out of a sense of duty or responsibility, the solution is less than satisfactory for both partners. In either case, he feels frustrated and deprived. He wants more than release from his own sexual tension; he wants her active involvement as well. Confronted with his ever-present readiness, she feels guilty:

I feel guilty and uncomfortable when he's always ready and I'm not, like I'm not taking care of him.

. . . coerced:

I feel like it hangs over my head all the time. He always wants it; twice a day wouldn't be too much for him. He says he doesn't want me just to give in to him, but if I didn't he'd be walking around horny all the time. If we waited for me to want it, it would never be enough for him.

. . . and also deprived:

Before I ever get a chance to feel really sexy, he's there and waiting. I'd like to know what it feels like sometimes to really want it that bad. Oh, sometimes I do. But mostly I don't get the chance.

Thus, she rarely has the opportunity to experience the full force of her own sexual rhythm, and with it the full impact of her sexuality. It is preempted by the urgency and frequency of his desires.

Finally, there is plenty of evidence that the battle between the sexes is still being waged in the marriage bed, and in very traditional ways. Several couples spoke of their early sexual adjustment problems in ways that suggest that the struggle was not over sex but over power and control. Often in the early years, when she wants sex, he's tired; when he wants sex, she's uninterested. For many couples, the pattern still repeats itself once in a while. For about one fifth of them, the scenario continues to be played out with great regularity and sometimes with great drama, as this story of one early-thirties couple illustrates.

In six months of premarital and ten years of marital coitus, the woman had never had an orgasm:

We had sex four or five times a week like clockwork all those years, and I just laid there like a lump. I couldn't figure out what all the noise was about.

Asked how he felt about her passivity during that period, her husband—a taciturn, brooding man, whose silence seemed to cover a wellspring of hostility—replied:

If she couldn't, she couldn't. I didn't like it, but I took what I needed. [*After a moment's hesitation.*] She's always been hard to handle.

A year ago, attracted by ideas about women's sexuality that seemed to her to be "in the air," she began to read some of the women's literature on the subject. From there, she moved on to pornography and one night, as she tells it:

The earth shook. I couldn't believe anything could be so great. I kept wondering how I lived so long without knowing about it. I kept asking Fred why he'd never made me understand before. [*Then, angrily.*] But you'll never believe what happened after that. My husband just lost interest in sex. Now, I can hardly ever get him to do it anymore, no matter how much I try or beg him. He says he's too tired, or he doesn't feel well, or else he just falls asleep and I can't wake him up. I can hardly believe it's happening sometimes. Can you imagine such a thing? I even wonder whether maybe I shouldn't have made such a big fuss about it. Maybe it scared him off or something.

Her husband refused my attempts to explore the issue with him, insisting that all is well in their sex life, but adding:

She's always asking for something or hollering about something. I don't have any control around this house anymore. Nobody listens to me.

It would seem, then, that as long as he could "take what I needed," he could feel he was asserting some control over his wife and could remain sexually active and potent. When she unexpectedly became an assertive and active participant in the sex act, the only possibility for retaining control was to move from the active to the passive mode. Thus, he fell impotent. His wife, now acutely aware of her sexual deprivation, is left torn between anger, frustration, and the terrible fear that somehow she is responsible for it.

A dramatic story? Certainly. But one whose outlines are clear in 20 percent of these marriages where three women complained about their husbands' impotence and seven about sexual withholding—not surprisingly, a problem most of the men were unwilling to talk about. In the three cases where the husband did address the issue at all, either he denied its existence, "It's no problem; I'm just tired;" or blamed his wife, "She doesn't appeal to me," or "She's too pushy." The last has been a subject of recent concern expressed publicly by psychologists and widely publicized in the mass media. The performance demands being laid on men are extraordinary, we are told, and women are cautioned that their emergent assertiveness—sexual and otherwise—threatens the sexual performance of their men. The time has come, these experts warn, to take the pressure off.

Nowhere, however, do we hear concern about the effects of the performance demand on women. Yet never in history have heavier demands for sexual performance been laid on them. Until recently, women were expected to submit passively to sex; now they are told their passivity diminishes their husbands' enjoyment. Until recently, especially among the less-educated working class, orgasm was an unexpected gift; now it is a requirement of adequate sexual performance.[5] These new definitions of adequacy leave many women feeling "under the gun"—fearful and anxious if they do not achieve orgasm; if it does not happen at the "right" moment—that is, at the instant of their husbands' ejaculation; or if they are uncomfortable about engaging in behaviors that feel alien or aberrant to them.[6] If anxiety about one's ability to perform adequately has an untoward effect on the male orgasm, is there any reason to believe it would not inhibit the female's as well?

In fact, the newfound concern with their orgasm is a mixed and costly blessing for many women. For some, it has indeed opened the possibility for pleasures long denied. For others, however, it is experienced as another demand in a life already too full of demands. Listen to this thirty-five-year-old woman who works part-time, takes care of a house, a husband, six children, and an aging, sick father.

It feels like somebody's always wanting something from me. Either one of the kids is hanging on to me or pulling at me, or my father needs something. And if it's not them, then Tom's always coming after me with that gleam in his eye. Then, it's not enough if I just let him have it, because if I don't have a climax, he's not happy. I get so tired of everybody wanting something from me all the time. I sometimes think I hate sex.

While it is undoubtedly true that more women have more orgasms more often than ever before—and that most of them enjoy sex more than women in earlier generations—it is also true that there are times when their husbands' wish for their orgasm is experienced as oppressive and alienating—when it seems to them that their orgasm is more a requirement of his pleasure than their own. We may ask: How rational are these thoughts? And we may wonder: Why should it be a matter of question or criticism if, in the course of pleasuring their wives, men also pleasure themselves? When phrased that way, it should not be questioned! But if we look at the discussion around female orgasm or lack of it a little more closely, we notice that it is almost invariably tied to male pleasure. If a woman doesn't have an orgasm, it is a problem, if not for her, then because both her man's pleasure and his sense of manhood are diminished. Can anyone imagine a discussion of male impotence centering around concern for women? In fact, when we talk about the failure of men to achieve erection or orgasm, the discourse takes place in hushed, serious, regretful tones—always in the context of concern about how those men experience that failure. How many of us have ever thought, "What a shame for his woman that he can't have an erection." Any woman who has shared that experience with a man knows that her concern was largely for him, her own frustration becoming irrelevant in that moment. Any man who has experienced impotence knows that his dominant concern was for the failure of his manhood.

It is not surprising, therefore, that several of the women I talked to were preoccupied with their orgasm, not because it was so important to them, but because their husbands' sense of manhood rested on it. Holding her head, one woman said painfully:

I rarely have climaxes. But if it didn't bother my husband, it wouldn't bother me. I keep trying to tell him that I know it's not his fault, that he's really a good lover. I keep telling him it's something the matter with me, not with him. But it scares me because he doesn't believe it, and I worry he might leave me for a woman who will have climaxes for him.

With these final words, she epitomizes the feelings of many women, whether orgasmic or not, at least some of the time: *her orgasm is for him, not for her.* It is his need to validate his manhood that is the primary concern—his need, not hers. For women of the working class, who already have so little autonomy and control over their lives, this may well be experienced as the ultimate violation.

To compound the anxiety, now one orgasm is not enough. One

woman, having read that some women have multiple orgasms, worried that her husband would soon find out:

It's really important for him that I reach a climax, and I try to every time. He says it just doesn't make him feel good if I don't. But it's hard enough to do it once! What'll happen if he finds out about those women who have lots of climaxes?

These, then, are some dimensions of sexual experience in the 1970s that are buried under the sensational reports of changing sexual mores. Undoubtedly, there is a loosening of sexual constraints for both women and men; undoubtedly, more people are enjoying fuller sexual experiences than ever before. Certainly it is important that these changes are discussed publicly, that the subject of sex has come out of the closet. But that is not enough. For we must also understand that such changes are not without cost to the individuals who try to live them out, who must somehow struggle past powerful early training to a new consciousness. For women especially—women of any class—that training in repressing and inhibiting their sexuality makes this a particularly difficult struggle.

It is both sad and ironic now to hear men complain that their wives are too cautious, too inhibited, or not responsive enough in bed. Sad, because the deprivation men experience is real; ironic, because these are the costs of the sexual limitations that generations of their forebears have imposed on women. Changing such historic patterns of thought and behavior will not be easy for either men or women. For certainly, many men are still not without ambivalence about these sexual issues with reference to their women—a subtlety that is not lost on their wives. But even where men unambivalently mean what they say about wanting their wives to be freer in the marriage bed, it will take time for women to work through centuries of socially mandated denial and repression:

All I know is, I can't just turn on so easy. Maybe we're all paying the price now because men didn't used to want women to enjoy sex.

. . . and probably will require their first being freer in other beds as well:

I was eighteen when we got married, and I was a very young eighteen.
I'd never had any relations with anybody, not even my husband, before
we were married. So we had a lot of problems. I guess I was kind of
frigid at first. But you know, after all those years when you're holding
back, it's hard to all of a sudden get turned on just because you got
married. I know it's not right, but sometimes I think we should have
had sex before we were married. Then maybe it wouldn't have been so
much trouble after.

Yes, it is "hard to all of a sudden get turned on just because you
got married." And as long as women's sexuality continues to be
subjected to capricious demands and treated as if regulated by an
on-off switch—expected to surge forth fully and vigorously at
the flick of the "on" switch and to subside quietly at the flick of
the "off"—most women will continue to seek the safest path—in
this case, to remain quietly someplace between "on" and "off."

CHAPTER

9

Work
and Its Meaning

Tell me something about the work you do and how you feel about it.

FOR THE MEN, whose definition of self is so closely tied to work, it's a mixed bag—a complex picture of struggle, of achievements and disappointments, of successes and failures. In their early work life, most move restlessly from job to job seeking not only higher wages and better working conditions, but some kind of work in which they can find meaning, purpose, and dignity:

God, I hated that assembly line. *I hated it.* I used to fall asleep on the job standing up and still keep doing my work. There's nothing more boring and more repetitious in the world. On top of it, you don't feel human. The machine's running you, you're not running it.

[*Thirty-three-year-old mechanic.*]

Thus, by the time they're twenty-five, their post-school work life averages almost eight years, and half have held as many as six, eight, or ten jobs.

Generally, they start out as laborers, operatives in an oil refinery, assembly-line workers in the local canneries, automobile or parts plants, warehousemen, janitors, or gas station attendants—jobs in which worker dissatisfaction is well documented. Some move on and up—into jobs that require more skill, jobs that still demand plenty of hard work, but which at least leave one with a sense of mastery and competence:

I'm proud of what I've done with my life. I come from humble origins, and I never even finished school; but I've gotten someplace. I work hard, but it's good work. It's challenging and never routine. When I finish a day's work, I know I've accomplished something. I'm damned good at what I do, too. Even the boss knows it.

[*Thirty-six-year-old steam fitter.*]

But the reality of the modern work world is that there are fewer and fewer jobs calling for such traditional skills. So most job changes don't mean moving up, but only moving on:[1]

When I first started, I kept moving around. I kept looking for a job I'd like. You know, a job where it wouldn't make you tired just to get up in the morning and have to go to work. [*With a heavy sigh.*] It took me a number of years to discover that there's not much difference—a job's a job. So now I do what I have to do, and maybe I can get my family a little security.

[*Twenty-seven-year-old mail sorter.*]

For some, the job changes are involuntary—due to lay-offs:

When I first got out of high school, I had a series of jobs and a series of lay-offs. The jobs lasted from three weeks to three months. Something always happened—like maybe the contract didn't come through —and since I was low man on the totem pole, I got laid off. A lot of times, the lay-offs lasted longer than the jobs.

. . . or industrial accidents—a common experience among men who work in factories, warehouses, and on construction sites:

I was working at the cannery about a week when my hand got caught in the belt. It got crushed, and I couldn't work for three months. When I got better, they wouldn't put me back on the job because they said I was accident-prone.

156

By the time they're thirty, about half are settled into jobs at which they've worked for five years. With luck, they'll stay at them for many more to come. Without it, like their fathers, they'll know the pain of periodic unemployment, the fear of their families doing without. For the other half—those still floating from job to job—the future may be even more problematic. Unprotected by seniority, with work histories that prospective employers are likely to view as chaotic and unstable, they can expect little security from the fluctuations and uncertainties of the labor market.

But all that tells us nothing about the quality of life on the job—what it feels like to go to work at *that* particular job for most of a lifetime—an experience that varies in blue-collar jobs just as it does in white-collar ones. For just as there are elite jobs in the white-collar work force, so they exist among blue-collar workers. Work that allows for freedom and autonomy on the job—these are the valued and high-status jobs, rare in either world. For the blue-collar worker, that means a job where he can combine skill with strength, where he can control the pace of his work and the order of the tasks to be done, and where successful performance requires his independent judgments. To working-class men holding such jobs—skilled construction workers, skilled mechanics, truck drivers—the world of work brings not only goods, but gratifications. The man who drives the long-distance rig feels like a free agent once he gets out on the road. It's true, there's a time recorder on the truck that clocks his stops. Still, compared to jobs he's had before in factories and warehouses, on this one, he's the guy who's in control. Sometimes the road's easy; sometimes it's tough. Always it requires his strength and skill; always he's master of the machine:

There's a good feeling when I'm out there on the road. There ain't nobody looking over your shoulder and watching what you're doing. When I worked in a warehouse, you'd be punching in and punching out, and bells ringing all the time. On those jobs, you're not thinking, you're just doing what they tell you. Sure, now I'm expected to bring her in on time, but a couple of hours one way or the other don't make no difference. And there ain't nobody but me to worry about how I get her there.

[*Twenty-eight-year-old trucker.*]

The skilled construction worker, too, finds challenge and reward in his work:

I climb up on those beams every morning I'm working, and I like being way up there looking down at the world. It's a challenge up there, and the work's hardly ever routine. You have to pay attention and use your head, too, otherwise you can get into plenty of trouble in the kind of work I do. I'm a good man, and everybody on the job knows it.

[*Thirty-one-year-old ironworker.*]

But most blue-collar men work at jobs that require less skill, that have less room for independent judgment—indeed, often expect that it will be suspended—and that leave their occupants with little freedom or autonomy. Such jobs have few intrinsic rewards and little status—either in the blue-collar world or the one outside—and offer few possibilities for experiencing oneself as a "good man." The men who hold these jobs often get through each day by doing their work and numbing themselves to the painful feelings of discontent—trying hard to avoid the question, "Is this what life is all about?" Unsuccessful in that struggle, one twenty-nine-year-old warehouseman burst out bitterly:

A lot of times I hate to go down there. I'm cooped up and hemmed in. I feel like I'm enclosed in a building forty hours a week, sometimes more. It seems like all there is to life is to go down there and work, collect your pay check, pay your bills, and get further in debt. It doesn't seem like the circle ever ends. Every day it's the same thing; every week it's the same thing; every month it's the same thing.

Some others respond with resignation:

I guess you can't complain. You have to work to make a living, so what's the use.

[*Twenty-six-year-old garage man.*]

... some with boredom:

I've been in this business thirteen years and it bores me. Its enough.

[*Thirty-five-year-old machine operator.*]

... some with alienation:

The one thing I like is the hours. I work from seven to three-thirty in the afternoon so I get off early enough to have a lot of the day left.
[*Twenty-eight-year-old assembly-line worker.*]

All, in fact, probably feel some combination of all these feelings. For the men in such jobs, bitterness, alienation, resignation, and boredom are the defining features of the work experience. For them, work is something to do, not to talk about. "What's there to talk about?"—not really a question but an oft-repeated statement that says work is a requirement of life, hours to be gotten through until you can go home.[2]

No big news this—at least not for readers of *The Wall Street Journal* and *Fortune* magazine, both aimed at the leaders of the industrial world. No big news either in the highest reaches of government where in 1972 the United States Senate sponsored a symposium on worker alienation.[3] When absentee and turnover rates rise, when wildcat strikes occur with increasing frequency—in short, when productivity falls off—the alienation of workers becomes a focal concern for both industrial managers and government. That concern increasingly is expressed both in the media and in the work of industrial sociologists, psychologists, and labor relations experts who more and more talk of plans for "job enrichment," "job enlargement," and "the humanization of work."

Despite the talk, however, the history of industrialization shows that as industry has become more capital intensive, the thrust has been toward technological developments which consistently routinize work and require less skill of the masses of workers. Today more than yesterday—because technology has now caught up with work in the office as well as the factory—most work continues to be steadily and systematically standardized and routinized; the skills of the vast majority of workers have been degraded. So profound is the trend that generally we are unaware that the meaning of "skill" itself has been degraded as well.[4] This, too, is no new phenomenon as even a casual glance at the historical record shows. For whether in 1875 or 1975, most of those concerned with the organization of work and with the qualities most desired in a work force talk not about skill but about "discipline" and "responsibility."⁵ The difference in these hundred years in what is required of the mass of workers is one of degree not of kind. Advancing technology means that there is less need than before for skill, more for reliability—that means workers who appear punctually and regularly, who work hard, who don't sabotage the line, and who see their own interests as identical with the welfare of the company. These are the "skills" such capital-intensive industries need. And these are the skills toward which—today as yesterday—training programs of the unemployed and underemployed so often are directed.⁶

In fact, there is no argument among most students of work in America that most work—whether in the factory or in the office—requires less skill than before. Rather the argument is heard around the *meaning* of the trend in the lives of those affected by it. In the United States, at least, most analysts insist upon the inevitability of the process, arguing that where technology exists it will be used—as if it had a force or a life of its own; where it doesn't exist, it will be invented. Human beings, such people argue, must invent their future; that is one essential meaning of being "human."⁷

That argument, however, fails to grapple with the fact that only a tiny minority of us ever are involved in inventing our present, let alone our future. Ordinary women and men—which means almost all of us—struggle along with received truths as well as received ways of being and doing. For such people, at least one half of the waking hours of each day are spent in doing work that is dull, routine, deadening—in a word, alienating and alienated labor. True, these analysts would say. But for those people, there are substitute gratifications to be found in the private sphere of life—that is, the family—and in their leisure hours.

But again, that formulation fails to deal with the degree to which the parts of human life are interrelated—each interacting with and acting upon the other—so that such a separation is nearly impossible. In fact, any five-year-old child knows when "daddy has had a bad day" at work. He comes home tired, grumpy, withdrawn, and uncommunicative. He wants to be left alone; wife and children in that moment are small comfort. When *every* working day is a "bad day," the family may even feel like the enemy at times. But for them, he may well think, he could leave the hated job, do something where he could feel human again instead of like a robot.

Over a century ago, in the early stages of industrialization, Karl Marx spoke to the profoundly important human consequences of alienation from work—of work that doesn't permit the development of skill, of a sense of mastery, of an understanding of the totality of the *process* of production, of a connectedness with its *product*. Those issues are no less real today. The overt brutalization of industrial workers is no longer with us. But the intensification of technological developments has given rise to dehumanization and alienation in the work world on a scale far greater than anything known before.

For the working-class men I met, these issues, while unarticulated in this way, are nevertheless real. Most are in a constant struggle to make some order and continuity out of the fragments of their lives. Thus, they come home after work and plunge into projects that offer the possibility for feeling useful, competent, whole again—fixing the car or truck, remodeling the kitchen, building something for the kids.[8] Others—those who seem already to have given up life and hope—collapse into a kind of numbed exhaustion from which they stir only to eat, drink, and watch television. Either way, the implications for family life are clear. Husbands and fathers are removed from active involvement— some because they are in a desperate struggle to retain some sense of their humanity, others because they have given it all up.

There are still a few who have fantasies of one day doing some other kind of work—owning a farm, a ranch, a small business are the most common of these dreams. No new phenomenon; for part of the American dream always has been to have a business of one's own. Rarely, however, are these dreams voiced spontaneously in the course of a discussion about work and their feelings about it. In that context, work tends to be seen as a given in life—more or less enjoyable, but ultimately unavoidable, thus not something to give much thought to. Only when the question itself has a dream-like and unreal quality does it encourage and get a fantasy response:

Would you fantasy for a minute about what you'd do if you suddenly inherited a million dollars?[9]

Most working-class people—men and women—are stopped cold by the question. Most say at once, "I've never thought about it." One thirty-two-year-old man added in wonder:

Most of my life I've been lucky to have ten dollars; thinking about a million—wow, that seems impossible.

When pushed to think of the question in terms of the work they'd like to do, slowly, thoughtfully, a few gave voice to their fantasies. But always the implicit understanding was there: both of us knew that *he knew* it was just a dream:

Well, I guess if I had a million dollars, I'd buy me a cattle ranch in the mountains and go live in the country. I like to hunt and fish. I like the country. I like animals. And I'd sure like to be my own boss and to work when I want to work. Oh, I know I'd have to work hard on a ranch, but it would be *my* work, and it would be on *my* time, and with me deciding what needed doing and doing it.
[Thirty-three-year-old delivery man.]

Like I said, my job is tedious. I'd actually be glad to quit it. I don't mean I'd quit work; nobody should ever do that. I might buy a goat farm and raise goats and pigs—just something where I could do something a person could care about. You know, something that was mine and that wasn't so tedious.
[Twenty-nine-year-old postal clerk.]

I guess if I was going to have a fantasy about anything, it would be to have a little sporting-goods store in the neighborhood, a place where all the kids on the local teams could come to get outfitted. I would feel a lot of satisfaction to have a store like that, and I think it would be a terrific business to be in. But it's just a dream. I'll never get enough money together to do it, and you can be sure there's nobody going to leave me no thousand dollars, let alone a million.
[Thirty-one-year-old night watchman.]

One twenty-seven-year-old warehouseman, after talking at length about the business he hoped he'd have some day, took a mental step back from our conversation, observed himself thoughtfully and said:

After all that talk, I really doubt I'll ever make any change. I'll probably stay where I am forever. Once you've been on the job seven years, look what you'd have to give up—good money, good benefits, seniority. What if I tried my own business and it didn't work? Then I'd have to come back and start all over again. No, I don't think I'll ever take that chance.

Paradoxically, then, the "good money, good benefits, seniority" that come with long tenure on the job also serve to limit his choices—to bind him to it, trading the dream for this stagnant stability. Perhaps, in the long run, that makes sense given the failure rate of small, independent businesses in America. In the immediate moment, there's pain and pathos when, at twenty-seven, he already knows his life choices largely are over.

Imagine the consequences to the shape and form of that human life. Imagine, too, an environment in which the same paucity of choices is the reality of most lives—no friends or relatives around who see a future with plenty of possibilities stretching before them; no one who expects very much because experience has taught them that such expectations end painfully. Such is the fertile field in which the fatalism, passivity, and resignation of the working class grow—qualities so often remarked upon by professional middle-class investigators. But it is not these qualities that are responsible for their humble social status. That is the illusion with which so many middle-class observers attempt to palliate their guilt about the inequalities in American life—inequalities that are at such odds with our most cherished ideological myth of egalitarianism. Rather it is their social status from which these qualities stem. No, these are not personal failings, nor are they outgrowths of character or personality deficiencies. They are, instead, realistic responses to the social context in which most working-class men, women, and children live, grow, and come to define themselves, their expectations, and their relationship to the world around them.

Would you fantasy for a minute about what you'd do if you suddenly inherited a million dollars?

For a few of the men, answering the fantasy question is easier; they know just what they would do. These are the half dozen who have some natural skill or talent in music or drawing and painting

—talents that are untutored and undeveloped, talents discovered accidentally:

I don't know how I know how to draw. I just know how. I guess I've been doing it since I was a little kid but nobody paid it any mind.

"Nobody paid it any mind"—unthinkable that such childhood demonstration of artistic abilities would go without attention and nurturance in most modern middle-class families. At the very least, such a boy would be encouraged to use those capabilities to become an architect, an engineer. But when you're one of ten children in a family where survival is the principal preoccupation, it seems quite natural that no one pays "any mind" to a boy who draws. No surprise, either, if you grow up without a family at all:

I was about sixteen the first time I held a banjo in my hands, and I just played it. It was the same thing later, the first time I sat down at a piano. I just taught myself how to play. I've wondered before about how that happened, but I don't know. One thing I remember from when I was little was I was a quiet, unhappy kid. Every time I moved to a new foster home, I'd be scared all over again, and I got quieter and quieter. I think what kept me from being panicked out all the time was the music I had in my head. It was like it kept me company. I used to make up songs and sing them to myself. And I used to pretend I was playing music on a great big piano in front of a hundred people. [*Laughing.*] I thought that was a lot of people then.

For these men, without exception, some part of the million would be spent on training—perhaps on becoming professionals—in their particular creative endeavor.

Whether the men like their work or not, whether it offers more gratification or less, whether they have active fantasies about another way of life or they accept what is without allowing dreams to intrude upon reality, the work they do powerfully affects the quality of family life. What happens during the day on the job colors—if it doesn't actually dictate—what happens during the evening in the living room, perhaps later in the bedroom. And the size of the weekly pay check is importantly related to how men feel about themselves, their work, and their responsibilities. Probably men of all classes experience those responsibilities with heavy weariness at times, but they seem to be felt more keenly among the working class where the choices are narrower and the rewards slimmer.[10]

Even before 1975 and early 1976, when the national unemployment rate consistently stood at more than 8 percent, and the California rate at 10 percent, the vision of the American worker supporting his family with ease and style was a palpable distortion, visible to any observer not blinded by the prevailing myth of his affluence. For just below that apparent affluence, working-class families have always lived with the gnawing fear of unemployment and underemployment—always aware that any cutback in overtime, any lay-off would send them over the edge into disaster. For most, it takes the combined incomes of wife and husband, plus a heavy load of overtime for him, just to stay even. In fact, even with those conditions met, few manage to keep up with all their bills:

Would you fantasy for a minute about what you'd do if you suddenly inherited a million dollars?

After the first surprised silence, both women and men answer with a regularity that quickly becomes predictable. "I'd pay off my bills," is the first thought that comes to 70 percent; for another 25 percent, it is the second thought. To the remaining few who don't give this evidence of financial stress, I remarked:

Most people I've talked to say they'd pay off their bills, and I'm wondering why that doesn't occur to you?

The answer is simple: they have no bills. These are the few families who buy only when they have cash in hand—a rare phenomenon in American life at any class level.

There is no issue in which the class differences are more striking, none which tells more about how differently families in the professional middle class experience financial pressures. For not one woman or man in the middle-class families talked about paying off their bills if they were suddenly to come into a large inheritance. It is not that such families don't have bills; indeed, they have very large ones—mortgages on expensive homes; cars, boats, vacations bought on credit; the bills from monthly charge accounts. Rather their failure to mention them stems from the relatively secure knowledge that annual incomes are high and climbing, and that professionals generally get hit last and least in the crunch of economic hard times.[11] In their mid-thirties, these professional men stand on the lower rungs of their career ladders. Barring a national economic catastrophe, a long climb up with steadily increasing earnings is assured.

At the same age and stage of the life cycle, working-class men generally are at the top of their truncated career ladders. Increased earnings can be anticipated only insofar as union negotiations are successful or in routine cost-of-living increases, which at best keep them barely even with the inflationary spiral. Moreover, even in the event of economic disaster, most men in the professional middle class can count on holding jobs or getting them more readily than their less educated working-class brothers. Recall the depression of the 1930s when college graduates displaced those with only a high-school diploma behind the counters in major department stores and at the gas pumps.

Would you fantasy for a minute about what you'd do if you suddenly inherited a million dollars?

Other interesting differences between the classes appear—differences that speak powerfully to their widely divergent early life experiences as well as to differences in their present life styles. Among the working-class families, for example, 34 percent said they would help their families:

First of all, I'd fix up my parents and Bob's so that none of them would ever have to worry again. Then I'd buy my sister and brother-in-law a house.

[*Thirty-year-old housewife.*]

I'd be able to help my mother and father and set them up so they wouldn't have to worry about anything anymore.
[*Twenty-seven-year-old carpenter's helper.*]

Almost identical words issuing from so many lips—"so they wouldn't have to worry anymore"—give testimony to the precariousness with which their parents and some of their siblings still live, to the continuing fragility of life in these families. Only one professional man exhibited a similar concern for his family—the only man from a working-class background. For the rest, there is no need to think about such things. Their parents can not only take care of themselves but usually can—and often do—help the children as well.

Finally, there are those—just over half and most often women —whose fantasies include buying some small services not now possible:

I'd get the TV fixed. It's not working right, but right now, it's hard to take the money to have it fixed. There's so many bills that *have* to be paid right now.

[*Thirty-six-year-old mother of four.*]

... getting some needed, but neglected, medical attention:

I'd make sure the kids would have everything they needed. Then I'd go to the dentist and get me some teeth where I've got some missing.

[*Twenty-nine-year-old father of two.*]

... or doing something special for the children—"special" usually defined in such a way as to highlight the scarcity of comforts that are taken for granted in most middle-class families:

I think I'd buy each of the kids a dozen pair of shoes. Poor little things, they only have one pair of shoes at a time. They're lucky to get that. It's practically a holiday when we go out to buy shoes for one of the kids. They get so excited.

[*Thirty-four-year-old mother of five.*]

I'd spend a lot of it on giving the kids a good time. We hardly ever have anything extra to take them to Kiddieland or something like that. Once this year we did, and they were so happy and excited. It made both of us feel good to see them that way.

[*Twenty-eight-year-old mother of three.*]

Under the pressures of these financial strains, 58 percent of the working-class wives work outside the home—most in part-time jobs.[12] Of those who stay at home, about two-thirds are happy to do so, considering the occupation of "housewife and mother" an important and gratifying job. Some are glad to work only in the home because jobs held earlier were experienced as dull and oppressive:

I worked as a file clerk for Montgomery Ward's. I hated it. There was always somebody looking over your shoulder trying to catch you in mistakes. Besides, it was boring; you did the same thing all day long. Now I can stop when I don't feel like doing something and play with the children. We go for walks, or we work in the garden.

. . . some, because life outside seems frightening:

No, I don't ever want to work again if I don't have to. It's really too hectic out there. Now when I'm home, I can go out to it when I want. I suppose it sounds like I'm hiding from something, or escaping from it. But I'm not. It's just that sometimes it's overwhelming.

. . . and some, just because they enjoy both the tasks and the freedom of work in the home:

I wouldn't work ever again if I didn't have to. I like staying home. I sew and take care of the house and kids. I go shopping. I'm my own boss. I like that. And I also like fixing up the house and making it look real nice. And I like cooking nice meals so Ralph is proud of me.

But few working-class wives are free to make the choice about working inside or outside the home depending only on their own desires. Most often, economic pressures dictate what they will do, and *even those who wish least to work outside the home probably will do so sometime in their lives.* Thus, for any given family, the wife is likely to move in and out of the labor force depending on the husband's job stability, on whether his overtime expands or contracts, on the exigencies of family life—a sick child, an aging parent.

The women I met work as beauticians, sales clerks, seamstresses, cashiers, waitresses, office clerks, typists, occasionally as secretaries and factory workers; and at a variety of odd jobs such as baby-sitters, school-crossing guards, and the like. Their work hours range from a few hours a week to a few—nine in all—who work full-time. Most—about three-quarters—work three or four days a week regularly.

Their attitudes toward their work are varied, but most find the work world a satisfying place—at least when compared to the world of the housewife. Therefore, although many of these women are pushed into the job market by economic necessity, they often stay in it for a variety of other reasons.

An anomaly, a reader might say. After all, hasn't it already been said that wives who hold jobs outside the home often are resentful because they also bear most of the burden of the work inside the home? Yet both are true. Women can feel angry and resentful because they are overburdened when trying to do both jobs almost single-handedly, while at the same time feeling that work outside the home provides satisfactions not otherwise available. Like men, they take pride in doing a good job, in feeling competent. They are glad to get some relief from the routines of housewifery and mothering small children. They are pleased to earn some money, to feel more independent, more as if they have some ability to control their own lives. Thus, they ask no more—indeed, a good deal less—than men do; the chance to do work that brings such rewards while at the same time having someone to share some of the burdens of home and family.

There is, perhaps, no greater testimony to the deadening and deadly quality of the tasks of the housewife than the fact that so many women find pleasure in working at jobs that by almost any definition would be called alienated labor—low-status, low-paying, dead-end work made up of dull, routine tasks; work that often is considered too menial for men who are less educated than these women. Nor is there greater testimony to the efficacy of the socialization process. Bored and discontented with the never-ending routine of household work, they seek stimulation in work outside the home. But a lifetime of preparation for housewifery and motherhood makes it possible to find gratification in jobs that require the same qualities—service, submission, and the suppression of intellectual development.[13]

No accident either that these traits are the ideal complements for the needs of the economy for a cheap, supplemental labor pool that can be moved in and out of the labor force as the economy expands and contracts. Indeed, the sex-stereotyped family roles dovetail neatly with this requirement of our industrial economy. With each expansion, women are recruited into the labor force at the lowest levels. Because they are defined primarily in their family roles rather than as workers, they are glad to get whatever work is available. For the same reason, they are willing to work for wages considerably below those of men. When the economy contracts, women are expected to give up their jobs and to return quietly to the tasks of housewifery and mothering.[14] Should they resist, they are reminded with all the force that society can muster that they are derelict in their primary duties and that those they love most dearly will pay a heavy price for their selfishness.

Tell me something about the work you do and how you feel about it?

A thirty-one-year-old factory worker, mother of five children, replies:

I really love going to work. I guess it's because it gets me away from home. It's not that I don't love my home; I do. But you get awfully tired of just keeping house and doing those housewifely things. Right now, I'm not working because I was laid off last month. I'm enjoying the lay-off because things get awfully hectic at work, but it's only a short time. I wouldn't like to be off for a long time. Anyhow, even now I'm not completely not working. I've been waiting tables at a coffee shop downtown. I like the people down there, and it's better than not doing anything.

You know, when I was home, I was getting in real trouble. I had that old housewife's syndrome, where you either crawl in bed after the kids go to school or sit and watch TV by the hour. I was just dying of boredom and the more bored I got, the less and less I did. On top of it, I was getting fatter and fatter, too. I finally knew I had to do something about it, so I took this course in upholstery and got this job as an upholstery trimmer.

"It gets me away from home"—a major reason why working women of any class say they would continue to work even apart from financial necessity. For most, however, these feelings of wanting to flee from the boredom and drudgery of housewifery are ambivalently held as they struggle with their guilt about leaving young children in someone else's care.

For all women, the issues around being a "working mother" are complex, but there are some special ones among the working class that make it both harder and easier for women to leave their homes to work. It is harder because, historically, it has been a source of status in working-class communities for a woman to be able to say, "I don't *have* to work." Many men and women still feel keenly that it's his job to support the family, hers to stay home and take care of it.[15] For her to take a job outside the house would be, for such a family, tantamount to a public acknowledgment of his failure. Where such attitudes still are held strongly, sometimes the wife doesn't work even when it's necessary; sometimes she does. Either way, the choice is difficult and painful for both.

On the other hand, it's easier for the wives of working-class men to override their guilt about leaving the children because the financial necessity often is compelling. On one level, that economic reality is an unpleasant one. On another, it provides the sanction for leaving the home and makes it easier for working-class women to free themselves from the inner voices that charge, "You're self-indulgent," that cry, "What kind of mother are you?"—as this conversation with a twenty-five-year-old working mother of two shows:

How do you feel about working?

I enjoy it. It's good to get out of the house. Of course, I wouldn't want to work full-time; that would be being away from the kids too much.

Do you sometimes wish you could stay home with them more?

Yeah, I do.

What do you think your life would look like if you could?

Actually, I don't know. I guess I'd get kind of bored. I don't mean that I don't enjoy the kids; I do. But you know what I mean. It's kind of boring being with them day after day. Sometimes I feel bad because I feel like that. It's like my mind battles with itself all the time—like, "Stay home" and "Go to work."

So you feel guilty because you want to work and, at the same time, you feel like it would be hard for you to stay home all the time?

Yeah, that's right. Does it sound crazy?

No, it doesn't. A lot of women feel that way. I remember feeling that way when my children were young.

You, too, huh? That's interesting. What did you do?

Sometimes I went to work, and sometimes I stayed home. That's the way a lot of women resolve that conflict. Do you think you'd keep on working even if you didn't need the money at all?

I think about that because Ed says I could stop now. He says we can make it on his salary and that he wants me home with the kids. I keep saying no, because we still need this or that. That's true, too. It would be really hard. I'm not so sure we could do it without my salary. Sometimes I think he's not sure either. I've got to admit it, though, I don't really want to stay home. I wouldn't mind working three days instead of four, but that's about all. I guess I really work because I enjoy it. I'm good at it, and I like that feeling. It's good to feel like you're competent.

So you find some real gratifications in your work. Do you also sometimes think life would be easier if you didn't work?

Sure, in some ways, but maybe not in others. Anyhow, who expects life to be easy? Maybe when I was a kid I thought about things like that, but not now.

Faced with such restlessness, women of any class live in a kind of unsteady oscillation between working and not working outside the home—each choice exacting its own costs, each conferring its own rewards. Another woman, thirty-two and with four children, chooses differently, at least for now:

Working is hard for me. When I work, I feel like I want to be doing a real good job, and I want to be absolutely responsible. Then, if the little one gets a cold, I feel like I should be home with her. That causes complications because whatever you do isn't right. You're either at work feeling like you should be home with your sick child, or you're at home feeling like you should be at work.

So right now, you're relieved at not having to go to work?

Yeah, but I miss it, too. The days go faster and they're more exciting when you work.

Do you think you'll go back to work, then?

Right now, we're sort of keeping up with the bills, so I probably won't.
When we get behind a lot again, I guess I'll go back then.

Thus, the "work–not work" issue is a lively and complicated one
for women—one whose consequences radiate throughout the
marriage and around which important issues for both the individuals and the marital couple get played out. Even on the question
of economic necessity, wives and husbands disagree in a significant minority of the families. For "necessity" is often a relative
term, the definition ultimately resting on differences between
wives and husbands on issues of value, lifestyle, sex-role definitions, and conjugal power. Thus, he says:

She doesn't have to work. We can get by. Maybe we'll have to take it
easy on spending, but that's okay with me. It's worth it to have her
home where she belongs.

She says:

My husband says I don't have to work, but if I don't, we'll never get
anywhere. I guess it's a matter of pride with him. It makes him feel
bad, like he's not supporting us good enough. I understand how he
feels, but I also know that, no matter what he says, if I stop working,
when the taxes on the house have to be paid, there wouldn't be any
money if we didn't have my salary.

In fact, both are true. The family *could* lower its living standard
—live in an apartment instead of a house; have less, do less. On
his income of about $11,500, they undoubtedly could survive. But
with all his brave words about not wanting his wife to work, he is
not without ambivalence about the consequences. He is neither
eager to give up the few comforts her salary supports nor to do
what he'd have to do in order to try to maintain them. She says:

He talks about me not working, then right after I went back this time,
he bought this big car. So now, I have to work or else who would make
the payments?

He says:

If she stops working, I'd just get a second job so we could keep up this place and all the bills and stuff.

How do you feel about having to do that?

Well, I wouldn't exactly love it. Working two jobs with hardly any time off for yourself isn't my idea of how to enjoy life. But if I had to, I'd do it.

What about the payments on the car? Wouldn't they get to be a big problem if she didn't work?

Yeah, that's what she says. I guess she's right. I don't want her to work; but even if I worked at night, too, I don't know how much I could make. She's right about if I work two jobs then I wouldn't have time to do anything with the family and see the kids. That's no life for any of us, I guess.

The choices, then, for this family, as for so many others, are difficult and often emotionally costly. In a society where people in all classes are trapped in frenetic striving to acquire goods, where a man's sense of worth and his definition of his manhood rest heavily on his ability to provide those goods, it is difficult for him to acknowledge that the family really does need his wife's income to live as they both would like. Yet, just beneath the surface of his denial is understanding—understanding that he sometimes experiences with pain, sometimes masks with anger. His wife understands his feelings. "It's a matter of pride with him," she says. "It makes him feel bad, like he's not supporting us good enough," she says. But she also knows that he, like she, wants the things her earnings buy.

It should be clear by now that for most women there are compensations in working outside the home that go beyond the material ones—a sense of being a useful and valued member of society:

If you don't bring home a pay check, there's no gauge for whether you're a success or not a success. People pay you to work because you're doing something useful and you're good at it. But nobody pays a housewife because what difference does it make; nobody really cares.
[*Thirty-four-year-old typist.*]

. . . of being competent:

In my work at the salon, it's really like an ego trip. It feels good when people won't come in if you're not there. If I go away for two weeks, my customers will wait to have their hair done until I come back. I'm not always very secure, but when I think about that, it always makes me feel good about myself, like I'm really okay.

[*Thirty-one-year-old beautician.*]

. . . of feeling important:

I meet all kinds of interesting people at work, and they depend on me to keep the place nice. When I don't go in sometimes, the place gets to be a mess. Nobody sweeps up, and sometimes they don't even call to have a machine fixed. It makes me feel good—you know, important—when I come back and everybody is glad to see me because they know everything will be nice again.

[*Twenty-nine-year-old manager
of a self-service laundromat.*]

. . . and of gaining a small measure of independence from their husbands:

I can't imagine not working. I like to get out of the house, and the money makes me feel more independent. Some men are funny. They think if you don't work, you ought to just be home every day, like a drudge around the house, and that they can come home and just say, "Do this," and "Do that," and "Why is that dish in the sink?" When you work and make some money, it's different. It makes me feel more equal to him. He can't just tell me what to do.

In fact, students of the family have produced a large literature on intra-family power which shows that women who work outside the house have more power inside the house.[16] Most of these studies rest on the resource theory of marital power—a theory which uses the language of economics to explain marital relations. Simply stated, resource theory conceptualizes marriage as a set of exchange relations in which the balance of power will be on the side of the partner who contributes the greater resources to the marriage.[17] While not made explicit, the underlying assumption of this theory is that the material contributions of the husband are the "greater resource." The corollary, of course, is the implicit denigration and degradation of the functions which women traditionally perform in the household—not the least of them providing the life-support system, the comfort, and the respite from the outside world that enables men to go back into it each day.

So pervasive is the assumption of the greater importance of the male contribution to the family, that generations of social scientists have unthinkingly organized their research around this thesis. Unfortunately, however, it is not the social scientists alone who hold this view. For women as well too often accept these definitions of the value of their role in the family and do, in fact, feel more useful, more independent, more able to hold their own in a marital conflict when they are also working outside the home and contributing some share of the family income. Such is the impact of the social construction of reality[18]; for, as the old sociological axiom says: "If men define situations as real, they are real in their consequences."

Indeed, it is just this issue of her independence that is a source of conflict in some of the marriages where women work. Mostly, when women hold outside jobs, there is some sense of partnership in a joint enterprise—a sharing of the experience of two people working together for a common goal. But in well over one third of the families, husbands complain that their working wives "are getting too independent." Listen to this conversation with a thirty-three-year-old repairman:

She just doesn't know how to be a real wife, you know, feminine and really womanly. She doesn't know how to give respect because she's too independent. She feels that she's a working woman and she puts in almost as many hours as I do and brings home a pay check, so there's no one person above the other. She doesn't want there to be a king in this household.

And you want to be a king?

No, I guess I don't really want to be a king. Well [*laughing*] who wouldn't want to be? But I know better. I just want to be recognized as an important individual. She needs to be more feminine. When she's able to come off more feminine than she is, then maybe we'll have something deeper in this marriage.

176

I'm not sure I know what you mean. Could you help me to understand what you want of her?

Look, I believe every woman has the right to be an individual, but I just don't believe in it when it comes between two people. A man needs a feminine woman. When it comes to two people living together, a man is supposed to be a man and a woman is supposed to be a woman.

But just what does that mean to you?

I'd like to feel like I wear the pants in the family. Once my decision is made, it should be made, and that's it. She should just carry it out. But it doesn't work that way around here. Because she's working and making money, she thinks she can argue back whenever she feels like it.

Another man, one who has held eight jobs in his seven-year marriage, speaks angrily:

I think our biggest problem is her working. She started working and she started getting too independent. I never did want her to go to work, but she did anyway. I don't think I had the say-so that I should have.

It sounds as if you're feeling very much as if your authority has been challenged on this issue of her working.

You're damn right. I feel the man should do the work, and he should bring home the money. And when he's over working, he should sit down and rest for the rest of the day.

And you don't get to do that when she's working?

Yeah, I do it. But she's got a big mouth so it's always a big hassle and fight. I should have put my foot down a long time ago and forced her into doing things my way.

The women respond to these charges angrily and defensively. The men are saying: be dependent, submissive, subordinate—mandates with which all women are reared. But for most white working-class women—as for many of their black sisters—there is a sharp dysjunction between the commandments of the culture and the imperatives of their experience.

The luxury of being able to depend on someone else is not to be theirs. And often, they are as angry at their men for letting them down as the men are at the women for not playing out their roles in the culturally approved ways. A thirty-two-year-old mother of two speaks:

I wish I could be dependent on him like he says. But how can you depend on someone who does the things he does. He quits a job just because he gets mad. Or he does some dumb thing, so he gets fired. If I didn't work, we wouldn't pay the rent, no matter what he says.

Another thirty-year-old mother of three says:

He complains that I don't trust him. Sure I don't. When I was pregnant last time and couldn't work, he went out with his friends and blew money around. I never know what he's going to do. By the time the baby came, we were broke, and I had to go back to work before she was three weeks old. It was that or welfare. Then he complains because I'm too independent. Where would we be if I wasn't?

Thus are both women and men stuck in a painful bind, each blaming the other for failures to meet cultural fantasies—fantasies that have little relation to their needs, their experiences, or the socio-economic realities of the world they live in. She isn't the dependent, helpless, frivolous child-woman because it would be ludicrously inappropriate, given her life experiences. He isn't the independent, masterful, all-powerful provider, not because he does "dumb" or irresponsible things, but because the burdens he carries are too great for all but a few of the most privileged— burdens that are especially difficult to bear in a highly competitive economic system that doesn't grant every man and woman the right to work at a self-supporting and self-respecting wage as a matter of course.

For those who hold to traditional notions that men are entitled to power and respect by virtue of their position as head of—and provider for—the family, a working wife may, in fact, be a threat. When, as is the case among the working-class families, a woman working part-time earns almost one fourth of the total family income, there is a shift in the power relations in the family—a shift which may be slight but with which, nevertheless, men of any class in this culture are likely to be uncomfortable. The fact that the professional middle-class men I met did not express these negative feelings about their wives working may be less related to their liberated attitudes about sex roles than to the fact that their wives' earnings comprise only 9 percent of the family income—a proportion so insignificant that it poses no threat to the traditional balance of power in the family.[19]

No surprise this, in a culture where "money talks" is a phrase embedded deep in the folklore. No surprise either that working-class men often feel forced into an arbitrary authoritarianism as they seek to uphold their authority in the family and to insist upon their entitlement to respect. Sadly, probably no one is more aware than they are that the person who must insist upon respect for his status already has lost it. That fact alone is enough to account for the seemingly arbitrary and angry demands they sometimes make upon wives and children. Add to that the fact that, unlike their professional counterparts, the family is usually the only place where working-class men have any chance of exercising authority, and their behavior—while often unpleasant—may no longer seem so unreasonable. Those realities of their husbands' lives also at least partly explain the apparent submissiveness of working-class wives who, understanding the source of their men's demands, often try to accede to them in a vain attempt to relieve their husbands' pain and restore their bruised egos.

Thus, in some families, husbands win the struggle to keep their wives from either working or going to school to prepare for a job. Sometimes the wife is compliant, as in this family:

I want to go back to school, but he doesn't want me to. He thinks I should just stay home with the children. But you know, I just can't stay home with them forever. After all, what am I going to do when they get to junior high school?

I always really wanted to be a teacher, and I thought now would be a good time to start. I could take classes while the children are in school and be home before they get back. I keep telling him that it wouldn't make any difference in the house. I'd still get all my work done. It wouldn't interfere with anything—not with the housework, or cooking the meals, or the kids, or anything. He wouldn't even know I was gone. By the time he'd get home, everything would be just like it always was.

I don't know what he worries about. Just because I want to go to school doesn't mean I'm going to go out and do anything. I guess he just doesn't want me getting too independent. We know some couples where the wife works, and then they get into fights over who should keep her money or what to spend it on. I wouldn't do that, but I guess he really isn't sure.

That seems like a real issue between you. How do you resolve such a conflict?

I keep talking to him, but I'm not getting anywhere yet. I'll keep trying, and maybe in a few years, he'll see it my way. Sometimes I understand how he feels, but sometimes I get mad because it doesn't seem fair that he can tell me no. I say to him, "It's my life; why can't I do what I want." And he says, "It's my life, too, and I say no." Then I get mixed up and I don't know what to say, so I just wait, and I'll try to talk to him again sometime when he's in a good mood.

The husband:

I don't want her to work, and I don't want her to go to school. What for? She doesn't have to. She's got plenty to keep her busy right here.

You feel strongly about that. Could you say why?

Mostly because of the kids. I think a mother should stay home with the kids. I told her when we first got married that I'd earn the money and she'd take care of the kids. I've never run across a family yet where the husband and wife work where there wasn't a lot of arguments and where the kids seem to grow up differently.

I understand that right now all she wants is to go to school.

Yeah, for five years and then eventually do something I don't want her to do anyhow. I told her she can't. Anyhow, I don't think she'd go all the way with it. Becoming a teacher, I don't know how many years you'd have to go to college for that. She wouldn't be able to go through with it.

If that's so, wouldn't it be worth letting her try so that she could find out for herself either that she couldn't or didn't want to do it?

No, not really. It would cause arguments between us, and the kids would be growing up with baby-sitters, and stuff like that. No, she can't do it.

I wonder, how far do you think you'd be willing to hold this position? If it threatened your marriage, would you be willing to go along with her even if you don't like the idea?

No, I wouldn't. I'd say this is the way it's going to be; it's the way I want it. If I was to back down because I feel it's not worth risking what I've got, what good would it be? I wouldn't have that much. She wouldn't be the same girl I married, so what would I be giving up?

So far, the stress of this struggle is not evident in the marriage. The battle lines are drawn, but the rules of war in this household are those of gentlepeople.

In other families, the battle is far more devastating and the victory a pyrrhic one—as the story of this couple, married thirteen years and parents of four, shows. Before the first word is spoken, the senses give evidence of the chaos in which they live. The front yard is a weed-infested patch, the porch cluttered and unswept. Inside, the house is dirty and disordered. My hostess matches the house—unkempt and uncared for. When she starts to speak, however, I am surprised. For here is an extremely articulate woman—her eyes bright, her voice lively and energetic. With a wave of her hand, she apologizes:

I know it's a mess, but somehow I just can't ever seem to get things organized. I know it doesn't look like it, but I really do work hard around here. It's just that I'm so disorganized that I never finish anything I start. So there's always a million things piled on top of one another.

She talks easily and brightly about one subject after the other. Finally, we get to the issue of work. Her voice flat, she says:

No, I don't work. My husband doesn't like me to work. He thinks a wife ought to be home taking care of the children and her husband.

You sound as if you wish it were otherwise.

[*Wistfully.*] Yes, I really enjoyed working. I used to work down at the bank and I really enjoyed it. I was the best girl in the office, too.

You know, it's funny, but I'm very organized when I work. I guess you wouldn't believe it, would you, but my desk was as neat as a pin. There was never a paper out of place. I even used to be more organized around the house when I was working.

Maybe it'll sound silly to you, but I still belong to the Business and Professional Women's Club here. When I get dressed to go to one of their meetings, it's the only time I feel like a whole individual. I'm not somebody's wife, or somebody's mother. I'm just Karen. I suppose that's why I liked working, too. When I'd be there, I could just be who I am—I mean, who I am inside me not just all those other things.

It seems as if you all pay a heavy price for your not working. Have you and your husband tried to reconcile that difference in some way that wouldn't be so costly to all of you?

We've tried, but we don't get anywhere. I understand his point, too. He wants me to be at home when he leaves and he wants me to be here when he comes home. It's because of his upbringing. He was sent from one foster home to another when he was growing up, and he has a pretty big thing about the family staying together and about mothers being home with their kids. I suppose I would, too, if my mother ran off and left me.

Here, then, we see expressed her yearnings for herself, her anger because she feels deprived of an important part of that self, and her insight into the source of her husband's unwillingness to compromise the issue. But while insight generates understanding, it does little to assuage the pain of deprivation she experiences every day of her life.

Her husband, a tall, thin man, with a shy, sensitive smile, also talks openly and easily, but with a great deal of bitterness about the state of the house:

I just don't understand. She works like a beaver around here and never gets anything done. [*Pointing to the litter of cans all over the kitchen.*] I don't know how to convince her that if you open a tin can, it's easier to put it right in the garbage instead of sticking it on the sink, then opening another one and putting it on top of the frig, then opening another one and putting it on the table. Eventually, you spend all your time cleaning up all the opened cans. I keep telling her, but I can't make a dent.

You sound very frustrated about that.

Sure, I hate to walk into the bathroom and try to shave with everything stacked up around me, or try to find a clean coffee cup, or try to find a place to sit down with junk all over everything, or to look in my drawer and not find any underwear for the fourth day in a row because it's still stacked up on a chair in the living room.

Karen says things were different around the house when she was working, that things were much more organized. Is that your recollection, too?

Oh yeah, when she's working, she's much better.

It sounds as if there might be a message in that for you. Don't you hear it?

Sure, I hear that message, but I'm a little stubborn myself. And from my background, I can't help wanting her home with my kids. Sometimes I think I'm nuts or something. I can't understand why a young woman who only wanted to get married can do such a poor job of being a housewife and such a good one at an occupation.

Since she does so much better a job at home when she's also working outside, maybe you could both get what you want if she felt free to do that.

[*Slamming his hand down on the table in anger.*] Dammit, no! A wife's got to learn to be number two. That's just the way it is, and that's what she better learn. She's not going to work. She's going to stay home and take care of the family like a wife's supposed to do.

And she does. But the wreckage of the struggle is strewn around the house, its fallout contaminating everything it touches —husband, wife, children, and the marriage.

Thus does work performed outside the house—the values associated with it and the stereotypic conceptions about who must do it—touch the core of life inside the house.[20] For the men, there is no real choice. Like it or not, they work—never seriously questioning how it came to be that way, why it must remain so. Despite the enormity of the burdens they carry, many men still feel they must do it alone if they are to fulfill their roles successfully. Often they cannot, as the soaring proportion of married women who work attests. For the working-class man, that often means yet another challenge to his already uncertain self-esteem—this time in the only place where he has been able to make his authority felt: the family. For his wife, it means yet another burden in the marriage—the need somehow to shore up her husband's bruised ego while maintaining some contact not only with her own desires but with family needs as well. For both wives and husbands, it means new adjustments, new ways of seeing themselves and their roles in the family—a transition that some make more successfully than others.

Who works? What kind of work do they do? Do they earn enough—either separately or together—to support the family in reasonable comfort? What are the objective conditions *and* the subjective experience of work? In the context of family life, these are the central questions around work and its meaning. The answers determine the quality not only of work but of leisure as well.

10

The Quality
of Leisure

Could you describe a typical evening in your family now?

ANOTHER DIFFICULT QUESTION—one that most often elicits a perplexed silence. Finally, an answer comes:

There's nothing to describe. We're just here, that's all.

What does that mean? What are you doing?

After the kids go to bed and things settle down, we're just here. I guess we watch TV or something. [*Angrily.*] What am I saying? It's not "or something"; that's what it is. It's the same every night; we're just here.

Being "just here," then, means that the family is gathered together in the house—father, mother, children. As in the families in which they grew up, dinner is typically early—between five and six. Father comes home, cleans up, and they eat:

What's the time at dinner like? Do you two get to share your day?

Not really. He says:

There's nothing much to say. I just been working all day.

She says:

Mostly it's the kids; nobody can get a word in when they're around.
If they're being good, then it's okay; we enjoy them. If not, it's a hassle
—you know, breaking up a fight. Or we're trying to teach them how
to eat and how to behave right.

After dinner, she does the dishes, cleans up the kitchen. If children are old enough, they help. In some families, at some times,
he helps. Mostly she does the job alone—children are too young;
he's too tired; it's not his job.

While she's doing that, in winter, he may be reading the newspaper, playing with the children, fixing something around the
house, or watching TV. In summer, he may be out on the street
talking to neighbors, out in the yard, or working on his car, truck,
camper, or boat. For about three-quarters of the men, such do-it-
yourself projects take up a good part of their time away from
work:

About twice a week, my buddy and I get out and fix cars. Between
us, we've always got a couple of cars we're working on. I usually have a
couple of projects around the house, too.
            [*Thirty-year-old warehouseman.*]

At night, I get involved in something. I've always got some projects
going—like some repairs around the house, or working on my truck.
            [*Thirty-one-year-old refinery worker.*]

For men whose days are spent at jobs that afford few personal
satisfactions, little sense of mastery, these projects offer more than
dollar savings. Indeed, such after-work jobs may be the only ones
they do that call upon them to use a wide range of skills and
competencies, in which they can take initiative and exercise
judgment:

I feel best about everything, including myself, when I can get to work
on something interesting after supper. I like to work on the house, or I

go down into the garage and fix the boat, or just play around with the engine of the pick-up. That seems to take the poisons out of my character.

[*Twenty-eight-year-old cannery worker.*]

An interesting expression—to "play around" with the engine—especially since working-class men often *work* very hard on those engines, putting out a great deal of time, energy, and money. It suggests that when people work at jobs that require the inhibition of imagination and creativity, any activity that permits those qualities—no matter how difficult or demanding—is experienced as play, not work. Thus, fixing, tinkering, "playing around" with these machines is a favored leisure activity, a source of much pride and pleasure.[1]

If his wife also works outside the house, there are after-dinner chores that demand her attention—straightening up the house, washing, ironing, a little sewing, tomorrow's lunches, perhaps a casserole for dinner the next day—all done under the pressure of guilt because she's not yet had any time with the children. Her body is there, but her attention is fixed on the tasks that need doing. In fact, she's resentful of the children's intrusions—sometimes churning inside with an anger that exacerbates her guilt. She knows she shouldn't be angry with them. "It's not their fault," she tells herself. But she can't help it. She's tired; there's still so much to be done; and there's no one to help.

If she doesn't have to go to a job the next day, after the clean-up, she may join the family at the TV, in the yard, or out front. In either case, by the time she gets the children in bed for the night, it's nine o'clock—not much left of the evening when people have to be up at five-thirty or six in the morning because their work day starts early.

Such evenings are experienced differently among women who work outside the home and those who don't. The former generally are glad that the day has come to an end, that there's a moment to rest quietly:

By the time I get the kids down, I'm glad if there's nothing else to do and I can just collapse on the couch and fall asleep watching TV like we did last night.

For those who have been home all day, it's a different story. They're more often bored and restless, feeling locked in by the walls of their houses, ready to get out—anyplace, just so long as it's out of the house. She says:

I know he's tired and that he's got all those projects he likes to do. But still, sometimes I feel like I'll go crazy if we don't go someplace. It doesn't have to be anything fancy or something special. I know we can't afford to go out to eat or even go to the movies very much. But we could just go for a little ride sometimes and maybe stop in and see his sister or my folks for a little while.

He says:

I've got things to do here, and if I don't feel like doing anything, I'm satisfied to relax and take it easy—you know, have a beer and watch TV. I guess I don't need much excitement like she does.

It's more than their differing requirements for "excitement," though. Rather, they experience different realities in their daily lives—she, home with the children, is relatively isolated from contact with other adults; he, out at work, is surrounded by them. Those differences mean that he's happy to get back into the peace and quiet of the house, while she's desperate to leave it. For him, the house is a haven; for her, a prison.

But in addition to those existential realities, there also are different psychological realities—differences that are rooted in the profoundly different ways in which women and men define themselves, and in the issues that preoccupy them when, as boys and girls, they struggle toward a definition of self that feels safe and comfortable.

Boys, seeking a masculine identity, learn early to repress their inner emotional and relational needs—to relate to the world in task-oriented, instrumental ways, to assert mastery and demonstrate competence. A man whose work day allows him little expression of those qualities often will seek them in his leisure pursuits. Middle-class men may be sportsmen—accomplished in golf, tennis, sailing. Working-class men are more likely to be "do-it-yourselfers"—fixing, building, making things with their hands.

These after-work activities help to affirm their identity, their sense of self, and their sense of worth.

On the other hand, girls, seeking a feminine identity, learn equally early that their singular area of expertise is to be the inner emotional and interpersonal one. It's true, they are taught the skills of homemaking. But, in general, these are skills that require little intelligence to master, that tap few special qualities of the individual, that offer limited outlets for intellectual and creative capacities. Moreover, no matter how well done by a woman, those few homemaking skills that do require creativity are validated largely as they are practiced in relation to the comfort and nurturance of others, in the setting of the home. A woman's cooking may be her crowning achievement—winning accolades from husband and friends, prizes at the county fair—but a chef is almost always a man, the assumption being that it takes a man to be *that* good.

Mastery, competence in the world of things and work—these are not issues that are supposed to concern little girls growing up. Indeed, these are the needs they are taught to suppress in the interest of developing in appropriately "feminine" ways.[2] It seems natural then that, when grown, their favored leisure pursuits would involve going places and seeing people—activities that call upon their relational and emotional acuity, and through which they affirm their identity, their sense of competence, and their self-worth.[3]

An ironic situation, this—one of life's bad jokes—for it means that day-by-day each sex is stuck with having to deny a fundamental part of self, and each night is spent in search of it.

Again the question presents itself: Is this so different from the lives of middle-class families? The answer: Not *so* different, but different enough to merit attention. The professional middle-class families I met have more active leisure lives on every count. They do more, go more, read more, have more friends, see more people. Partly, that's due to financial differences; the professional middle class can better afford to entertain themselves regularly both inside and outside the house. On an income of $25,000 a year, a baby-sitter, a movie, a dinner out don't feel like major investments. Whether separately or together, there's more money to do more things—a family vacation, a weekend without children for wife and husband, at least occasional household help for the most onerous chores, a baby-sitter one afternoon a week so a house-bound mother can have some time to herself.

But that's only part of the story. The other part lies in the difference in the quality of the daily work lives of the men, which makes for important differences in the quality of home life. For if there is one crucial difference between the lives of professional men and blue-collar men, it is that the professionals' lives are not so profoundly cleft between work and leisure. Indeed, a major problem in professional families may be just this issue—that is, work time and off-work time are so fused as to leave little room for free time that is not also spent in work. And while that is no small issue in these families, at least one member—the professional husband—does not suffer the malaise of work alienation which so dominates the lives of most working-class men.

For the professional, the fragmentation of which I spoke earlier doesn't exist. There is not the separation between working and living that so often characterizes the working-class experience. Work and life—which also means play—are part and parcel of each other. Their friends are often colleagues or other profession-als in similar or related fields. Evenings spent with them mean that the ideas that engage them at work also involve them at play. Social life is almost always a coupled affair, a shared experience of husband and wife.

It's true—especially when she's "just a housewife"—that *she* is sharing *his* experience; he has little to do with hers. But for most women in that class, that is the reality of their lives; and at least until now, they have not dared to complain much or loudly about their satellite status. In fact, even with the feminist movement at its height, not one professional wife with whom I spoke discussed this aspect of the family social life as if she thought anything was amiss. Without doubt, she would like him more involved in her life and concerns as well. And she often says so. But that doesn't mean she wants to bow out of his. There are gains for her—the excitement of meeting people and doing things, the sense that she's important in the advancement of his career, the admiration she gets for doing her job well.

This is not to suggest that life in these professional families is somehow ideal. Far from it. But whatever the problems they have, there is a greater continuity between the day and the night, a sense of connectedness between the various parts of life that is almost wholly lacking in most working-class families. That difference, together with the greater financial ease, makes for differences in the quality of leisure which are highlighted on these and the following pages:

When you have free time in the evening, what do you like best to do?

By far, the most common answer of working-class husbands and wives is—"just relax." Internally, that may mean different things to each of them. In practice, it usually means watching television. For the women, that may be combined with some kind of needlework. For the men, it's "just watching":

I'm watching, that's all. I'm not thinking about things or anything like that. I sit down and I'm just watching. That's what I do most nights. I come home and die in front of the TV.

Just as the women are captivated by daytime television with its attractive soap opera characters who support their romantic fantasies, so the men are mesmerized by nighttime television with its heroic images of the tough cop or cowboy, the action of a baseball, football, basketball, or hockey game. The flickering screen serves well to block out life's painful realities and to drain off the tensions it produces:[4]

It's relaxing. I can just sit there watching *Mannix* and forget about it all. If it's been a lousy day, or that damn foreman was riding me, or Linda's been bugging me—I can just forget about it.

Although 30 percent of the men and 42 percent of the women spend some time reading, for most of them, it's an activity infrequently undertaken and relatively unimportant in the fabric of their lives. Only two women and two men—not in the same families—spontaneously mentioned reading as a valued leisure activity. Fifteen—nine women and six men—had read a book in the preceding year, usually recalling it only under the stimulus of close questioning. For the rest of the men who read, that generally means the newspaper or, less frequently, a sports or technical magazine; for the women, it most often means women's magazines.[5]

Do you ever have a night out alone with just your friends?

Occasionally either a husband or a wife—more often a husband —answers yes, but it's rarely a part of the routine of life. The days of the regular "night-out-with-the-boys" seem to be past—gone with the compliant "little woman" who would sit patiently and wait for his return. One young husband puts it this way:

Sure, I'd like to go out with the fellas one night a week, but Josie wouldn't stand for it. If I did it, she'd do it, too, and I wouldn't like that. I've thought about it a lot, and I always end up thinking, well, if I could do it, why can't she? That would only be fair, wouldn't it? So I figure, it's no use to have all that trouble. Oh, I go out with the fellas once in a while, but not much.

Using almost identical words, a woman in another family says:

I wouldn't stand for him going out with his friends. I don't believe in a guys' night out and a girls' night out. If he was going to go out and have a guys' night out, you can be sure I'd have a girls' night out, because if one does it, the other can. Even if I had to go sit at my mother's house, I'd make him know what it was like to think I was out.

For most, the issue of his "night out" was a part of the early years of the marriage—a struggle engaged, and usually compromised, within the first few years. One common way in which men handle that constraint is by "stopping off for a beer with the guys" on the way home from work. Few women like the idea, and the practice is the source of a great deal of conflict. Some wives complain:

I don't like him coming in and smelling like the bottom of a beer barrel.

. . . others:

I come right home from work, so why can't he. I'd like to sit down and rest awhile when I get off, but I can't. So why's it coming to him?

Those who don't work outside the house argue:

If anybody needs to get out, it's me, not him. He's been away all day. I've been right here taking care of the kids, washing and cleaning and cooking. You'd think he'd be glad to come home and just be here with us.

I get maddest because he won't even call up to say he'll be late for supper. He says, "What would it look like if I've got to call my wife every time I want to stop off?" I understand that, and I don't want to embarrass him in front of his friends. But he could go do it quietly, and they wouldn't have to know.

Others, who have seen the devastating effects of alcoholism on the family, worry:

Both of us had fathers who were alcoholics, and drinking really scares me. I never drink—never; and I'd be a lot happier if he didn't either. He says it's just a social drink with the guys, but it's three, four times a week. Even though he won't admit it, I know it's more than one.

Generally, the men tune out their wives' complaints on this issue, insisting that "it's harmless," arguing that "everybody does it," or charging her with being "too possessive."

If week nights generally are taken with men's projects, women's chores, and TV, and if husbands and wives no longer go their separate ways, what does social life in working-class families look like now? Mostly, it happens on the weekend, and mostly, the activities include the whole family.

Perhaps the most popular social activity is bowling. Over one third of the couples bowl regularly every Friday night. And while it's the parents who bowl, children beyond the toddler age usually go along and spend the evening in the baby-sitting center that most neighborhood bowling alleys now provide free. As one mother tells it:

The kids love to go to the bowling alley with us because they know all the other kids there by now. Everybody who bowls in a Friday night league brings their kids, so they're all good friends.

Less than one fourth of the couples go out without the children as often as one Saturday night a month. Such evenings out usually include dinner or a movie—sometimes with another couple, sometimes not—but almost always the outings are neighborhood-based, close to home. Although for most, San Francisco is no more than a half hour's drive, few could remember the last time they had been to the city for an evening's entertainment. Typically, the comments about going to the city sound like this:

There's nothing there we don't have right here in the area, so why would I go over there with all them people and crowds?

. . . or:

We like to be closer to home so we can get back in a hurry if we have to.

Undoubtedly, there's truth in both those explanations, but one senses another truth as well—a vague, unarticulated fear of wandering too far from familiar territory; a sense of discomfort with the manners and mores of The City with which they—especially the men—fear they would be out of place; and an angry dislike for "all those hippies and freaks" who, they imagine, dominate its streets.

In fact, the fears, fantasies, and anger they harbor about this alien world run so deep that they manage to avoid contact even when it is right on their doorstep. Thus, although about half the families live minutes away from the city of Berkeley—with its large university-based population—so few ever go there that it might as well be on another planet. They say they don't like the children exposed to that environment, that they're afraid of the "crazy people" on the street there. But underlying that is another fear and a deeper anger. They are angry at the university students and their supporters—a privileged minority who cavalierly dismiss and devalue a way of life these working-class people have struggled so hard to achieve. And they are afraid to be in the presence of such a fundamental challenge to that traditional lifestyle and its values—afraid that such a permission-giving environment might bring their own conflicts and questions about their lives more readily to the surface. They already have trouble enough keeping those conflicts in check—remonstrating with themselves for feelings that seem dangerous and untoward. Thus, over and over, both women and men disavowed the wish for some desired activity—whether to spend some time alone, to develop some personal interest, or to see more of same-sex friends—with the comment that they don't want to get into "bad habits." Speaking of her wish to go out with her women friends once in a while, one twenty-eight-year-old woman reasons:

I think about it sometimes. It would be fun to go with my girlfriends sometimes—you know, not to do anything wrong, but to have some fun. But then I worry what would happen if I did? I might get to like it. Then I get afraid, and I think I don't know if I want to taste that life. You know, sometimes when you taste something like that, then you start requiring it. My life is really my husband and my children and my home. I wouldn't want to risk taking any chances of losing them. If I started to go out, and then I liked it, I might want to do more and more. [*Firmly.*] No! I don't think it's a good idea, not at all.

A man, thirty-three years old, says:

I'd like to have time for myself, just to do what I want. I don't know for sure what it would be, but it would be only mine. But I wouldn't like to make a habit of it. It can be dangerous to have habits like that, so I wouldn't want to do it a lot.

Entertaining adults who are not family members seems to be on the increase in working-class families; more than one third say they do so at least four to six times a year.[6] But the dinner party— that backbone of middle-class social life—is almost nonexistent:

On holidays, we have the family to dinner or we go there. I've never given a dinner party. I don't know that I've ever been to one. You know, every now and then—it isn't often, because it costs too much and besides it's too much trouble—I just have people down for dinner, but it's not what you'd call a dinner party.

"It costs too much and besides it's too much trouble"—major reasons why working-class women rarely look forward to entertaining at home. Whether their full-time occupation is housewife, or they work both inside and outside the house, these women rarely get away from the chores of cooking and cleaning. Thus, another night in the kitchen—one even more demanding than usual because you're cooking for company—is a far less enticing prospect than going out for the evening where, at least for the moment, someone is waiting on you.

Those who do entertain adult friends at home are most likely to be young couples with very small children for whom going out is both difficult and expensive. Some miss the good times of dancing and partying of just a few years earlier. Unable to afford the cost of a visit to places that provide such diversions, they invite friends in late on Saturday night—after the children are asleep—for some drinking and dancing. Others just yearn for adult companionship. The friends they invite often bring their children along and put them to sleep while the adults visit:

We don't have the money to go out hardly at all, but I get lonely to see some friends without the kids around sometimes. So once in a while, we invite them over, and we play some cards and have a little beer and a snack.

Except for holidays which almost always include big family dinners in which everyone participates—parents, siblings, sometimes aunts, uncles, and cousins all sharing both cost and preparation—most entertaining at home is of the casual, drop-in sort, and is likely to happen more often in the summer when evenings are long and children don't have to be up early in the morning for school. Thus, a family—a couple and their children—may go for a walk or a ride on a summer evening, and stop to visit a friend, a sibling, or a parent for an hour or so. Since it's still daylight outside, the children can be sent out to play giving the adults some time to themselves.

Neighboring is also an important part of life, especially for the women who do not have jobs outside the house. By day, these women may drink coffee together, take their children to the park together, sometimes even go shopping together—thus easing their isolation and loneliness. But these relationships are seldom incorporated into family social life. In fact, although they clearly fill a need for sociability, they seem more important as mutual aid relationships. If a child is sick, if someone needs a lift, if, occasionally, a mother needs a baby-sitter, there's usually a neighbor who can be counted on to lend a hand. The men, too, may share a beer together on a summer evening, go down to the lumber yard together, share tools and expertise. But these interactions remain between the men and generally stop at the front door unless someone is called in for some expert counsel on a project.

Generally, it is the relationships with extended family—parents and siblings—that are at the heart of working-class social life. Parents and married children exchange casual visits regularly throughout the year, with the parents most often visiting the children. Such visits allow the grownups to exchange news, to play cards, to watch TV together without disrupting the regular routines of small children. In fact, even in mobile California, the importance of extended kin among working-class families is striking. These are the people who are seen most often and most regularly, whose lives are shared both emotionally and socially. These are the people with whom intimacies are maintained, who can be trusted with the care of young children on the rare occasion when a couple takes an evening out alone, perhaps to celebrate a birthday or an anniversary. For it is not only the cost of baby-sitters that keeps most working-class couples from going out alone together— although that is indeed a very large factor—but the suspicion of strangers and the fear that no one but family can properly care for the children.

Partly this close involvement with extended family inhibits joint friendships with outsiders since it fills both the time available and the need for social relationships. But partly, also, these family relationships are reinforced by the early and difficult years in the marriage when a major concern of the young wife was to break her new husband's attachment to his high-school peer group— those buddies with whom he used to "hang out," to whom he fled when they had a fight:[7]

I didn't like those friends of his. They used to do things that aren't right. Jimmy knows that, too. They'd run around and get drunk and pick up girls. They were a bad influence on him. Some of them were married, and I could never figure out how their wives put up with their cheating ways. Eventually, I got him to break away from them. But we used to have a lot of fights over it. It's no problem now. We both have big families and with all the kids' birthdays and holidays and all that stuff, it keeps us too busy for much else.

The husband, too—perhaps partly in retaliation for her response to his friends, perhaps also because he genuinely feels uncomfortable with hers—complains often that he doesn't like her high-school girlfriends or that their husbands aren't his "idea of a guy I want to bother with."

The implicit bargain that's generally struck, then, is that they both give up their old friends—although if she isn't working, she may continue to see hers during the day. That leaves them with only the family for company and with few possibilities for establishing joint friendships outside the neighborhood. It's true that they both may make new friends on the job, but those friendships are infrequently brought into the home—partly because it's difficult for four people all to get on equally well; but mostly because sharing friends and entertaining at home still is not a commonly accepted part of working-class life.

These, then, are the nights—week days and weekends. What about the days? During the week, all the men and many of the women work. The women who stay home usually still have infants or pre-schoolers in the house. Consequently, social life is confined largely to the neighborhood. The few women with school-aged children who don't work outside the home may go out with a friend, a neighbor, a sister, or a mother one morning a week— bowling and shopping being the favored activities.

Weekends, when the whole family is home, are somewhat different while also being very much the same—more like a variation on a theme than a different tune. There are still the chores; but there's more time for them so they create less tension. There are the ubiquitous projects around the house. There are the shopping expeditions—for groceries and sundries—that often involve the whole family and take on the air of an outing. There are the sporting events on television on Saturday and Sunday afternoons that claim male attention. There are the Sunday visits with the family. For about one fourth of the men, there's also something else: a day off—sometimes once a week, sometimes once a month —to ride motorcycles with their buddies:

One weekend a month, a bunch of us guys go out and take a big bike ride. The girls get mad, so maybe once a year we take them with us just to keep them in good spirits.

. . . or, for the five who own them, to get the boat out on the water:

We got this boat, see, and with the kids, we can't go out together anymore. So I take it out—mostly on Sundays—and she takes the kids and goes over to her family.

Sometimes wives are understanding about these activities of their husbands, especially if they also work and have been away from the children for a good part of the week:

He works hard and that boat gets him through. I could go with him; I used to. But I really feel guilty now about leaving the kids all week and then leaving them again for that. So I stay home. I don't mind; I like to spend the time with the kids. And I understand that he really needs the time off.

Sometimes—especially if they've been home all week—wives feel angry, exploited, and neglected:

He gets up early on Saturday and takes off with a buddy of his, and they just ride their motorcycles. It makes me mad because I don't want to just stay here while he's riding around. It's especially irritating when he comes home after a whole day out like that and complains that the living room is a mess because the kids left a couple of toys out.

I like to go up to Tahoe on the bus with my sister. He doesn't like me to do that, though, because I go away early in the morning and I come back late at night. He says he feels like he's doing my job, so I hardly ever do it. But why is it okay for him to go away early every Saturday and just leave me baby-sitting?

Over one-fourth of these families have campers and/or boats, bought with the fantasy that these possessions would help them live the good life. In reality, however, they find themselves stuck with large payments for goods they can seldom use. To meet those payments, most men must work overtime, leaving them with relatively little free time for such leisure pursuits as camping:

We bought the camper because we thought it would be a cheap way to get away weekends. There's nothing I like more than going up to Clear Lake with the family—fishing, swimming. But Christ, I've been working every Saturday for the last sixteen months, so there's no chance to use the damn thing.

To compound the bind, when overtime stops, it's not a blessed relief that allows more time for pleasure, but a frightening worry about how the bills—including those for the camper—will be paid:

Don't get me wrong. We're not complaining about the overtime. We sure need it. There's lots of bills to pay around this place that just wouldn't get paid without it. [*Sighing with perplexity.*] I guess you can't win. If I had the time to get out of here, there wouldn't be any money.

Thus, most camper owners use their vehicles two or three times a year, usually when the husband is on vacation. But even vacations are not universally taken. Among those who have the option, half the men reported that they "take the pay without taking off"—an arrangement that puts an extra two or three weeks wages in the family coffers even while it keeps him working on the job without a break.

Most do take vacation time, however, although the weeks usually are spent close to home—occasional daily excursions with the kids, two or three days at a nearby lake, the norm. Again, it happens this way not because it's preferred, but because a long trip—no matter how inexpensively planned and executed—costs more than most families can afford. Indeed, high on the list of fantasies of most working-class women and men is travel, rarely to the exotic, far-away places of Europe, Asia, and Africa that occupy the dreams of the professional middle class, but to the fabled places of the American West—the gold country, the Mojave desert, Disneyland, the Grand Canyon, Yellowstone or Glacier National Parks.

Finally, there's the issue of participation in community activities and extra-family organizations:

Do you belong to any organizations or participate in any activities in the community?

Surprisingly, in a group of fifty families where 42 percent are Protestant, 18 percent Catholic, and 22 percent are mixed Protestant-Catholic marriages (18 percent claim no religious affiliation at all), the organization that claims most working-class women as members is not the church but the P.T.A. Almost all claim to believe in God and think religion is important—especially as a vehicle around which to teach children right from wrong—but few actually are members of a church. Of those who are, only five families—three Protestant, two Catholic—attend with any regularity.

To the degree that women are active or involved outside the home, those activities are concentrated around the children's school. Thus, almost all the mothers with school-aged children belong to the P.T.A., even though only a small minority of them are actively engaged in the organization or ever even go to a meeting.

Among the men, of course, it is union membership that is the most common affiliation—although, as with the women in the P.T.A., there's a wide gap between belonging and involvement.[8] Only three ever go to a union meeting at all—one of the three is a shop steward, the other aspires to be an officer in his local one day. Moreover, unlike P.T.A. membership, union affiliation is not really voluntary—a point about which at least some of the men make note:

I belong to the union because I have to keep my job. Nobody works unless you belong to the union. So I belong.

While there's some acknowledgment of the benefits derived from union membership—mostly around issues of job security—more commonly the men gripe about it.[9] Some complain about the rules:

I guess it's a necessary evil. It's crazy; they say I can't use my own truck on the job without getting paid for it. Well, the truth is I work steady because I bend and I'm not a strict union man. And these days, a guy needs any edge he can get.

. . . some about the corruption:

They're just a bunch of god-damned crooks, out for themselves. Our wages aren't bad, but look at those fat cats on top. They're living it up, for sure.

Apart from these organizations, here and there a woman is a Camp Fire Girl leader, a man a Boy Scout leader; a woman belongs to a sewing club, a man to a motorcycle club; a proposal to institute a busing plan in the local school district involves some couples in an anti-busing campaign for a few months; an election very occasionally claims the attention of a man or a woman. But that's the sum of it. Active participation in the community and its organizations is rare—almost nonexistent—unless, as in the case of the struggle around busing in the schools, an issue arises that is perceived as a threat to the family, its way of life, and its values.

With all, then, the leisure hours generally are quiet ones—spent mostly with the family or in family-related activities. Husband and wife probably get away on their own without the children more often than their parents did. And, in general, their leisure hours are more often spent together than in the rigidly sex-segregated activities of earlier generations. Despite those changes, most still are frankly ambivalent about the quality of their leisure lives, often expressing a deep longing for more—for the freedom and fun that was the implicit promise of the adulthood they sought so eagerly:

I sometimes feel like I'm just sitting home becoming an old woman—like a picture of the old woman who lived in the shoe.

. . . says one twenty-seven-year-old. And a thirty-two-year-old man:

I get to thinking sometimes that there isn't any fun in life anymore. I used to look at my folks and think, "I'm not going to live like that." And here I am, doing the same thing. I understand my Dad a lot more now. I mean, the way he'd get drunk and how he'd fly off the handle. It was probably the only way he could stand it.

Of course, people *do* find ways to "stand it," ways to tolerate the dullness and the disappointments—small compensations, wrought sometimes at the expense of a mate, that make life easier to swallow. Meanwhile, they dream of the future—the time when the children will be grown or gone, when the responsibilities and expenses will be less, when there will be time both for separate and together activities and a little more money around to support both.

Worlds of Pain

SOME TOPICS lend themselves to conclusions; they have a beginning, a middle, and an end. This one does not. For it is about life and the people who live it. And life is a process that, until death, does not lend itself to endings.

What I have drawn here is a portrait—a still picture, a frame abstracted from a movie that continues to run long after the viewer leaves the theater. So it is with the people who live on these pages. Their lives continue to "run"; they continue to live, grow, change, and struggle.

Still, there are things left to be said—loose ends to be tied together, themes to be highlighted, questions not yet answered satisfactorily. First among those tasks is to restate clearly what every line of the book implies: the affluent and happy worker of whom we have heard so much in recent decades seems not to exist. True, the median income of these families is $12,300. Not bad, many will say. But focusing on the statistical median obscures the fact that fully one-half fall below it, some very far below. In fact, almost one third of the families I met earn between $6,900 and $10,500 a year—not much money on which to support a family of at least four.

Where, then, does the myth of affluence come from? Why is it so persistent? It is the illusion of a society that mistakes the acquisition of consumer items with a good life. In fact, while some of those possessions *do* make life easier—especially for the women who do most of the work around the house—they also add burdens. Each purchase is bought "on time," each adds "just a few dollars a month" to the cost of living. But together, the car payment, appliance payments, mortgage payments, payments on charged purchases, perhaps payments for a truck, a camper, a small boat, add up to an enormous chunk of family income—all requiring payment before the first dollar is spent on food or medical care, whether the pay check comes in each week or not. Thus, buying the goods may be easy; keeping and paying for them is another problem—one that preoccupies the men and women I met, that sticks them with a nagging anxiety from which there is no relief:

Would you fantasy for a minute about what you'd do if you suddenly inherited a million dollars?

No wonder the first words that come to most of their lips are, "I'd pay off my bills." For, in fact, they live precariously perched on the edge of financial disaster; any lay-off, any cut-back in overtime threatens to plunge them into the abyss. For more than a few working-class families throughout America, that threat has become a reality during the last two years.

Until now, at least, all the families I met could be counted among the settled-living. Yes, almost all were poor in the early years of marriage. Yes, there was some drinking, some angry explosions. But they were also very young then, just starting out—a time when no one expects to have much, when people assume they will have to struggle, have to find ways to "make do" with little. Their childhoods—from which they had only just emerged—had prepared them well for that. But those early years were also something more—a time of hope, a time when they dreamed dreams of a life different from the one they'd known, when they believed they could "make it" in a way their parents had not.

For most—even those whose earnings have been consistently below the average—some part of that dream seemed to come true. Despite the hardships and problems they confronted, their lives *did* seem easier than their parents' lives. That's one reason why they complain so little about living conditions that seem so difficult and oppressive to a middle-class observer.

For most, work was more readily available; wages were rising and prices had not yet climbed so high as to wipe out each increase; there was plenty of credit around so they could buy those things that would make life a little more comfortable, a little more fun. Each new purchase was also an affirmation of self and a confirmation of their well-being, of their status—a statement to the world that they were "doing okay." For they, after all, are part of this culture and buy its illusions; they, too, believed these goods would bring with them the good life.

For most, too, there has been less drinking and less violence in the family, more companionship, and more shared leisure moments than anything their parents had known. Maybe none of it matches the fantasies with which they entered marriage, but it is, in fact, so much more than they saw in their own pasts that over and over again both women and men try to still their doubts, their fears, and their anger with reminders that they have no right to complain. "My folks had it so much worse than we do, and I never heard them complaining. So what right do I have to complain?"

But things change when an economy begins to contract. Because I have kept in touch with many of the families and, through them, heard about others, I already know of some of those changes. In the current economic crunch, over half the men have lost the overtime that made it possible to pay the bills for the goods they bought in their more optimistic moments; some have had extended periods of unemployment; at least three of the fifty families have been divorced in the two years since we met; and four—two women and two men—who had incipient drinking problems two years ago have developed full-fledged ones. Thus, at least for some, hard times probably will bring hard-living in their wake—periods when the gains they made over their parents will be lost, when despair will conquer hope, when the game won't seem worth the candle.

Most, however, retain their settled-living ways and probably will continue to do so for all or most of their lives. Life will get a little harder as inflation pushes the cost of living up. But they're used to it; somehow they'll manage. Those wives who already are working outside the home will increase their time where possible; those who aren't will begin to look for jobs. The lucky ones will find them, making it just a little easier, a little more likely that they'll come out closer to even at the end of the month. But a shrinking economy is not a good time for women to enter the labor market; so most won't be so lucky. Adjustments will be made, new possessions not acquired, near-new ones sold or repossessed. Old dreams will be laid to rest; there won't be many new ones to take their place.

What hope is left will be invested in the next generation. The most commonly heard wish: "I want my kids to be happy." But what does it mean?

I don't know; I just want them to be happy, that's all. I want them to have everything they want, all the things we couldn't have.

Even now, it's hard for working-class adults to imagine what it means to "be happy," hard to imagine a life that's very different from the one being lived. The alternatives they perceive still are limited—limited now not just by their childhood experiences but by the cumulative effect of their adulthood as well; limited not just in dreams for personal life but in occupational life as well:

Do you hope your children will go to college?

Most aren't sure. "If they want to," is the reply most often heard. Indeed, less than 20 percent of the families answered with a firm and unequivocal "yes"—even that small proportion almost always referring only to sons not daughters. The meaning of that "yes," however, is not self-evident. For as the conversation continues, it becomes clear that few working-class parents have any real idea about the cost of a college education—most guessing it to be "maybe a few hundred dollars a year or so."

Partly that's naïveté; but partly, also, it's because they don't discriminate between the local junior college and the unversity. Thus, very often, "going to college" means the two-year community college in the neighborhood.

Under any circumstances, the cost of a college education, even at the state university where it is relatively low, is a distant issue for most of these parents. For most assume that the only help they'll give their children will be to let them live at home without cost. The rest, the children will have to do for themselves—an attitude that rests not on their callousness or their unwillingness to help, but on their conviction that to give the children more, even were it possible, would be to spoil them, to encourage them to take the opportunity lightly, to "spend their time partying and running around the streets."

It was hard not to wonder, as I heard those words repeated again and again, how much of what they were saying was part of beliefs and values deeply held, how much a defensive response to the realization that no matter what their wish, there was no way they'd be able to give their children more, no way they could support one or more children through four years of a college education. Whatever the mix, there's heartache in that realization and pain in knowing that their children probably won't be much better off than they. For under such circumstances, only the hardiest, the most ambitious, the most motivated toward some specific occupational goal will ever get through college. For the parents, however, there's some compensation as well: the reassurance that the children won't be lost to an alien way of life, a way of life that parents can't and don't want to understand.

In fact, there's not much danger of that—at least not within the next few generations. For upward mobility does, indeed, depend largely upon at least a college education these days, and most people simply aren't going to get it. It's true that the proportion of adults over twenty-five who have completed four years or more of college doubled between 1950 and 1973. But before we join in the self-congratulatory huzzahs and hosannas that greet those educational statistics, let's see what they mean.

In 1950, just over 6 percent of the over-twenty-five population had completed four years or more of college; by 1973, it was somewhat over 12 percent.[1] At best, that's one in eight. Jumping ahead to 1990, the United States Census Bureau projects that 20 percent of the same aged population will have reached similar educational heights.[2] Even if we don't challenge the optimism that underlies that projection, it still means only one in five.

But, the argument can be made, those figures still represent a social achievement worthy of pride, one that ought not to be cast aside lightly and cynically. Perhaps so. But if we insist on pride, we must insist also on understanding—on knowing just what it is we're to be proud of. In this case, that means a hard look at the fact that such statistics make no distinction between one school and another, the quality of education received there, and the opportunities for mobility they offer. It means that four years at Teachers' Normal is counted as the same as four years at Harvard or Dartmouth; the tables make no distinctions. In real life, however, we all know that equation is an absurdity. In real life, even when the children of working-class families do go to a four-year college, most go to schools that, at best, will track them into lower-middle-class jobs through which they will live lives only slightly better than their parents'.

Still, on the average, the difference between a college and a high-school diploma is worth a lot. In 1972, the lifetime earnings of the person who had four years or more of college was calculated at $758,000; of the high-school graduate, $479,000.[3] That means that in his lifetime, the average college graduate will earn almost 60 percent more than the average high-school graduate—this despite the fact that the high-school graduate is at work at a regular job by eighteen while most of those who go to college don't enter the full-time labor market until after graduation at twenty-two. But even figuring on the same forty-seven-year work life for both—that is, from eighteen to sixty-five—the high-school graduate can count on an annual income of just over $10,000; the college graduate on just over $16,000—the difference between some measure of comfort and a substantial measure of deprivation.

Again, a word of caution about statistical averages. Many—probably more than half—of the college graduates will earn considerably less than the $16,000 annual average; many will earn considerably more. Notice, too, that the census category in which the story of their lifetime earnings is told lumps together all those with "four years or more" of college, thus making no distinction between the person with a bachelor's degree and the one with an M.D. It takes little ingenuity to figure out that those who earn less most likely will come from the lower strata in the society, will go to the less prestigious schools, will have only the four years required to get a bachelor's degree, and, at best, will spend their lives at some middle-level bureaucratic job. The high earners generally will fall into the "or more" part of the census category. They will be the professional and high-level executives, most of whom will come from professional middle-class families, and will graduate with advanced degrees from the top universities and professional schools in the country. In sum, even with a college degree, the child of a working-class home is likely to live in considerably less affluence than his middle-class counterpart.

At the beginning of this book, I said that my main concern was with the quality of working-class family life and centered on whether working-class life has a rationale and integrity of its own, a quality of life that is distinctly related to class position. The entire book, it seems to me, has been devoted to answering that question. It comes out a resounding yes. For the economic realities of working-class life and the constraints they impose upon living are the common ingredients from which a world of shared understandings arises, from which a consciousness and a culture grows that is distinctly working class. Whether in ways of being in the family, in childrearing patterns, in orientations toward work and leisure—common experiences create common adaptations, all responses to a particular set of life circumstances. Thus, what I said somewhat speculatively at the beginning seems quite true at the end:

. . . the family is a product of its time and place in the hierarchy of social institutions [and] American families [are] both similar and different—similar in that they share some common experiences, some elements of a common culture by virtue of being part of the same society; different in that class, race, and ethnic differences give a special cast to the shared experience as well as a unique and distinctly different set of experiences.

Until those socio-economic realities of class are changed, until working-class families face a new and different set of circumstances which require new and different adaptations, we can expect those subcultural differences to persist.

But those realities make us uncomfortable; they seem to call the lie to the mobility myth we cherish so dearly. Consequently we proliferate "people changing" programs—programs with which we hope to change the manners, the mores, and the lifeways of the poor and the working class. Then, we tell ourselves and them, they will be able to move into the more privileged sectors of the society. A comforting illusion! But one that avoids facing the structured reality that there's no room at the top and little room in the middle; that no matter what changes people or groups make in themselves, this industrial society requires a large work force to produce its goods and service its needs—a work force that generation after generation comes from working-class families. These families reproduce themselves not because they are somehow deficient or their culture aberrant, but because there are no alternatives for most of their children. Indeed, it may be the singular triumph of this industrial society—perhaps of any social order—that not only do we socialize people to their appropriate roles and stations, but that the process by which this occurs is so subtle that it is internalized and passed from parents to children by adults who honestly believe they are acting out of choices they have made in their own lifetime.

Epilogue

AS I FINISH THIS BOOK, I am mindful of a poem I read some years ago—a poem by a woman who had grown up poor and black:[1]

> *childhood remembrances are always a drag*
> *if you're Black*
> *you always remember things like living in*
>   *Woodlawn*
> *with no inside toilet*
> *and if you become famous or something*
> *they never talk about how happy you were to have*
>   *your mother*
> *all to yourself and*
> *how good the water felt when you got your bath*
>   *from one of those*
> *big tubs that folk in chicago barbecue in*
> *and somehow when you talk about home*
> *it never gets across how much you*
> *understood their feelings*
> *as the whole family attended meetings about*
>   *Hollydale*
> *and even though you remember*
> *your biographers never understand*

your father's pain as he sells his stock
and another dream goes
and though you're poor it isn't poverty that
concerns you
and though they fought a lot
it isn't your father's drinking that makes any
*   difference*
but only that everybody is together and you
and your sister have happy birthdays and very
*   good christmases*
and I really hope no white person ever has cause
*   to write about me*
because they never understand Black love is Black
*   wealth and they'll*
probably talk about my hard childhood and never
*   understand that*
all the while I was quite happy

Fearful that the people whose lives I have described here in such grim terms might one day say the same, I asked a few to read the book before it went into print. It was not an easy experience— either for them or for me. We were both anxious. I, about their response; they, about what they might read about themselves. It was hard for them, too, to believe they could offer me anything. They were shy, embarrassed, unbelieving that I cared, that anything they could say would count:

Me? How could I tell somebody like you what to write?
How would I know?

I reminded them all:

It's your life I've been writing about. You're the only one who could tell me whether I understood it or not, whether the picture I've drawn is a true one.

They were surprised and pleased by my response, and more than a little frightened. None had ever seen a book in creation; most had not even read one since high school. And I asked a good deal of them—not only that they read the manuscript, but that they discuss their responses with me. "Suppose I don't have anything to tell you?" some worried. I reassured them, "This isn't a test; it's a favor you're doing for me."

It took a long time for them to read the book—none less than two months. During that time, they were apologetic if we met. "It's hard to find the time," they said. But there was clearly more than that. It was also painful. One woman, half way through the book, commented about the chapter describing their families:

I was depressed to read it. It sounded just like the families so many of my friends had.

Surprised that she did not include herself since parts of her life are prominently reproduced in that chapter, I asked:

Did any of it seem at all like your own family?

She looked startled, somewhat confused. Finally, haltingly, she replied:

Yes, I suppose so. But I really don't like to think about it. I guess nobody does. Bobby, he read that chapter and got mad at those alcoholic people, and just ranted and raved around about them. I thought he was off because he didn't recognize his own father there. I did, but he didn't. I told him, and at first he got mad at me. But he calmed down. I guess it just hurt him too much to be mad at his own father now that he's dead and all that.

These responses were typical—attempts to avoid re-experiencing the pain. If it can be externalized or denied, dealt with as a familiar experience but not one's own, it's easier to read about, easier to bear.

After a wait that seemed agonizingly long to me, we met and talked. Their comments added depth to my understanding, helped me to grasp meanings that had eluded me. Thus, they added to and deepened what I had already written; no one quarreled with any of it. The lives they read about seemed real to them all—hard to take sometimes, but real:

It's hard to read about it, but everything you said is really true.

Are there good times? Yes: a birthday remembered with joy, a happy Christmas, a loving and tender moment between wife and husband. But they stand out in memory as unique and treasured events, monumentally important because they happen so seldom, because they are so little a part of daily experience. Yes, those moments are real. But as people talk about their lives, such small events become insubstantial, slipping away before a more compelling reality. For, in fact, in the working class, the process of building a family, of making a living for it, of nurturing and maintaining the individuals in it "costs worlds of pain."

NOTES

CHAPTER 1

1. For an informed and sophisticated analysis of the ideological currents in the American society which have distorted the vision of students of social stratification, see Pease, Form, and Huber (1970). Also Aronowitz (1973); Braverman (1974); Hamilton (1972); Massey (1975); Parker (1972); Rinehart (1971) for excellent recent discussions and refutations of the thesis of the affluence and the *embourgeoisement* of the working class.

2. See Thernstrom (1972:57–79) for an outstanding historical analysis of the promise of mobility in the New World during the mid-nineteenth century, when the notion that talent "finds a sure reward [was] a central cultural theme in America." Analyzing the function of this mobility ideology for the upper classes, Thernstrom argues that it served

> ... to integrate workmen into the social order, minimizing discontent and directing it against targets other than society itself. The repetition of success stories would have nurtured the hope that opportunity was just around the corner—if not this week, then next; if not for oneself, then for one's children. Were belief in mobility widespread, the failure to succeed in the competitive race would have seemed proof of individual inadequacy rather than social injustice. Politically explosive resentment would thus have been transformed into guilt and self-depreciation.

See also Wohl (1953) for an interesting analysis of the Horatio Alger novels and the "rags to riches" theme in American ideology. For a more recent examination of the impact of the ethic of individualism and the mobility ideology on working-class consciousness, see Sennett and Cobb (1973).

3. Cf., Thernstrom (1972:115–137) for an insightful discussion of the impact of "property mobility" on the lives of the working class and on the development of class consciousness. Although his assertion that property is a "dimension of social mobility which has received too little attention in the literature of social stratification" fails to take account of the theory of the *embourgeoisement* of the working class which has found great popularity among American social scientists and which *defines* class in terms of possessions, lifestyle, and spending patterns, the discussion is nevertheless valuable in that it shows the historical continuity of the ideology. In the mid-nineteenth century, any man with a bank account was said to be a capitalist; in the mid-twentieth century, it was any man with a share of General Motors. In both centuries as well, despite the fact that the sons of working-class fathers generally became fathers of working-class sons (Blau and Duncan, 1967; Goyder and Curtis, 1975; Lipset and Bendix, 1964), the accumulation of personal possessions has served to sustain the belief among working-class people that

Notes

they were indeed fulfilling the promise of the American dream and getting ahead. For some examples of both sides of the debate around the thesis of the *embourgeoisement* of the working class, see Aronowitz (1973); Bell (1965); Berger (1968); Bonjean (1966); Braverman (1974); DeFronzo (1973); Dobriner (1963); Galbraith (1958); Goldthorpe, et al. (1968a, 1968b, 1969); Hamilton (1964, 1972); Handel and Rainwater (1964); Kohn (1969); Lockwood (1966); Massey (1975); Mayer (1963); Miller and Riessman (1961a, 1961b, 1964); Nisbet (1959); Parker (1972); Pease, Form, and Huber (1970); Rainwater (1971); Rinehart (1971); Sexton and Sexton (1971); Shostak (1969); Wilensky (1964, 1966).

4. By 1973, just over 50 percent of married women (husbands present) with children between 6–17 years, and almost 33 percent with children under six, were in the labor force (U. S. Bureau of the Census, 1974). Cf., Hamilton (1972:370–371, Table 10.2) who shows that "affluent working-class families are not like equivalent middle-class families." In 93 percent of the families of manual workers it took two incomes to reach the "$10,000 or More" bracket. In nonmanual families at the same income level, only 31 percent were dependent upon that second income.

5. Howell (1973); Sennett & Cobb (1973); Shostak (1969) are welcome exceptions. See U.S. Department of Health, Education, and Welfare (1973b:34–35) for a recent good discussion of the negative images of blue-collar workers held in the culture.

> We must also recognize that manual work has become increasingly denigrated by the upper middle class of this nation. The problems of self-esteem inherent in these changing attitudes are further compounded by the impact of the communications media. For example, the images of blue-collar workers that are presented by the media (including school textbooks) are often negative. Workers are presented as "hard-hats" (racists or authoritarians) or as "fat cats" (lazy plumbers who work only twenty-hour weeks yet earn $400.00 a week). The view of the worker in the mass media is that he is the problem, not that he *has* problems.

We may question only the notion that this denigration of manual labor is a recent phenomenon or represents a change in attitudes from the past. What David Lockwood (1958) wrote of English society, applies to America equally well.

> Working with one's hands was associated with other attributes—lack of authority, illiteracy, lowly social origins, insecurity of livelihood—which together spelt social depreciation. The dominant values underlying differences in social worth were those of the entrepreneurial and professional middle classes. The most widely influential criteria of prestige therefore were those which expressed the occupational achievement of the individual. The education required for the job, the rewards and responsibilities offered, the fact that it was clean and nonmanual, and therefore "respectable," gradually established themselves as the key determinants of a person's social standing over a wide range of the society. . . .

6. Komarovsky (1962).

7. In her study of the religious conversion experiences of early New England women at two different time frames—one when the entire household was an integral part of the productive forces, the other when production was split off from the home—Easton (1975) examines the relationship between the ideology of motherhood and the needs of emergent capitalism. See also Ariès (1962) whose classic work on the history of the family traces the emergence of the *idea* of childhood.

Notes

8. Although most current writing about the working class focuses on ethnic differences, this book will not deal with ethnicity. Undoubtedly, no such work coming out of the northeastern part of the United States would ignore ethnic differences in favor of class, but life in the West (and, I suspect, in most of the Midwest and South as well) suggests that class, not ethnicity, should be our major focus. In fact, I would argue that it is because Americans are so resistant to acknowledging the class-bound nature of this society that ethnic rather than class differences are at the center of so many of the analyses of our social conflicts. A recent study of ethnic mobility undertaken by the National Opinion Research Center in Chicago lends support to my argument. In a representative sample of 18,000 Americans, the NORC researchers were surprised to find that "even among whites in the metropolitan areas of the North, the ethnics have higher incomes than do native Protestants—indeed higher than the most aristocratic Protestant denomination, the Episcopalians." Yet, whenever there is a conflict—especially in the eastern half of the United States—the class nature of the conflict is buried under sensational reports of the anger of one ethnic group or another.

This is not to say that ethnic differences are not real and worthy of our attention. It is, however, to insist that the major issue is class, not ethnicity, and that it is possible to see the issue more clearly in the West where ethnic lines generally—although not always—tend to be more blurred than in the East. The reasons for that difference between East and West seem to be quite straightforward. The West Coast never felt the full force of the European migration since most immigrants ended their arduous journey somewhere in the eastern half of the country. Those who did find their way west generally came later and in much smaller numbers. Furthermore, when they arrived, they found much more space so that settlements were not so densely packed as in the East and contacts between individuals could be more limited.

We might speculate as well about the nature of the differences between those newcomers who huddled together in their Eastern ghettoes and those who had the tenacity, independence, courage—however we might label it—to break free and travel west. The ability to take that step in itself probably suggests a loosening of the ethnic and family bonds for those individuals, perhaps even a wish to be free of the constraints of the close-knit community. If true, it makes sense that ethnic ties in the new place of settlement would be attenuated.

These speculations aside, the fact is that ethnicity is not nearly so central an issue in the white working class in the West as it seems to be in the East. Thus, unlike Boston, with its high concentration of Irish working class, when the city of Richmond, California, erupted into controversy about school busing, no ethnic group stood in the forefront to blur the class nature of that struggle. My detailed study of that community conflict showed no ethnic issues, no groups of participants who could be identified as white ethnics. Almost all the leaders of the anti-busing forces, in fact, were third-, fourth-, or fifth-generation working-class Americans whose families generally came to California from the Midwest and Southwest (Rubin, 1972). Even in San Francisco, a city with a relatively large white ethnic population, the schisms on the busing issue had little relationship to ethnicity. Except for the Chinese, with whom there were important issues of subcultural integrity—including the potential disruption of instruction in the Chinese language—the white ethnics were no more heavily represented among the protesters and boycotters, no more monolithic in their opposition, than others in the white working class.

In the present study, the proportion of families with acknowledged ethnic backgrounds probably is quite small when compared to what one would expect to find in the metropolitan Northeast in a similarly selected sample. Ninety-two percent of the parents and 58 percent of the grandparents of the working-class respondents were reported as native born. Three percent didn't know where their parents were born, and 15 percent knew nothing of their grandparents' origins. Interestingly, there is a smaller proportion of native-born parents and grandparents among the professional middle-class families—82 percent of the parents and 46 percent of the grandparents in that group were born in the United States.

9. See Hamilton (1972) and Parker (1972), both of whom make a very persuasive case for this proposition.

10. Rubin (1972).

11. Professional readers quickly remind me that the current recession has hit professionals very hard. While that obviously is true, it is those who man the machines in the factories, those who work in construction, those who provide services, who are the hardest hit. It is the blue-collar worker who has been unemployed and underemployed in the largest numbers in this recession; it is he who has the fewest options. The unemployed physicist makes front-page news when he turns bartender. But where do the unemployed bartenders, auto workers, carpenters, and electricians go? To jobs even further down the wage scale or to the unemployment line.

12. In his otherwise outstanding analysis of the quality of work life in America, Braverman (1974:34) argues that not only has the status and prestige of white-collar work been degraded but that income as well often lags behind blue-collar workers. To support that thesis, he cites income figures which show that "the average weekly pay for clerical workers in 1969 was $105.00 per week, while blue-collar production workers were taking home an average of $130.00 per week."

This argument fails to hold up on two counts. First, a comparison of weekly wages between hourly and salaried workers makes little sense since salaried workers are not as subject to lost wages from layoffs, sickness, and the like as are hourly workers. To know whether the income differences that Braverman cites are *real* differences, we would have to know the annual income figures for both classes of workers. Second, even using the weekly income figures, the comparison between clerical workers and production workers is inapt since clerical workers are at the lowest level of the white-collar hierarchy while production workers are in the middle of the blue-collar pyramid. A more reasoned comparison would be between clerical workers and operatives—a comparison which shows that the *weekly* wage rate in 1973 was almost identical—$132.00 for operatives vs. $131.00 for clerical workers (U.S. Bureau of the Census, 1974).

13. Cf., Hamilton (1972), who presents convincing evidence on this point.

14. While the experience of the immigrant working class is somewhat different from the nonimmigrant's—that is, it's harder for the immigrant child to believe he's like everybody else in the face of such obvious differences as the foreign accent, the exotic foods, the alien customs of his home—there are important similarities in the experiences as well. Today's child of a working-class home knows, just as I did, that his or her parents are not successful in the ways our society rewards, that the culture of his home is devalued by his middle-class teachers at school, that his "ways" are somehow different from theirs, and less estimable.

CHAPTER 2

1. See Caplovitz (1967) for convincing documentation of the thesis that "the poor pay more."

2. One male colleague with years of research experience among working-class men objected that my argument here is unconvincing, insisting that "male camaraderie is legendary and intimate talk among shopmates is well documented." But as we discussed the matter further, the difference between us turned out to rest on a rather typical male-female difference about the definition of intimacy.

"I've heard any number of guys confiding their problems to a workmate," he argued.

"What kinds of problems?" I asked.

"For example, they'll talk about the fact that their car is a lemon," he replied.

"You call that intimate talk?" I asked.

"Sure," he answered, "in the sense that the guy reveals something about himself and his lack of judgment in getting stuck like that. It threatens his manly image, the pose that he can always take care of himself, that nobody can get the best of him."

"Granted," I replied, "but does he tell his workmate that he's worried about his sexual performance; that he has nightmares that his wife might leave him; that he's just found out she's having a love affair with another man? That's the kind of sharing I'm talking about. It's of a different order than the things you call intimate."

"Okay, I get your point," he answered. "We *are* talking about different things when we use the word 'intimacy.' Of course, the guys I'm talking about don't talk about those kinds of very personal things to each other."

In a study seeking to investigate just this issue—that is, whether psychological intimacy in males is experienced in cross-sex or same-sex relationships—Komarovsky (1974) found that for the overwhelming majority of the male college students she studied, a female friend is the preferred confidante. Moreover, those from lower-class backgrounds were even more inclined to self-disclosure to female friends than those from higher-class backgrounds.

CHAPTER 3

1. Although well aware of the problems of defining alcoholism, I use the word here because that is the way my respondents described what they saw in their families. Under any circumstances, from the evidence they presented, there is little doubt that they were describing problem drinkers according to the generally accepted definitions in the field. See, for example, Plaut (1967:37–38) who describes problem drinking as "a repetitive use of beverage alcohol causing physical, psychological, or social harm to the drinker or to others."

While the 40 percent problem drinkers reported here seems shockingly high, the figure actually is congruent with findings from national studies which sampled the

Notes

household population—that is, which excluded the institutionalized, the homeless, and the skid-row derelicts. For example, in several such national samples in which the researchers also controlled for class, Don Cahalan and his associates (1967) found that among men aged twenty-one to fifty-nine, one half reported some drinking problem within the last three years, and one third had some fairly severe problems during that period. Their findings lead them to conclude, moreover, that "men of lower social status have more severe problems, and a higher ratio of interpersonal problems to alcohol intake." And, further, that "the primary independent correlates of drinking problems appear to be socio-economic status, large city residence, age, childhood deprivations, race, and religion." All together, then, the findings of their very comprehensive work support my own, and suggest that the proportion of problem drinkers in all strata of the population is even higher than the gross national statistics suggest, and highest among those at the lower levels of the socio-economic order. See also U.S. Department of Health, Education, and Welfare (1971:28) which presents an occupational breakdown of drinking patterns. Among male manual workers who drink at all, 25 percent of the craftsmen, 36 percent of the semi-skilled, 28 percent of the service workers, and 27 percent of the laborers are classified as heavy drinkers.

2. Presently, over half the teenage marriages in the United States end in divorce. Schoen (1975) examined the California divorce statistics for 1969 and found a strong inverse relationship between the age at first marriage and the likelihood of divorce—that is, the lower the age at first marriage for both males and females, the higher the chance that the marriage would end in divorce. Thus, the California divorce rates imply that three out of seven first marriages undertaken by males between eighteen and twenty-five and females between sixteen and twenty-four will end in divorce. For those who marry at the lower end of these age ranges, however, the risk of divorce is *twice as great* as it is for those who marry at the higher end of the ranges.

The proportion of such young marriages is highest among those who do not go to college, which generally means young people of the working class. Shostak (1969:175) writes: "Oriented toward early marriages, the blue-collar accommodators are heavily represented among the half-million or more seventeen-year-old young women who marry before their eighteenth birthday, a bloc equal to 25 percent of all seventeen-year-old females. They are also disproportionately found among half of all young women who marry before they are twenty years of age." If this is true of the present generation about which Shostak writes, it probably was even more true a generation ago before the boom in college attendance in all sectors of the population.

Among the respondents in this study, the median age of the women at *first marriage* was 18.1. Given the trend data—that is, the increase in the median age at first marriage over the last two decades (U.S. Bureau of the Census, 1974:66)—it is a reasonable assumption that their mothers generally were married somewhat younger. Indeed, often enough, by way of explaining a divorce or a mother who left her children, I was told that, "My mother was just a kid herself when she got married—only fifteen."

3. In no way are these words intended to give support and legitimacy to the traditional role divisions in the family. They are simply a statement of fact about the structure of family relations—that is, given women's traditional role in the family, *they* are likely to take the heat of a child's anger, to be blamed when a child feels less than adequately nurtured and loved. If the structure of roles in the

222

family were changed so that men had the primary nurturing tasks, then it would be fathers instead of mothers who would be the source of disappointment and the target of hostility.

4. For a poignant, first-hand story of life in such a family, see Sharon Isabell's (1974) autobiographical novel. Also Cottle (1976) for a compelling account of a mother and child's ambivalent love-hate feelings toward each other—the mother, because she can't protect her child from the pain and suffering of poverty; the child, because she wants that protection so desperately yet understands her mother's inability to give it to her.

5. Howell (1973). Others have made parallel and equally useful distinctions. Bernard (1966) speaks of the "externally adapted" and the "acculturated"; Gans (1962) describes the "action seekers" and the "routine seekers"; Rainwater (1970) distinguishes between the "expressive" and the "instrumental" lifestyles; and Shostak (1969) makes the tripartite distinction among the "rebels," the "accommodators," and the "achievers." Rather than add another set of terms to those that already exist, I have chosen to use Howell's "hard-living–settled-living" distinction primarily because his referent is families while, except for Bernard (1966), the other work cited here refers to individuals, usually to men. Shostak (1969:169–184) does have a brief chapter entitled, "Blue-Collar Daughters" in which ". . . particular attention [is] paid to the vast bulk of white urban daughters of blue-collarites who appear to be accommodators—now and forevermore." Forever is, of course, a very long-term prediction.

6. Shostak (1969:54–57) remarking upon the same phenomenon, writes: "Blue-collarites begin and end the workday with the knowledge that their employ could hardly have less status . . . They may earn enough to 'command respect,' but the low blue-collar origins of their high earnings may undermine both their self-esteem and the respect they command from others."

7. Sennett & Cobb (1973:171–172) insist that "no more urgent business in a life can exist than establishing a sense of personal dignity." In this society, they argue, the quest for personal dignity is at the root of consumerism. "In consuming . . . men are not trying to keep capitalism alive, nor have they arrived at that identification with the Establishment that Marcuse depicts." Rather, their consuming behavior is in the interest of "personal restoration." Ironically, these "manifold acts of personal restoration added to one another . . . become transformed into a force that keeps the wounding society powerful."

8. Lipset and Bendix (1964:197–199). In an early but still relevant study, Hollingshead (1949:267–287) analyzes the ways in which family influence and prestige (or lack of it) determine job prospects for adolescents. Cf., also Blau and Duncan (1967); Goyder and Curtis (1975); Rogoff (1953).

9. For the seminal article on the deferred gratification pattern, see Schneider and Lysgaard (1953). Miller, Riessman, and Seagull (1965) offer an excellent critique. For the related literature on the culture of poverty, see Coser (1969); Davis (1946); Hyman (1953); Knupfer (1947); Lewis (1968); Liebow (1966); Miller (1958); Moynihan (1965); Riessman (1962). Criticisms of culture of poverty theory are to be found in Billingsley (1968); Carper (1968); Coles (1968); Gans (1968); Gladwin (1967); Lewis (1967); Mackler and Giddings (1967); Miller and Riessman (1964, 1968); Rainwater (1966, 1970); Rainwater and Yancy (1967); Riessman (1966); Rodman (1965); Valentine (1968, 1971).

10. For others who have observed the unrealistic fantasy-like aspirations of lower-class adolescents, see Danserau (1964); Furstenberg (1971); Hollingshead

Notes

(1949); Howell (1973); Kerchkoff (1972); Kohn (1969); Lipset and Bendix (1964); Nagasawa (1971).

11. Cf. Komarovsky (1962); Rainwater, Coleman, and Handel (1959); Shostak (1969).

12. Komarovsky (1962:24–26) also points to the "marriage as liberation" theme in the lives of working-class youth, both female and male.

13. See Collins (1971); Gillespie (1972).

14. In a case study of a high school, Cicourel and Kitsuse (1963) present a vivid account of how *routine* decisions of school guidance and counseling personnel reinforce and perpetuate the existing class distinctions. Greer (1972), confronting the persistent American myth that schools are the primary agency of upward mobility, argues that the real achievement of the schools in America has been their ability to train children to accept the prevailing class structure and their fate as workers in the industrial system. Katz (1968, 1971, 1975), analyzing the roots of educational reform movements, also digs beneath the ideology to show the same reality. Wilson and Portes (1975) also challenge those studies which argue for the primacy of family influence and attitudes and other social psychological variables in determining educational attainment. Instead, their examination of a national sample shows that "personal influences and subjective orientations are of less significance than the structural effects of parental resources and the bureaucratic evaluation of ability."

For other expositions of the ways schools serve the class structure of America, see Bowles (1972); Bowles and Gintis (1973, 1976); Clark (1965); Coleman, et al. (1966); Dennison (1969); Dentler, et al. (1967); *Harvard Educational Review* (1969, 1973); Hentoff (1966); Herndon (1965); Hollingshead (1949); Jencks, et al. (1972); Kozol (1967); Leacock (1969); Miller and Riessman (1968); Parenti (1973); Rist (1970); Rosenthal (1973); Rosenthal and Jacobson (1968); Rubin (1972); Schafer, et al. (1970); Schrag (1968); Sexton (1964); Stein (1971); U.S. Commission on Civil Rights (1967).

15. The figures cited here are taken from the U.S. Bureau of the Census (1974:340). See also Dahlstrom and Liljestrom (1971); Myrdal and Klein (1956); Peterson (1967); U.S. Department of Labor, Women's Bureau (1968).

CHAPTER 4

1. Divorce statistics are complex, and a directly comparable figure is almost impossible to find. Scanzoni (1972:6–28) offers a fine critique of the use of both crude and refined divorce statistics as well as the marriage-divorce ratio. "One suspects," he writes, "that there is a circle of 'analysts' who quote each other on divorce statistics and whose quotes are in turn disseminated to millions of people through the media, but that no one (including the experts) bothers to check the validity of anyone else's sources."

The most reliable and valid divorce rate, he argues, would come from following a national sample of marriages undertaken in any given year until either divorce or death end them—an ambitious, lengthy, and expensive project that has never yet been undertaken. Barring that, Scanzoni controlled the refined divorce rate for such variables as age, education, occupation, and income, and found that *age at the time of marriage is the critical factor in divorce*, followed closely by education, occupation, and income. Thus, in 1965 when the median age at marriage for women was 20.6 years, almost half—48 percent—of all wives involved in divorce had been married before age 20. Moreover, by itself, age at the time of marriage is a good predictor of the other variables since young marriages generally occur among those with lower levels of education and lower status occupations with less income—a portrait of the families I talked to. This, then, is the most divorce-prone segment of the American population. See also Chapter 3, Note 2.

In contrast, the professional middle-class couples in this study were married considerably later. Only two women were married before their twentieth birthdays, one of them because she was pregnant. And true to the picture Scanzoni suggests, the group of college-educated professionals shows a strikingly lower divorce rate. Only two women and one man had been divorced.

2. In a profile of juvenile delinquents prepared by the California Youth Authority, 56 percent of the males come from what is described as a "below average socio-economic environment," and 36 percent from an "average socio-economic environment." For females, the parallel figures are 51 percent and 40 percent respectively. See also Sellin and Wolfgang (1969) whose study in Philadelphia showed similarly high juvenile delinquency rates among young people from "the lower socio-economic areas of the city." In fact, much of the literature on delinquency points to the relationship between juvenile crime and low socio-economic status. Some investigators argue persuasively, however, that, at least in part, that relationship is an artifact of the more intense police activity in poor and working-class neighborhoods, insisting that young people from the poorer socio-economic areas are more closely observed and more readily apprehended by police than those from more middle-class neighborhoods. For an excellent review of the literature on delinquency, see Gibbons (1970).

3. For discussions of childrearing practices as related to class, see Bronfenbrenner (1966); Grey (1969); Havighurst and Davis (1969); Kohn (1959, 1963, 1969); Pearlin and Kohn (1966); White (1969); Zunich (1969).

4. See U.S. Department of Health, Education, and Welfare (1973b:34–35), where it is argued that:

> Today, there is virtually no accurate dramatic representation—as there was in the 1930s—of men and women in working class occupations . . . Research shows that less than one character in ten on television is a blue-collar worker, and these few are usually portrayed as crude people with undesirable social traits. Furthermore, portrayals tend to emphasize class stereotypes: lawyers are clever, while construction workers are louts. But it is not only the self-image of the worker that is being affected; television is conveying to children superficial and misleading information about work in society. If children do, indeed, learn from television, they will "learn" that professionals lead lives of carefree leisure, interspersed with drama and excitement . . . and that blue-collar workers are racist clods who use bad grammar and produce little of use for society.

5. Sennett and Cobb (1973).

6. For the famous study of the authoritarian personality, see Adorno, et al. (1950); also Arendt (1958); Fromm (1941); Lederer (1940) for other writers who showed an early concern about the political consequences of authoritarianism; Lipset (1963) for his widely read and debated exposition of working-class authoritarianism; and Miller and Riessman (1961a) and Lipsitz (1965) for critiques of Lipset. For more recent empirical tests of Lipset's thesis of the authoritarianism of

the working class, see Hamilton (1972); Korpi (1971); Ransford (1972); Rubin (1972); Wright (1972). For a review of the literature on the authoritarian personality, see Kirscht and Dillehay (1967).

7. Cf., Komarovsky (1962:24–26).

8. See Note 2 above.

9. Citing a United States Public Health Service study published in 1970, Scanzoni (1972:21) writes: "Some rather convincing evidence for the association between premarital conception, age at marriage, and disadvantaged economic position has been gathered by the U.S. Public Health Service for the years 1964–1966"—precisely the years when many of the couples in my study were married. Operating on the assumption that a birth any time within the first eight months of marriage was conceived before the marriage, the Public Health Service study found that during those calendar years, 42.4 percent of all legitimate births to married women aged fifteen to nineteen were premaritally conceived—very close, indeed, to the 44 percent in my study. See also U.S. Department of Health, Education, and Welfare (1973a) which estimates that almost 60 percent of the babies born to teenage mothers in 1968 were conceived out of wedlock.

10. Among the college-educated middle-class women, their present spouse was their first and only sexual partner in just over half the cases; among the high-school-educated working-class women, this was true for 36 percent. Explaining similar differences in other studies, Gagnon and Simon (1974:224–225) note "that the patterns of premarital coitus are relatively similar for females across the social-class spectrum, but there exists a minority of females . . . primarily from working- and lower-class origins, who serve as sexual targets for fairly large numbers of males and at fairly high rates of contact . . ."

11. Cf., Miller (1973) who investigated the sexual attitudes and practices in two San Francisco Bay Area high schools—"one predominantly white and middle class, the other racially and ethnically mixed and lower class." He found that 48 percent of the girls in the lower-class school admitted to having sexual intercourse, while 42 percent said they believed premarital coitus was unacceptable behavior. Among the girls in the middle-class school, 58 percent were having intercourse and only 25 percent believed that girls should wait until marriage. Unfortunately, the investigators did not ask how the young women who were having sexual intercourse felt about their behavior, so we cannot make any direct comparisons. Still, it is not without significance that among the lower-class girls, about as many thought it was wrong as were engaging in sexual intercourse—a reflection of the greater ambivalence with which values about premarital chastity are held among working-class girls compared to those in the middle class.

12. Given the reports of various public-opinion polls showing high levels of support for abortion in all strata of the society, this finding seems anomalous. But the trend data presented by Yankelovich (1974) help make sense of it. According to that study, in 1969, 64 percent of noncollege youth believed that abortion was morally wrong. By 1973, five years after the passage of California's therapeutic abortion law and the same year the Supreme Court handed down its decision which effectively legalized abortion (410 US 113 *Roe* v. *Wade*), the proportion dropped to 48 percent. Since most of the pregnancies in this study happened in the early or middle 1960s, we can assume that attitudes then were even more restrictive about abortion than in 1969. Add to that, the fact that often the reason for the pregnancy—albeit unspoken and dimly understood, if at all—was the desire to

marry, and we can see why people responded so negatively to a question about abortion. In fact, several women did qualify their remarks about abortion with comments that suggested they might act differently today—eight or ten years later.

CHAPTER 5

1. For the formulation of the notion of a psycho-social moratorium and the consequences both for individual development and social behavior, see Erikson (1950, 1968); Keniston (1968).

2. See Chapter 3, Note 9 for references to the debate around the deferred gratification pattern and the related literature on the culture of poverty.

3. Komarovsky (1962:28–32) also writes of the "pull of the male clique" and its role in supporting male resistance to assuming the new roles and responsibilities demanded by marriage.

4. See Rossi's (1968) excellent article analyzing the readjustments that must take place when couples move from childlessness to parenthood. Bernard (1973) and Lopata (1971) also found that the arrival of the first child often has a less than salutary effect on the marriage. Bernard (1973:70) writes:

> The effect may be traumatizing. There is a drop in all the indexes of marital
> satisfaction. Diverging interests—the wife's in her maternal and household
> responsibilities, the husband's in his professional career—can produce a drop
> in daily companionship. The marital interaction pattern seems to be muted.

On November 20, 1974, *The New York Times* reported that a research team headed by Angus Campbell, Philip Converse, and Willard Rodgers (of the University of Michigan's Institute for Social Research) found that the proportion of people who were satisfied with marriage was highest among childless couples, lowest where young children were still in the home. And Rollins and Cannon (1974) argue that marital satisfaction is lowest at those periods in the life cycle where role strain is highest—that is, when a high level of stress is generated by a high number of intense and demanding social roles which place conflicting and/or incompatible demands on the individual. The early childraising phase of marriage is just such a period.

5. See Chodorow (1977 forthcoming).

6. Cf., Gans (1962:242–249), who describes the subcultural differences in family lifestyles. The professional middle-class style, which he describes as "adult directed" and centered on individual self-expression and development, is comparable to those professional families I spoke with. His description of the family style of the working-class subculture, however, seems more suited to the ethnic style of the Italians he studied than to the working-class families I met or to working-class families in general. See Handel and Rainwater (1964); Miller (1964b); Miller and Riessman (1964) who also have noted the heterogeneity in working-class lifestyle and have pointed to the fact that it is in a state of flux—changing from what Handel and Rainwater call the "traditional" to the "modern" lifestyle, categories that are roughly equivalent to what Gans calls the working-class and the middle-class lifestyle.

The families I met, in fact, seem to live in a style that is an amalgam of both but leans more heavily toward Gans's middle-class style, especially in their view of

Notes

childrearing and the child-centered nature of family life. Therefore, when the arrival of children brings with it problems, conflicts, and pain, it is especially difficult to bear—or even to acknowledge—since such feelings are incongruent with the romanticized version of the joys of parenthood that is so prevalent among those families.

In contrast, although children are equally important in the professional middle-class families, their adult-directed lifestyle permits more emphasis on the adults as a couple rather than simply as parents, more of an ongoing struggle to keep the marriage relationship primary, and more concern with individual development *apart* from the family for both adults and children.

7. For an analysis of the class-based nature of a community in struggle over its schools, see Rubin (1972, 1976). The controversy in West Virginia around school textbooks also divides along class lines, as Paul Cowan argues in a fine article in *The Village Voice* (December 9, 1974).

8. See Joffe (1974); Rubin (1972, 1976) for discussion of the class-related issues that lie at the heart of much of the controversy around early childhood education.

9. There is a growing recognition among childcare experts that, given the subcultural variation in values in American life, institutional facilities are not the only—perhaps not even the primary—answer to childcare needs. In December, 1974, the Ford Foundation in New York sponsored a conference on working-class women at which both researchers and working women were invited to exchange views. Those of us who acknowledged that we understood the subcultural variations around preferred childcare arrangements and who argued for flexibility in childcare program planning were encouraged and applauded by the working-class women and union representatives who were present.

CHAPTER 6

1. Lopata (1971:123) also notes that "white working class women . . . consider themselves lucky if their husbands are 'good to them,' do not use physical violence, and bring home a paycheck."

2. *The Prime of Ms. America* (New York: Putnam's, 1975):127.

3. See, for example, Blood and Wolfe (1960), a much-cited study that has achieved the status of a classic in the field, in which the word "class" does not appear in the text.

4. Cf., Bernard (1973) who presents a review and re-analysis of the literature and data on marriage and concludes that, on the whole, marriage is less satisfying and contains within it more "structured strain" for women than for men.

5. Papanek (1973).

6. See Walker (1969, 1970) whose time-budget data show that, in the aggregate, husbands contribute the same amount of time to the family—about 1.6 hours a day—whether their wives work or not. Furthermore, husbands' family time remains independent of wives employment when age, class, and number of children are controlled for. See also Pleck (1975) for a fine analysis of the sex-patterned relationship between work and family roles; and Cook (1975) for a cross-national analysis of the problems of working mothers.

7. Cf., Lopata (1971:113–122) who telegraphs her findings by the subheading

of this section of her book, "The Division of Labor and Husband's *Help* in the Home." [*emphasis mine*] On the issue of childcare as well, Lopata comments: "the fact that so many respondents feel that their husbands 'help with the children' is significant, even when stated as a form of praise. It suggests that *childcare is not part of the role of father and is done as a favor to the wife* . . ." [*emphasis mine*]

8. Cf., Holmstrom (1972:68) who studied two-career professional families and found that "the tasks most likely to be done by the husband were emptying the garbage and trash, repair work, and heavy yard work."

9. Although there may be some changes from the findings of earlier eras (see, for example, Blood and Wolfe, 1960; Komarovsky, 1962), my data for both working-class and professional middle-class families strongly support his contention. Cf., also Lopata (1971) and Epstein (1971), whose findings also support those reported here. In fact, in her study of husband-and-wife law partnerships, Epstein (1971) found that, even among those where the language of equality is most frequently heard, the wife has the major responsibility for house and children. Even more striking, the division of labor in the law practice generally broke down along traditional female-male lines.

After a careful and perceptive examination of the literature, Bernard (1973:140–175), too, argues that there is no research proof that egalitarianism has been increasing between husbands and wives. "Talking a good egalitarian game," she comments acidly, "does not . . . prove that we are playing it." Cf., Nye (1974) who, in a study of 210 couples, reports that while there are some changes taking place in the functions of the family, the traditional role divisions (where wives are expected to assume responsibility for socialization and childcare and husbands for providing for the family) still are adhered to strongly. For an insightful exposition of the struggle between husbands and wives on this issue, see Mainardi (1970).

10. For a recent critical review of the family-power literature and the resource theory of family power which has dominated the field since its formulation by Blood and Wolfe (1960), see Safilios-Rothschild (1970a). For critical comments on her review, see Bahr (1972) and Safilios-Rothschild (1972a) for her rejoinder.

11. See for example, Bahr (1974); Blood and Hamblin (1958); Blood and Wolfe (1960); Heer (1958, 1962); Hoffman (1960); Olson and Rabunsky (1972); Sprey (1972); Turk and Bell (1972). Larson (1974) also argues that a major methodological weakness in family studies is the reliance on the response of one family member—usually the wife—from which inferences about family power and decision-making are made. His recent study shows that perceptions of family power vary systematically by both sex and age—that fathers, mothers, sons, and daughters tend to perceive "family reality" differently. Cf., Safilios-Rothschild (1969) who aptly describes family research as "wives' family sociology."

CHAPTER 7

1. Historian Barbara Easton (1975, 1976) presents a compelling account of the change in family ideology in America. In her fascinating work, she demonstrates the link between the technological developments that made obsolete the relationship between the household and the productive forces and the emergence of the ideology which holds women responsible for the social-emotional content of the

Notes

marriage relationship and men for the economic-instrumental side. For other historical perspectives on the relationship between the family and the economy—its evolution from the public to the private sphere—and the consequent changes in the roles and responsibilities that were defined as women's, see Ariès (1962); Lasch (1974); Lazerson (1975); Shorter (1975); Zaretsky (1973).

See also Balswick and Peek (1974) who write about the tragic consequences to modern marriage of the "inexpressive male."

2. See Broverman, et al. (1972) for an intriguing study which shows that practicing psychotherapists (both male and female) hold a different standard of mental health for women and men and that, among others, they divide on these very traits to which I refer here. The study shows that for these clinicians, the definitions of a healthy adult and a healthy male are identical; the definition of a healthy female is exactly the opposite from the other two.

3. The recent literature on sex-role socialization, both scientific and journalistic, is rich and abundant. For an excellent review as well as a fine bibliography, see Hochschild (1973). In a particularly interesting study, Johnson, et al. (1975) reexamine the expressive-instrumental distinction and distinguish between a negative and positive pole on each attribute. After examining the self-ratings of four hundred female and male college students, the authors conclude that:

> . . . men associate independence with negative expressiveness. While the
> women in our sample were able to incorporate positive expressiveness, positive
> instrumentalness, and independence in their self-pictures, the men in our
> sample could not include expressiveness with independence and instru-
> mentalness. This supports the theory that developmnt of masculinity in-
> volves the rejection of femininity. The young boy becomes a man not by
> accepting masculine traits but by rejecting feminine ones.

For further development of this theme, see Stockard (1975); also Balswick and Peek (1974); Broverman, et al. (1972); Chodorow (1971).

4. See Shostak (1971, 1973) for a moving description of the bewilderment with which blue-collar husbands face these new demands from their wives.

5. Chodorow (1977 forthcoming).

6. For rich descriptions of the earlier patterns of interaction and communication between working-class couples, see Komarovsky (1962); Rainwater, Coleman, and Handel (1959); Shostak (1969, 1971).

7. Cf., Shostak (1971).

8. Bogart (1964:417).

9. Shostak (1969:188–190) writes: "In a very important way TV is essentially a confirmatory exercise. By exercising discrimination at channel-switching, blue-collarites are able to expose themselves only, or especially, to a particular brand of TV fare (a phenomenon much in effect like visiting only with members of one's extended family or old neighborhood) . . . Undesired themes and values are screened out, the blue-collarite gaining only resonance of cultural commonplaces from a media that seems itself intent at times on deserting its own potential to challenge, stir, and inform."

10. Komarovsky (1962).

11. See U. S. Department of Health, Education, and Welfare (1973b:34–35) and Chapter 4, Note 4.

12. See Kohn (1959, 1963, 1969) for some of the most important work in the field on class differences in childrearing patterns. Also Bronfenbrenner (1966); Grey (1969); Pearlin and Kohn (1966).

13. See Joffe (1974) and Rubin (1972) for empirical studies showing the class differences in educational values.

14. From the famous Coleman (1966) study onward, analysts have documented this point and variations on the theme over and over again. To mention a few, Bowles (1972); Bowles and Gintis (1973); Jencks (1972, 1976); Rist (1970); Rosenthal (1973); Rosenthal and Jacobson (1968); Rubin (1972); Schafer, et al. (1970); Sexton (1964, 1967); Wilson and Portes (1975).

15. Rubin (1972).

16. Cf., Kohn (1969).

CHAPTER 8

1. Hunt's (1974) study, conducted for *Playboy* magazine, included a representative sample of urban and suburban adults, of whom 982 were men and 1,044 were women. Seventy-one percent of the sample were married (not to each other), 25 percent were never married, and 4 percent had been married.

2. For a good description of this stereotype, see Shostak (1971). See also Komarovsky (1962:82–111) who, while noting that the stereotype applies to "only a small minority" of the families she studied, found that only 30 percent of the women said they were very satisfied with their sexual relations. And some of the data she presents do, indeed, validate the stereotype more forcefully and very much more often than among my sample where it is practically nonexistent.

3. Cf., Simon and Gagnon (1969:733–752) and Gagnon and Simon (1973) whose work is a major contribution toward understanding the differences in male-female sexuality as an expression of the differential socialization patterns for women and men, and who also point to the masculine tendency to separate love and sex and the feminine tendency to fuse them. They suggest, in fact, that the male "capacity for detached sexual activity, activity where the only sustaining motive is sexual . . . may actually be the hallmark of male sexuality in our culture."

For an exploration of the ways in which social structure and personality intersect from a psychoanalytic perspective, see Chodorow (1977 forthcoming) who argues that the root of the differences in male-female personality, and the concomitant differences in the development of psychosexual needs and responses, lie in the social structure of the family.

See also Barker-Benfield (1973) for a portrait of nineteenth-century definitions of male and female sexuality and the fear and abhorrence with which men viewed female sexuality in that era.

4. It is for this reason that studies relying on the recollection of only one spouse for their data—as most do—risk considerable distortion. Thus, for example, when Hunt (1974) reports that almost 26 percent of the married women ages twenty-five to thirty-four report having sexual intercourse between 105-156 times a year, we know only that this is the wife's perception, and we can assume that the recollection is filtered through her *feelings* about the frequency of the sexual encounter.

5. Again, Hunt's (1974) data, while not controlled for class, are suggestive. Using the 1948 Kinsey data as a comparative base, he reports that marital coitus has increased in frequency at every age and educational level. Comparing the Kinsey sample with his own at the fifteenth year of marriage, Hunt reports "a

Notes

distinct increase in the number of wives who always or nearly always have orgasm (Kinsey: 45 percent; *Playboy*: 53 percent) and a sharp decrease in the number of wives who seldom or never do (Kinsey: 28 percent; *Playboy*: 15 percent)."

6. For a rebuke of the self-styled male "experts" on women's sexuality that is both wonderfully angry and funny as it highlights the absurdity of their advice to women, see Frankfort (1973:172–180). She opens this section of her book, entitled "Carnal Ignorance," by saying:

> For the longest time a woman wasn't supposed to enjoy sex. Then suddenly a woman was neurotic if she didn't achieve orgasm simultaneously with her husband. Proof of a woman's health was her ability to come at the very moment the man ejaculated, in the very place he ejaculated, and at the very rate ordained for him by his physiology. If she couldn't, she went to a male psychiatrist to find out why.

CHAPTER 9

1. In his fine treatise on the nature of work in modern industrial society, Braverman (1974) argues that while short-term trends in rapidly growing industries may open the way for the advancement of a few, the lower skill requirements that characterize the largest majority of jobs mean that there are fewer and fewer opportunities to move into skilled work. This suggests even more serious limitations on upward mobility than the American society heretofore has known since, as Thernstrom (1972) persuasively argues, to the degree that upward mobility existed in the working class, it was *intra*stratum mobility—that is, men moving up within the class from less skilled to more skilled labor. If work itself has been and will continue to be stripped of skill requirements, then, as Braverman asserts, that avenue of upward mobility will be largely closed off. Cf., Aronowitz (1973) who also deals with this issue in his analysis of the forces that are shaping working-class consciousness in America.

2. This is, of course, not a new finding. Dubin (1956) long ago argued that work is not a "central life interest" for most industrial workers. Chinoy (1955) studied automobile workers and found that success and gratification were defined primarily in non work-related terms. And Herzberg (1959) and Herzberg, et al. (1959) made essentially the same observation that I make here—that is, that most blue-collar workers are neither satisfied nor dissatisfied with their work. They do their jobs because they must and try to think as little as possible about whether they're happy, satisfied, or interested in their work.

Criticizing such work-satisfaction studies, Braverman (1974:28–29) argues that the appropriate matter for concern ought not to be with how workers feel about their jobs but with the nature of work itself. He charges that by the methods they use (i.e., survey research) and the questions they ask "sociologists [are] measuring not popular consciousness but their own." The sociologist, he asserts, shares with management the conviction that the existing organization of the process of labor is necessary and inevitable. "This leaves to sociology the function, which it shares with personnel administration, of assaying not the nature of the work but the degree of adjustment of the worker. Clearly, for industrial sociology the problem does not appear with the degradation of work, but only with the overt signs of dissatisfaction on the part of the worker."

3. See U.S. Senate Committee on Labor and Public Welfare (1972) for the hearings on SB 3916, a bill brought before the United States Senate whose purpose was: "To provide for research for solutions to the problems of alienation among American workers in all occupations and industries and technical assistance to those companies, unions, State and local governments seeking to find ways to deal with the problem . . ." See also the U.S. Department of Health, Education, and Welfare report entitled *Work in America* (1973). For other recent studies on the consequences of alienation from work on life both on and off the job, see Levitan (1971); Meissner (1971); Seashore and Barnowe (1972); Shepard (1970); Sheppard (1971); Sheppard and Herrick (1972). For a more radical view of the alienation of American workers and their developing class consciousness, see Aronowitz (1973) and Braverman (1974).

4. See Aronowitz (1973) and Braverman (1974) for excellent recent discussions of this phenomenon and its consequences.

5. See Blauner (1964:169) who comments that "the shift from skill to responsibility is the most important historical trend in the evolution of blue-collar work." For an historical analysis of continuity and change in the ideologies of management in the course of industrialization, see Bendix (1963). Bremer (1970) presents a documentary history of the early reform movements in America and their view of the poor and working classes. Threaded throughout, one finds expressions of concern about the unruliness of the masses and their consequent unfitness for the world of work. Even a casual examination of such early documents leaves the clear impression that one important—if not explicitly articulated—goal of the reformers was to turn the masses into docile and disciplined Americans who could be counted on to work every day in the factories for which they were destined. Cf., Bendix (1963) who shows that Sunday schools were introduced in eighteenth-century England as a means of governing the poor and training them for what was considered their appropriately subordinate place. In his outstanding analysis of the origins of early school reform in Massachusetts, Katz (1968) argues that this was precisely the function of the developing public-school system and compulsory attendance regulations.

6. Punctuality, regularity, cleanliness, and orderliness have long been the focus of training for the industrial work world. Cf., Greer (1972) and Katz (1968) for excellent analyses of the historical function of the schools in providing this training. More recently, national manpower-training programs and state programs sponsored by the Human Resources Development Agency also have focused heavily on training the poor, the unemployed, and the underemployed in those traits.

7. See, for example, the publications of the Harvard University Program on Technology and Society established in 1964 by a grant from International Business Machines Corporation. Also Burke (1966); Theobald (1967); Torbert (1963). For a fine critique of the technology-as-progress view, see Ellul (1967).

8. Discussing the trivialization of labor in modern capitalist society, Aronowitz (1973:130) comments on the same point:

> Under modern conditions, the self is only realized in the world of leisure, which now becomes the location for autonomy rather than work . . . That is why, with few exceptions, workers expect nothing intrinsically meaningful in their labor, and satisfy their desire for craftsmanship in the so-called "private realm." For example, tens of thousands of young people have become "car freaks." The automobile is invested with much more than reified status or power. It has become a vital means for the realization of the

Notes

frustrated need to make a direct link with the totality of production for youth who are condemned to either the fragmented labor of the factory or the office or the truncated learning of the school.

9. For three decades now, a popular question used in surveys seeking to determine work satisfaction asks the respondent whether he would continue to work if he had enough money to live comfortably without working. See, for example, Kaplan and Tausky (1972); Morse and Weiss (1955); Tausky (1969); Veroff and Feld (1970). The question I asked also was designed to tap attitudes about work. I chose the more ambiguous wording, however, in order that it might be more in the nature of a projective test which gives the respondent fewer cues toward which to direct an answer. The question, therefore, tapped not only attitudes toward work, but also gave me data on the issues that preoccupy the people in this study and their fantasied solutions.

In a challenge to attitude surveys and the traditional questions in work-satisfaction studies, Kaplan and Kruytbosch (1975) made a "behavioral test of the commitment to work" by studying lottery winners in New York and New Jersey. They found that while commitment to *work* was pervasive, commitment to one's *job* was not, and that the greater the amount of the winnings, the greater was the number of quits and job changes. The authors conclude:

> The most significant finding of this study is that many people when given a real opportunity to choose between keeping their present jobs and quitting or changing, choose the latter. When the economic necessity to work is removed [in fact, not in fantasy], as in the case of the millionaires, eight out of ten quit their jobs . . . If there are lessons to be learned from this research it is that attitudinal questions about satisficing states are intriguing but not necessarily conducive to an accurate interpretation of social reality. Asking workers whether they are satisfied with the work they do and finding that most say they are is like asking a horse that has always been fed hay if he likes his diet. The opportunities for a change of work or diet are closed, unknown or impractical . . . But when people had a chance, they knew what to do. They got out—not of *work* . . . but of their *jobs* which they viewed as dull, dirty and dead-end.

10. For the last two decades, social scientists have argued about whether the work force has become increasingly proletarianized or increasingly middle class. Mills (1951), for example, argues for the increasing proletarianization of white-collar workers as their traditional status edge over blue-collarites disappears as office work requires less and less specialized skill and training. Wilensky (1964, 1966), one of the foremost proponents of the other side of the argument which rests on the diminution of observed lifestyle differences between the classes, developed the notion of the "middle mass" to reflect his view of the homogenization of the upper working class and the lower middle class. In recent years, Marxist theorists have developed a theory of the "new working class" which takes as its starting point the fact that not only are white-collar workers divorced from the means of production as are manual workers, but that they, too, have been systematically dispossessed of their skills, their status, their prestige, and their historical advantage in earnings over blue-collar workers. Aronowitz (1973); Braverman (1974); Smith (1974) persuasively develop and argue various facets of new working-class theory.

These provocative formulations, while pointing to some important core truths about the *process* of work in America, still leave us with some dilemmas about how to define class in this advanced industrial society, and about the differences in life situation between what traditionally has been known as the working class and the middle class. While it is patently absurd to hold tenaciously to these traditional distinctions, there still remains an important difference between the mass of hourly workers and the mass of salaried workers in their vulnerability to economic fluctuations. Despite the fact that some white-collar occupations have been hard hit by the current recession, the burden of unemployment and underemployment still is carried most heavily by the hourly workers in the factories, the trades, and the service sector of the economy. In 1974, for example, the rate of unemployment among male professional and technical workers, age 25–44, was 1.5 percent compared to 5.3 percent for operatives and 4.5 percent for transport equipment operators (U. S. Department of Labor, *Handbook of Labor Statistics*, 1975).

11. A recent article in the San Francisco *Chronicle* (December 25, 1975) reported the research of Eugene Hammel and Virginia Aldrich, who studied the job fate of 5,550 University of California, Berkeley, students who received the Ph.D. degree between 1967 and 1974. Expressing irritation at the press stories about Ph.D.'s who can't find work, Hammel said, "Sure, you can always find a taxi-driving physicist somewhere . . . but that just isn't typical." In fact, the research found that *at least* 97.6 percent of these women and men found work in their chosen fields, indicating an unemployment rate of "no higher than 2.4 percent and maybe as low as 1.1 percent." While it may be true that the job market is less favorable to professionals from less prestigious schools, it still is a far cry from the unemployment rate of, for example, automobile workers.

12. In 1973, the labor force participation of all married women (husbands present), regardless of class, with children under six was 32.7 percent; with children between six and seventeen, it was 50.1 percent. (U.S. Bureau of the Census, 1974).

13. The literature on the socialization of women to "femininity" is vast. For some recent analyses of particular interest, see Bardwick and Douvan (1971); Bem and Bem (1972); Broverman, et al. (1972); Brun-Gulbrandsen (1971); Chafetz (1974); Chodorow (1971, 1977 forthcoming); Freeman (1974); Oakley (1972); Shainess (1972); Weisstein (1971); Weitzman, et al. (1972). Hoffman (1972) and Horner (1972) are particularly interesting on the issue of achievement-related conflicts in women. In a study of urban natives in Alaska, Jones (1975) also argues that one reason why native women adapt more readily than men to low-status demeaning jobs is because the women are so well socialized to passivity and subordination.

14. See Aronowitz (1973); Braverman (1974); Holter (1971); Sokoloff (1975); Zaretsky (1973) for discussion and analysis of the importance of women as a reserve labor force in the economy.

15. See Easton (1975, 1976) for a picture of the historical development of the woman's-place-is-in-the-home ideology and its relationship to the economic requirements of the burgeoning industrial society. Cf., also Lazerson (1975); Sokoloff (1975).

16. For a comprehensive review of the literature on working mothers and family power along with an extensive and up-to-date bibliography, see Hoffman and Nye (1974). Chapter 7, written by Stephen J. Bahr is of particular interest. For a fine critique of this literature and its unspoken assumptions, see Gillespie (1972).

17. For an early and comprehensive statement, see Blood and Wolfe (1960). In a more recent formulation, Scanzoni (1972:66–70) writes:

Notes

In simplified form, we may suggest that *the husband in modern society exchanges his status for marital solidarity*. If we accept as given that expressive satisfactions (companionship, physical affection, empathy) are the obvious goals of modern marriage, and that the major latent goal is status and economic well-being, then we may say that the latent goal influences the attainment of the manifest goal. *Specifically, the greater degree of the husband's integration into the opportunity system (the more his education, the higher his job status, the greater his income), the more fully and extensively is the interlocking network of marital rights and duties performed in reciprocal fashion. The economic rewards he provides motivate the wife to respond positively to him, and her response to him in turn gives rise to a continuing cycle of rectitude and gratitude.* [emphasis mine]

For other similar analyses, see Bahr (1972, 1974); Blood and Hamblin (1958); Heer (1958, 1962); Hoffman (1960).

18. See Berger and Luckman (1967).

19. At the time of this study, the range of income among working-class women was $400 to $8,000 annually. Median income for part-time workers was $2,900; for full-time workers (only nine in number), $6,000, with those women who worked full-time found in the lower family income levels. Assuming even that the income in a family where a woman works full-time was at the median of $12,300, that woman would be contributing very close to half the total family income. In contrast, median wages of part-time women workers in the professional middle-class families was $2,000, or 9 percent of family income. Only one wife in those families worked full-time. With earnings of $15,000 a year, she still contributed only 27 percent of the total family income which was $54,000.

The literature which compares class differences in family power is slim, indeed. Still, what exists supports the argument I make here. Bahr (1974) reviewed that literature and concluded that "Working-class wives gain more power through employment than middle-class wives." Cf., also Scanzoni (1972:66–70) who examines the tools for measuring family decision-making and shows that regardless of the methodology or the instrument used, "husbands are more powerful than wives in routine family decisions as well as in conflict resolution, and higher status husbands generally have the greatest amount of family authority." See also Note 17 above for a further statement of his argument.

20. See Terkel (1974) for some compelling vignettes about the ways in which a person's work life, the social value placed on a particular kind of work, and the internalization of that value affect off-work life. Also Sennett and Cobb (1973) for an analysis of these issues.

CHAPTER 10

1. See Chapter 9, pp. 155–161 and Note 8 for a fuller discussion of the degradation of work in modern industrial society and its impact on off-work activities.

2. For references regarding the socialization of women to "femininity," see Chapter 9, Note 13.

3. See Chodorow (1977 forthcoming) and the summary of her work presented in Chapter 7, pp. 115–119, for an analysis of how the psychodynamic processes of

the individual intersect with the social structure of the family to produce this outcome in women.

4. Cf., Shostak (1969:188–190).

5. Here, as with most of the other leisure issues in this chapter, my findings (although not always my interpretation and analysis) are in essential agreement with Shostak (1969:187–210). One major difference between us is in his comment that blue-collar workers "are often avid . . . pocketbook readers." I find no evidence to support this assertion, and since he provides none either, it is impossible even to speculate on the nature and cause of our differences.

6. Cf., Komarovsky (1962:311–329) who details the limited joint social relationships of the working-class couples she studied. Among the families I met, there was clearly more of a joint social life, both inside and outside the house, than she found fifteen years earlier.

7. Cf., Komarovsky (1962:28–32) for her discussion of relationships in the male clique and the struggle of the young couples around this issue.

8. Despite the widespread belief that most American workers are unionized, less than half of all blue-collar workers are union members (Levitan, 1971:23). The proportion in this study is a little higher—58 percent work in union shops—probably because one of the criteria for the sample was that the husband be stably employed.

9. See Aronowitz (1973) for an outstanding study of the labor movement and an important analysis of the hostility and suspicion with which modern workers generally view their unions. Also Shostak (1969:79–101) for discussion of the dilemmas of blue-collar unionists.

CHAPTER 11

1. U.S. Bureau of the Census (1974:116, Table 186).
2. U.S. Bureau of the Census (1974:117, Table 189).
3. U.S. Bureau of the Census (1974:120, Table 194).

EPILOGUE

1. Cade (1970:15).

BIBLIOGRAPHY

Adorno, T. W., et al. *The Authoritarian Personality.* New York: Harper & Brothers, 1950.

Aldous, Joan. "The Making of Family Roles and Family Change." *The Family Coordinator* 23 (1974):231–236.

Altbach, Edith Hoshino, ed. *From Feminism to Liberation.* Cambridge. Mass.: Schenkman Publishing, 1971.

Amundsen, Kirsten. *The Silenced Majority.* Englewood Cliffs, N. J.: Prentice-Hall 1971.

Andreas, Carol. *Sex and Caste in America.* Englewood Cliffs, N. J.: Prentice-Hall, 1971.

Anspach, Donald, and George A. Rosenberg. "Working Class Matricentricity." *Journal of Marriage and the Family* 34 (1972):437–441.

Arendt, Hannah. *The Origins of Totalitarianism.* New York: Meridian, 1958.

Ariès, Philippe. *Centuries of Childhood: A Social History of Family Life.* New York: Vintage Books, 1962.

Arnott, Catherine C. "Husbands' Attitude and Wives' Commitment to Employment." *Journal of Marriage and the Family* 34 (1972):673–684.

Aronowitz, Stanley. *False Promises.* New York: McGraw-Hill, 1973.

Aronson, Harvey. "Life with Cappelli on $101 a Week." In *The White Majority,* edited by Louise Kapp Howe. New York: Vintage Books, 1970.

Babcox, Deborah, and Madeline Belkin, eds. *Liberation Now!* New York: Dell, 1971.

Bahr, Stephen J. "Comment on 'The Study of Family Power Structures: A Review 1960–1969.' " *Journal of Marriage and the Family* 34 (1972):239–243.

———. "Effects on Family Power and Division of Labor in the Family." In *Working Mothers,* edited by Lois W. Hoffman and F. Ivan Nye. San Francisco: Jossey-Bass, 1974.

Ball, Donald. "The Family as a Sociological Problem: Conceptualization of the Taken-for-Granted as Prologue to Social Problems Analysis." In *Intimacy, Family, and Society,* edited by Arlene Skolnick and Jerome Skolnick. Boston: Little, Brown, 1974.

Balswick, Jack O. "Attitudes of Lower Class Males Toward Taking a Male Birth Control Pill." *The Family Coordinator* 21 (1972):195–200.

Balswick, Jack, and Charles Peek. "The Inexpressive Male: A Tragedy of American Society." In *Intimacy, Family, and Society,* edited by Arlene Skolnick and Jerome Skolnick. Boston: Little, Brown, 1974.

Bardwick, Judith M., and Elizabeth Douvan. "Ambivalence: The Socialization of Women." In *Woman in Sexist Society,* edited by Vivian Gornick and Barbara K. Moran. New York: Basic Books, 1971.

Barker-Benfield, Ben. "The Spermatic Economy: A Nineteenth-Century View of

Bibliography

Sexuality." In *The American Family in Social-Historical Perspective*, edited by Michael Gordon. New York: St. Martin's Press, 1973.

Bartz, Karen W., and F. Ivan Nye. "Early Marriage: A Propositional Formulation." *Journal of Marriage and the Family* 32 (1970):258–268.

Bassett, Marion. "The Double Standard." In *The Family and the Sexual Revolution*, edited by Edwin M. Schur. Bloomington: Indiana University Press, 1964.

Baude, Annika, and Per Holmberg. "The Positions of Men and Women in the Labour Market." In *The Changing Roles of Men and Women*, edited by Edmund Dahlström. Boston: Beacon Press, 1971.

Bell, Daniel. *The End of Ideology*. New York: Free Press, 1965.

Bell, Robert R. *Premarital Sex in a Changing Society*. Englewood Cliffs, N. J.: Prentice-Hall, 1966.

———, ed. *Studies in Marriage and the Family*. New York: Thomas Y. Crowell, 1968.

Bem, Sandra L., and Daryl J. Bem. "Training the Woman to Know Her Place." In *The Future of the Family*, edited by Louise Kapp Howe. New York: Simon and Schuster, 1972.

Bendix, Reinhard. *Work and Authority in Industry*. New York: Harper Torchbooks, 1963.

Bendix, Reinhard, and Seymour Martin Lipset, eds. *Class, Status, and Power*. New York: Free Press, 1953.

———. *Class, Status, and Power*. 2d ed. New York: Free Press, 1966.

Benét, Mary Kathleen. *The Secretarial Ghetto*. New York: McGraw-Hill, 1972.

Berg, Ivar. *Education and Jobs: The Great Training Robbery*. Boston: Beacon Press, 1971.

Berger, Bennett. *Working-Class Suburb: A Study of Auto Workers in Suburbia*. Berkeley: University of California Press, 1968.

Berger, Peter L., and Thomas Luckman. *The Social Construction of Reality*. Garden City, N. Y.: Anchor Books, 1967.

Bernard, Jessie. *Marriage and Family Among Negroes*. Englewood Cliffs, N. J.: Prentice-Hall, 1966.

———. "Changing Family Life Styles: One Role, Two Roles, Shared Roles." In *The Future of the Family*, edited by Louise Kapp Howe. New York: Simon and Schuster, 1972.

———. *The Future of Marriage*. New York: Bantam Books, 1973.

Bernard, Jessie. *The Future of Motherhood*. Baltimore: Penguin Books, 1975.

Billingsley, Andrew. *Black Families in White America*. Englewood Cliffs: Prentice-Hall, 1968.

Binzen, Peter. *Whitetown, USA*. New York: Random House, 1970.

Bird, Caroline. *Born Female*. New York: Pocket Books, 1969.

Blake, Judith. "Coercive Pronatalism and American Population Policy." In *The Family: Its Structures and Functions*, edited by Rose Laub Coser. New York: St. Martin's Press, 1974.

Blau, Peter M., and Otis D. Duncan. *The American Occupational Structure*. New York: John Wiley, 1967.

Blau, Zena Smith. "Maternal Aspirations, Socialization, and Achievement of Boys and Girls in the White Working Class." *Journal of Youth and Adolescence* 1 (1972):35–57.

Blauner, Robert. *Alienation and Freedom*. Chicago: University of Chicago Press, 1964.

Blood, Robert O., Jr., and Robert M. Hamblin. "The Effect of the Wife's Employment on the Family Power Structure." *Social Forces* 36 (1958):347–352.

Blood, Robert O., Jr., and Donald M. Wolfe. *Husbands and Wives: The Dynamics of Married Living*. New York: Free Press, 1960.

Blum, Alan. "Social Structure, Social Class, and Participation in Primary Relationships." In *Blue-Collar World*, edited by Arthur Shostak and William Gomberg. Englewood Cliffs, N. J.: Prentice-Hall, 1964.

Bogart, Leo. "The Mass Media and the Blue-Collar Workers." In *Blue-Collar World*, edited by Arthur Shostak and William Gomberg. Englewood Cliffs, N. J.: Prentice-Hall, 1964.

Bonjean, Charles M. "Mass, Class, and the Industrial Community: A Comparative Analysis of Managers, Businessmen, and Workers." *American Journal of Sociology* 72 (1966):149–162.

Bowles, Samuel. "Getting Nowhere: Programmed Class Stagnation." *Society* 9 (1972):42–49.

Bowles, Samuel, and Herbert Gintis. "I.Q. in the U.S. Class Structure." *Social Policy* 3 (1973):65–96.

———. *Schooling in Capitalist America*. New York: Basic Books, 1976.

Bowman, Claude. "Mental Health in the Worker's World." In *Blue-Collar World*, edited by Arthur Shostak and William Gomberg. Englewood Cliffs, N. J.: Prentice-Hall, 1964.

Braverman, Harry. *Labor and Monopoly Capitalism: The Degradation of Work in the Twentieth Century*. New York: Monthly Review Press, 1974.

Bremer, Robert H., ed. *Children and Youth in America*, vols. 1 and 2. Cambridge, Mass.: Harvard University Press, 1970.

Broderick, Carlfred B., and Jessie Bernard, eds. *The Individual, Sex, and Society*. Baltimore: Johns Hopkins Press, 1969.

Bronfenbrenner, Urie. "Socialization and Social Class Through Time and Space." In *Class, Status, and Power*, 2d ed., edited by Reinhard Bendix and Seymour M. Lipset. New York: Free Press, 1966.

———. "Who Cares for America's Children." In *The Future of the Family*, edited by Louise Kapp Howe. New York: Simon and Schuster, 1972.

Broverman, Inge K., et al. "Sex-Role Stereotypes: A Current Appraisal." *Journal of Social Issues* 28 (1972):59–78.

Brown, Judith. "A Note on the Division of Labor by Sex." In *Intimacy, Family, and Society*, edited by Arlene Skolnick and Jerome Skolnick. Boston: Little, Brown, 1974.

Bruce, John Allen. "The Role of Mothers in the Social Placement of Daughters: Marriage or Work?" *Journal of Marriage and the Family* 36 (1974):492–497.

Brun-Gulbrandsen, Sverre. "Sex Roles and the Socialization Process." In *The Changing Roles of Men and Women*, edited by Edmund Dahlström. Boston: Beacon Press, 1971.

Buff, Stephen. "Greasers, Dupers, and Hippies: Three Responses to the Adult World." In *The White Majority*, edited by Louise Kapp Howe. New York: Vintage Books, 1970.

Burke, John, ed. *The New Technology and Human Values*. Belmont, Calif.: Wadsworth Publishing, 1966.

Cade, Toni, ed. *The Black Woman*. New York: Signet Books, 1970.

Cahalan, Don. "Problem Drinking Among American Men Aged 21–59." Paper delivered at the Thirtieth International Congress on Alcoholism and Drug Dependence, Amsterdam, The Netherlands, September 1972.

Bibliography

————, Iris Crisin, and Helen Crossley. *American Drinking Patterns. Report No. 3.* Publication of the Social Research Group, George Washington University, Washington, D.C., 1967.

California Department of the Youth Authority, Health, and Welfare Agency. *Annual Report: Program Description and Statistical Summary.* 1973.

Caplowitz, David. "The Problems of Blue-Collar Consumers." In *Blue-Collar World*, edited by Arthur Shostak and William Gomberg. Englewood Cliffs, N. J.: Prentice-Hall, 1964.

————. *The Poor Pay More.* New York: Free Press, 1967.

Carper, Laura. "The Negro Family and the Moynihan Report." In *Poverty: Views from the Left*, edited by Jeremy Larner and Irving Howe. New York: William Morrow, 1968.

Cavan, Ruth Shonle, ed. *Marriage and Family in the Modern World*, 3d ed. New York: Thomas Y. Crowell, 1969.

Chafetz, Janet Saltzman. *Masculine/Feminine or Human?* Itasca, Ill.: F. E. Peacock, 1974.

Chilman, Catherine S. "Some Psychological Aspects of Female Sexuality." *The Family Coordinator* 23 (1974):123–131.

Chinoy, Eli. *Automobile Workers and the American Dream.* New York: Random House, 1955.

Chodorow, Nancy. "Being and Doing: A Cross-Cultural Examination of the Socialization of Males and Females." In *Woman in Sexist Society*, edited by Vivian Gornick and Barbara K. Moran. New York: Basic Books, 1971.

————. *The Reproduction of Mothering: Family Structure and Feminine Personality.* Berkeley: University of California Press, forthcoming, 1977.

Christensen, Harold, and Christina Gregg. "Changing Sex Norms in America and Scandinavia." In *Intimacy, Family and Society*, edited by Arlene Skolnick and Jerome Skolnick. Boston: Little, Brown, 1974.

Cicourel, Aaron V., and John Kitsuse. *The Educational Decision-Makers.* Indianapolis: Bobbs-Merrill, 1963.

Clark, Kenneth. *Dark Ghetto.* New York: Harper & Row, 1965.

Clavan, Sylvia. "Changing Female Sexual Behavior and Future Family Structure." *Pacific Sociological Review* 15 (1973):295–300.

Cohen, Bernard. "The Delinquency of Gangs and Spontaneous Groups." In *Delinquency: Selected Studies*, edited by Thomas Sellin and Marvin Wolfgang. New York: John Wiley, 1969.

Coleman, James, et al. *Equality of Educational Opportunity.* Washington: U.S. Government Printing Office, 1966.

Coles, Robert. *Children of Crisis.* New York: Delta Books, 1968.

Collins, Randall. "A Conflict Theory of Sexual Stratification." *Social Problems* 19 (1971):3–21.

Cook, Alice H. *The Working Mother.* Ithaca: New York State School of Industrial and Labor Relations, Cornell University, 1975.

Coser, Lewis A. "Unanticipated Conservative Consequences of Liberal Theorizing." *Social Problems* 16 (1969):263–272.

Coser, Rose Laub, ed. *The Family: Its Structures and Functions*, 2d ed. New York: St. Martin's Press, 1974.

————, and Gerald Rokoff. "Women in the Occupational World: Social Disruption and Conflict. In *The Family: Its Structures and Functions*, edited by Rose Laub Coser. New York: St. Martin's Press, 1974.

242

Cottle, Thomas J. "Angela: A Child-Woman." *Social Problems* 23 (forthcoming, 1976).

———. *A Family Album: Portraits of Intimacy and Kinship.* New York: Harper Colophon, 1974.

Cowan, Paul. "Holy War in West Virginia: A Fight Over America's Future." *The Village Voice,* 9 December 1974, pp. 19–23.

Cuber, John, and Peggy Harroff. "Five Types of Marriage." In *Intimacy, Family, and Society,* edited by Arlene Skolnick and Jerome Skolnick. Boston: Little, Brown, 1974.

Curtis, Russell, and Louis Zurcher. "Voluntary Associations and the Social Integration of the Poor." *Social Problems* 18 (1971):339–357.

Dahlström, Edmund, ed. *The Changing Roles of Men and Women.* Boston: Beacon Press, 1971.

Dahlström, Edmund, and Rita Liljeström. "The Family and Married Women at Work." In *The Changing Roles of Men and Women,* edited by Edmund Dahlström. Boston: Beacon Press, 1971.

D'Amico, Debby. "To My White Working-Class Sisters." In *Marriage and the Family,* edited by Carolyn Perucci and Dena B. Targ. New York: David McKay, 1974.

Dansereau, H. Kirk. "Work and the Teen-Age Blue-Collarite." In *Blue-Collar World,* edited by Arthur Shostak and William Gomberg. Englewood Cliffs, N. J.: Prentice-Hall, 1964.

Davis, Allison. "The Motivation of the Underprivileged Worker." In *Industry and Society,* edited by William F. Whyte. New York: McGraw-Hill, 1946.

Davis, Ethelyn. "Careers as Concerns of Blue-Collar Girls." In *Blue-Collar World,* edited by Arthur Shostak and William Gomberg. Englewood Cliffs, N. J.: Prentice-Hall, 1964.

DeFronzo, James. "Embourgeoisement in Indianapolis?" *Social Problems* 21 (1973): 269–283.

Dennison, George. *The Lives of Children.* New York: Vintage Books, 1969.

Dentler, Robert A., et al., eds. *The Urban R's.* New York: Praeger, 1967.

Dobriner, William M. *Class in Suburbia.* Englewood Cliffs, N. J.: Prentice-Hall, 1963.

Dowdall, Jean A. "Women's Attitudes Toward Employment and Family Roles." *Sociological Analysis* 35 (1974):251–262.

Duberman, Lucille. *Marriage and Its Alternatives.* New York: Praeger, 1974.

Dubin, Robert. "Industrial Workers' World: A Study of the Central Life Interests of Industrial Workers." *Social Problems* 3 (1956):131–141.

Dyer, William. "Family Reactions to the Father's Job." In *Blue-Collar World,* edited by Arthur Shostak and William Gomberg. Englewood Cliffs, N. J.: Prentice-Hall, 1964.

Easton, Barbara Leslie. "Women, Religion, and the Family: Revivalism as an Indicator of Social Change in Early New England." Ph.D. dissertation, University of California, Berkeley, 1975.

———. "Industrialization and Femininity: A Case Study of Nineteenth Century New England." *Social Problems* 23 (forthcoming, 1976).

Ellul, Jacques. *The Technological Society.* New York: Vintage Books, 1967.

Endleman, Robert. "Moral Perspectives of Blue-Collar Workers." In *Blue-Collar*

World, edited by Arthur Shostak and William Gomberg. Englewood Cliffs, N. J.: Prentice-Hall, 1964.

Engels, Frederick. *The Origin of the Family, Private Property, and the State*. New York: International Publishers, 1942.

Epstein, Cynthia Fuchs. "Law Partners and Marital Partners." *Human Relations* 24 (1971):549–564.

———. "Reconciliation of Women's Roles." In *The Family: Its Structures and Functions*, edited by Rose Laub Coser. New York: St. Martin's Press, 1974.

Epstein, Cynthia Fuchs, and William Goode, eds. *The Other Half: Roads to Women's Equality*. Englewood Cliffs, N. J.: Prentice-Hall, 1971.

Epstein, Gilda F., and Arline Bronzaft. "Female Freshmen View Their Roles as Women." *Journal of Marriage and the Family* 34 (1972):671–672.

Erikson, Erik. *Childhood and Society*. New York: W. W. Norton, 1950.

———. *Identity: Youth and Crisis*. New York: W. W. Norton, 1968.

Farber, Bernard. "Kinship and Class." In *The Family: Its Structures and Functions*, edited by Rose Laub Coser. New York: St. Martin's Press, 1974.

Farrell, Warren. *The Liberated Man*. New York: Bantam Books, 1975.

Fasteau, Marc Feigen. *The Male Machine*. New York: McGraw-Hill, 1974.

Felson, Marcus, and David Knoke. "Social Status and the Married Woman." *Journal of Marriage and the Family* 36 (1974):516–521.

Firestone, Shulamith. *The Dialectic of Sex*. New York: Bantam Books, 1971.

Fisher, Seymour. *Understanding the Female Orgasm*. New York: Bantam Books, 1973.

Flacks, Richard. "Growing Up Confused: Cultural Crisis and Individual Character." In *Intimacy, Family, and Society*, eds. Arlene Skolnick and Jerome Skolnick. Boston: Little, Brown, 1974.

Frankfort, Ellen. *Vaginal Politics*. New York: Bantam Books, 1973.

Freedman, Lawrence. "Psychopathology and Poverty." In *Blue-Collar World*, edited by Arthur Shostak and William Gomberg. Englewood Cliffs, N. J.: Prentice-Hall, 1964.

Freeman, Jo. "The Social Construction of the Second Sex." In *Intimacy, Family, and Society*, edited by Arlene Skolnick and Jerome Skolnick. Boston: Little, Brown, 1974.

———, ed. *Women: A Feminist Perspective*. Palo Alto, Calif.: Mayfield Publishing, 1975.

Fried, Marc. *The World of the Urban Working Class*. Cambridge, Mass.: Harvard University Press, 1973.

Friedenberg, Edgar Z. "An Ideology of School Withdrawal." In *Blue-Collar World*, edited by Arthur Shostak and William Gomberg. Englewood Cliffs, N. J.: Prentice-Hall, 1964.

Fromm, Erich. *Escape from Freedom*. New York: Avon Books, 1941.

Furstenberg, Frank F., Jr. "The Transmission of Mobility Orientation in the Family." *Social Forces* 49 (1971).

Gagnon, John H., and William Simon. *Sexual Conduct: The Social Sources of Human Sexuality*. Chicago: Aldine Publishing, 1973.

Galbraith, John K. *The Affluent Society*. Boston: Houghton Mifflin, 1958.

Galenson, Marjorie. *Women and Work: An International Comparison*. Publication of the New York School of Industrial and Labor Relations, Ithaca, New York, 1973.

Gans, Herbert J. *The Urban Villagers: Group and Class in the Life of Italian-Americans.* New York: Free Press, 1962.

———. *People and Plans.* New York: Basic Books, 1968.

———. "Mean Streets: A Study of the Young Working Class." *Social Policy* 4 (1974):61–62.

Garskof, Michele Hoffnung, ed. *Roles Women Play: Readings Toward Women's Liberation.* Belmont, Calif.: Wadsworth, 1971.

Garson, Barbara. "Women's Work." *Working Papers for a New Society* 1 (1973): 5–16.

Gecas, Viktor, and F. Ivan Nye. "Sex and Class Differences in Parent-Child Interactions: A Test of Kohn's Hypothesis." *Journal of Marriage and the Family* 36 (1974):742–749.

Geisel, Paul. "Meaning of Work and Mental Illness." In *Blue-Collar World*, edited by Arthur Shostak and William Gomberg. Englewood Cliffs, N. J.: Prentice-Hall.

Gerald, Patricia. "The Three Faces of Day Care." In *The Future of the Family*, edited by Louise Kapp Howe. New York: Simon and Schuster, 1972.

Gibbons, Don. *Delinquent Behavior.* Englewood Cliffs, N. J.: Prentice-Hall, 1970.

Giele, Janet Z. "Changes in the Modern Family: Their Impact on Sex Roles." In *The Family: Its Structures and Functions*, edited by Rose Laub Coser. New York: St. Martin's Press, 1974.

Gillespie, Dair. "Who Has the Power? The Marital Struggle." In *Family, Marriage, and the Struggle of the Sexes*, edited by Hans P. Dreitzel. New York: Macmillan, 1972.

Ginzberg, Eli. "The Long View." In *Blue-Collar Workers*, edited by Sar Levitan. New York: McGraw-Hill, 1971.

Gladwin, Thomas, *Poverty U.S.A.* Boston: Little, Brown, 1967.

Glaser, Barney G., and Anselm L. Strauss. *The Discovery of Grounded Theory: Strategies for Qualitative Research.* Chicago: Aldine-Atherton, 1967.

Glazer-Malbin, Nona, ed. *Old Family/New Family.* New York: Van Nostrand, 1975.

Glazer-Malbin, Nona, and Helen Youngelson Waehrer, eds. *Woman in a Man-Made World.* Chicago: Rand McNally, 1973.

Goldthorpe, John H., et al. "The Affluent Worker and the Thesis of Embourgeoisement." *Sociology* 1 (1967):11–31.

Goldthorpe, John H., et al. *The Affluent Worker: Industrial Attitudes and Behavior.* Cambridge: Cambridge University Press, 1968a.

Goldthorpe, John H., et al. *The Affluent Worker: Political Attitudes and Behavior.* Cambridge: Cambridge University Press, 1968b.

Goldthorpe, John H., et al. *The Affluent Worker in the Class Structure.* Cambridge: Cambridge University Press, 1969.

Goode, William J. *Women in Divorce.* New York: Free Press, 1956.

———. *World Revolution and Family Patterns.* New York: Free Press, 1963.

———. "Force and Violence in the Family." In *Intimacy, Family, and Society*, edited by Arlene Skolnick and Jerome Skolnick. Boston: Little, Brown, 1974.

Gordon, David M. "From Steam Whistles to Coffee Breaks." *Dissent* 19 (1972): 197–210.

Gordon, Michael, ed. *The American Family in Social-Historical Perspective.* New York: St. Martin's Press, 1973.

Gordon, Michael, and Penelope Shankweiler. 1974. "Different Equals Less: Female Sexuality in Recent Marriage Manuals." In *Intimacy, Family, and Society*, edited by Arlene Skolnick and Jerome Skolnick. Boston: Little, Brown, 1974.

Gordon, Milton, and Charles Anderson. "The Blue-Collar Worker At Leisure." In *Blue-Collar World*, edited by Arthur Shostak and William Gomberg. Englewood Cliffs, N. J.: Prentice-Hall, 1964.

Gornick, Vivian, and Barbara K. Moran, eds. *Woman in Sexist Society*. New York: Basic Books, 1971.

Gough, Kathleen. "The Origin of the Family." In *Intimacy, Family, and Society*, edited by Arlene Skolnick and Jerome Skolnick. Boston: Little, Brown, 1974.

Goyder, John C., and James E. Curtis. "A Three-Generational Approach to Trends in Occupational Mobility." *American Journal of Sociology* 81 (1975):129–138.

Greeley, Andrew. "White Against White: The Enduring Ethnic Conflict." In *The White Majority*, edited by Louise Kapp Howe. New York: Vintage Books, 1970.

Greeley, Andrew M. "Marginal But Not Alienated Confessions of a Loudmouthed Irish Priest." *Social Policy* 5 (1970):4–11.

Greer, Colin. *The Great School Legend*. New York: Basic Books, 1972.

Grey, Alan L., ed. *Class and Personality in Society*. New York: Atherton Press, 1969.

Grønseth, Erick. "The Breadwinner Trap." In *The Future of the Family*, edited by Louise Kapp Howe. New York: Simon and Schuster, 1972.

Gross, Ronald. "The Future of Toil." In *Blue-Collar World*, edited by Arthur Shostak and William Gomberg. Englewood Cliffs, N. J.: Prentice-Hall, 1964.

Hadden, Jeffrey K., and Marie L. Borgatta, eds. *Marriage and the Family*. Itasca, Ill.: F. E. Peacock, 1969.

Hamill, Pete. "The Revolt of the White Lower-Middle Class." In *The White Majority*, edited by Louise Kapp Howe. New York: Vintage Books, 1970.

Hamilton, Richard. "The Behavior and Values of Skilled Workers." In *Blue-Collar World*, edited by Arthur Shostak and William Gomberg. Englewood Cliffs, N. J.: Prentice-Hall, 1964.

Hamilton, Richard F. "Black Demands, White Reactions, and Liberal Alarms." In *Blue-Collar Workers*, edited by Sar Levitan. New York: McGraw-Hill, 1971.

———. *Class and Politics in the United States*. New York: John Wiley, 1972.

Handel, Gerald, and Lee Rainwater. "Persistence and Change in Working-Class Life Style." In *Blue-Collar World*, edited by Arthur Shostak and William Gomberg. Englewood Cliffs, N. J.: Prentice-Hall, 1964.

Harbeson, Gladys E. *Choice and Challenge for the American Woman*, rev. ed. Cambridge, Mass.: Schenkman Publishing, 1971.

Harris, Fred R. "Hot Under the Blue Collar." In *Blue-Collar Workers*, edited by Sar Levitan. New York: McGraw-Hill, 1971.

Harris, Janet. *The Prime of Ms. America: The American Woman at 40*. New York: G. P. Putnam's, 1975.

Harvard Educational Review, eds. *Equal Educational Opportunity*. Cambridge, Mass.: Harvard University Press, 1969.

———. *Perspectives on "Inequality: A Reassessment of the Effect of Family and Schooling in America."* Cambridge, Mass.: Harvard University Press, 1973.

Hausknecht, Murray. "The Blue-Collar Joiner." In *Blue-Collar World*, edited by Arthur Shostak and William Gomberg. Englewood Cliffs, N. J.: Prentice-Hall, 1964.

Havighurst, Robert J., and Allison Davis. "A Comparison of the Chicago and Harvard Studies of Social Class Differences in Child Rearing." In *Class and*

Personality in Society, edited by Alan L. Grey. New York: Atherton Press, 1969.

Hedges, J. N. "Women at Work: Women Workers and Manpower Demands in the 1970's." *Monthly Labor Review* 93 (1970):19–29.

Heer, David M. "Dominance and the Working Wife." *Social Forces* 36 (1958): 341–347.

———. "Husband and Wife Perceptions of Family Power Structure." *Marriage and Family Living* 24 (1962):65–77.

Henshel, Anne Marie. "Swinging: A Study of Decision Making in Marriage." *American Journal of Sociology* 78 (1973):885–891.

Hentoff, Nat. *Our Children Are Dying*. New York: Viking Press, 1966.

Herndon, James. *The Way It Spozed To Be*. New York: Simon and Schuster, 1965.

Herzberg, Frederich. *Work and the Nature of Man*. Cleveland: World Publishing, 1966.

Herzberg, Frederich, et al. 1959. *The Motivation to Work*. New York: John Wiley, 1959.

Hochschild, Arlie Russell, ed. "The American Woman." *Trans-action* 8 (1970).

———. "A Review of Sex Role Research." *American Journal of Sociology* 78 (1973):1011–1029.

Hoffman, Lois Wladis. "Effects of the Employment of Mothers on Parental Power Relations and the Division of Household Tasks." *Marriage and Family Living* 22 (1960):27–35.

———. "Early Childhood Experiences and Women's Achievement Motives." *Journal of Social Issues* 28 (1972):129–155.

Hoffman, Lois Wladis, and F. Ivan Nye. *Working Mothers*. San Francisco: Jossey-Bass, 1974.

Hoggart, Richard. *The Uses of Literacy*. New York: Oxford University Press, 1970.

Hollingshead, August B. *Elmtown's Youth*. New York: John Wiley, 1949.

Hollingshead, August B., and Frederick C. Redlich. *Social Class and Mental Illness: A Community Study*. New York: John Wiley, 1958.

Holmstrom, Lynda L. *The Two-Career Family*. Cambridge, Mass.: Schenkman Publishing, 1972.

Holter, Harriet. "Sex Roles and Social Change." *Acta Sociologica* 14 (1971):2–12.

Horner, Matina S. "Toward an Understanding of Achievement-Related Conflicts." *Journal of Social Issues* 28 (1972):157–175.

Howe, Louise Kapp, ed. *The White Majority: Between Poverty and Affluence*. New York: Vintage Books, 1970.

———. *The Future of the Family*. New York: Simon and Schuster, 1972.

Howell, Joseph T. *Hard Living on Clay Street*. Garden City, N. Y.: Anchor Books, 1973.

Huber, Joan, ed. *Changing Women in a Changing Society*. Chicago: University of Chicago Press, 1973.

Hunt, Morton. *Sexual Behavior in the 1970's*. Chicago: Playboy Press, 1974.

Hurvitz, Nathan. "Marital Strain in the Blue-Collar Family." In *Blue-Collar World*, edited by Arthur Shostak and William Gomberg. Englewood Cliffs, N. J.: Prentice-Hall, 1964.

Hyman, Herbert H. "The Value Systems of Different Classes: A Social Psychological Contribution to the Analysis of Stratification." In *Class, Status, and Power*, edited by Reinhard Bendix and Seymour Martin Lipset. New York: Free Press, 1953.

Bibliography

Isabell, Sharon. *Yesterday's Lessons*. Oakland, Calif.: Women's Press Collective, 1974.

Jacoby, Susan. "What Do I Do for the Next Twenty Years?" In *Intimacy, Family, and Society*, edited by Arlene Skolnick and Jerome Skolnick. Boston: Little, Brown, 1974.

Jencks, Christopher, et al. *Inequality: A Reassessment of the Effect of Family and Schooling in America*. New York: Basic Books, 1972.

Joffe, Carole E. "Child Care: Destroying the Family or Strengthening It?" In *The Future of the Family*, edited by Louise Kapp Howe. New York: Simon and Schuster, 1972.

————. "Marginal Professions and Their Clients: The Case of Childcare." Ph.D. dissertation, University of California, Berkeley, 1974.

Johnson, Miriam, et al. "Expressiveness Reevaluated." *School Review* 83 (1975): 617–644.

Jones, Dorothy. *Urban Native Men and Women: Differences in Their Work Adaptations*. Publication of I.S.E.G.R., University of Alaska, Fairbanks, Alaska, 1975.

Jordan, Joan. "The Exploitation of Women Workers." In *The White Majority*, edited by Louise Kapp Howe. New York: Vintage Books, 1970.

Kantor, David, and William Lehr. *Inside the Family*. San Francisco: Jossey-Bass, 1975.

Kaplan, H. Roy, and Curt Tausky. "Work and the Welfare Cadillac: The Function of and Commitment to Work Among the Hard-Core Unemployed." *Social Problems* 19 (1972):469–483.

————, and Carlos E. Kruytbosch. "Sudden Riches and Work Behavior: A Behavioral Test of the Commitment to Work." Delivered at the Seventieth Annual Meeting of the American Sociological Association, San Francisco, California, August 25–29, 1975.

Karabel, Jerome. "Protecting the Portals: Class and the Community College." *Social Policy* 5 (1974):12–20.

Kasschan, Patricia L., Edward H. Ransford, and Vern L. Bengston. "Generational Consciousness and Youth Movement Participation: Contrasts in Blue Collar and White Collar Youth." *Journal of Social Issues* 30 (1974):69–94.

Katz, Michael B. *The Irony of Early School Reform: Educational Innovation in Mid-Nineteenth Century Massachusetts*. Cambridge, Mass.: Harvard University Press, 1968.

————. "The Present Movement in Educational Reform." *Harvard Educational Review* 41 (1971):342–359.

————. *Class, Bureaucracy, and Schools*. 2d ed. New York: Praeger Publishers, 1975.

————. *The People of Hamilton, Canada West: Family and Class in a Mid-Nineteenth-Century City*. Cambridge, Mass.: Harvard University Press, 1975.

Keller, Suzanne. "Does the Family Have a Future?" *Journal of Comparative Family Studies* (1971):1–14.

Keniston, Kenneth. *The Young Radicals*. New York: Harcourt, Brace, 1968.

Kerckhoff, Alan. *Socialization and Social Class*. Englewood Cliffs, N. J.: Prentice-Hall, 1972.

Kinsey, Alfred, W. Pomeroy, and C. Martin. *Sexual Behavior in the Human Male*. Philadelphia: W. B. Saunders, 1948.

248

——. *Sexual Behavior in the Human Female.* Philadelphia: W. B. Saunders, 1953.

Kirscht, John P., and Ronald C. Dillehay. *Dimensions of Authoritarianism: A Review of Research and Theory.* Lexington: University of Kentucky Press, 1967.

Knudsin, Ruth B., ed. *Women & Success: The Anatomy of Achievement.* New York: William Morrow, 1974.

Knupfer, Genevieve. "Portrait of the Underdog." *Public Opinion Quarterly* 11 (1947):103–114.

Koedt, Anne, Ellen Levine, and Anita Rapone, eds. *Radical Feminism.* New York: Quadrangle Books, 1973.

Kohlberg, Lawrence. "A Cognitive-Developmental Analysis of Sex-Role Concepts." In *Intimacy, Family, and Society*, edited by Arlene Skolnick and Jerome Skolnick. Boston: Little, Brown, 1974.

Kohn, Melvin. "Social Class and Parental Values." *American Journal of Sociology* 64 (1959):337–351.

——. "Social Class and Parent-Child Relationships." *American Journal of Sociology* 68 (1963):471–480.

——. *Class and Conformity.* Homewood, Ill.: Dorsey Press, 1969.

Kolb, Trudy M., and Murray Straus. "Marital Power and Marital Happiness in Relation to Problem-Solving Ability." *Journal of Marriage and the Family* 36 (1974): 756–766.

Komarovsky, Mirra. "A Functional Analysis of Sex Roles." *American Sociological Review* 15 (1950):508–516.

——. *Blue-Collar Marriage.* New York: Vintage Books, 1962.

——. "Learning the Feminine Role." In *The Family and the Sexual Revolution*, edited by Edwin M. Schur. Bloomington: Indiana University Press, 1964.

——. "Blue-Collar Marriages and Families." In *The White Majority*, edited by Louise Kapp Howe. New York: Vintage Books, 1970.

——. "Cultural Contradictions and Sex Roles: The Masculine Case." *American Journal of Sociology* 78 (1973):873–884.

——. "Patterns of Self-Disclosure of Male Undergraduates." *Journal of Marriage and the Family* 36 (1974):677–686.

Kornblum, William. *Blue Collar Community.* Chicago: University of Chicago Press, 1974.

Korpi, Walter. "Working Class Communism in Western Europe: Rational or Nonrational." *American Sociological Review* 36 (1971):971–984.

Kozol, Jonathan. *Death at an Early Age.* Boston: Houghton Mifflin, 1967.

Kremen, Bennet. "No Pride in This Dust." *Dissent* 19 (1972):21–28.

Kreps, Juanita. "Do All Women Want to Work? The Economics of Their Choice." In *The Future of the Family*, edited by Louise Kapp Howe. New York: Simon and Schuster, 1972.

Labor-Mental Health Conference. *Helping Blue-Collar Workers in Trouble.* Publication of the Sidney Hillman Health Center Mental Health Rehabilitation Project, New York City, 1969.

Lane, Robert. "The Fear of Equality." In *The White Majority*, edited by Louise Kapp Howe. New York: Vintage Books, 1970.

Larson, Lyle E. "System and Subsystem Perception of Family Roles." *Journal of Marriage and the Family* 36 (1974):123–138.

Lasch, Christopher. "Divorce and the Decline of the Family." In *The World of Nations*, edited by Christopher Lasch. New York: Vintage Books, 1974.

Bibliography

Laslett, Barbara. "The Family as a Public and Private Institution: An Historical Perspective." In *Intimacy, Family, and Society*, edited by Arlene Skolnick and Jerome Skolnick. Boston: Little, Brown, 1974.

Lasson, Kenneth. *The Workers*. New York: Bantam Books, 1971.

Lazerson, Marvin. "Social Change and American Families: Some Historical Speculations." Xerox, 1975.

Leacock, Eleanor Burke. *Teaching and Learning in City Schools*. New York: Basic Books, 1969.

Lederer, Emil. *State of the Masses*. New York: W. W. Norton, 1940.

Leggett, John C. "Sources and Consequences of Working Class Consciousness." In *Blue-Collar World*, edited by Arthur Shostak and William Gomberg. Englewood Cliffs, N. J.: Prentice-Hall, 1964.

Lerner, Michael. "Respectable Bigotry." In *The White Majority*, edited by Louise Kapp Howe. New York: Vintage Books, 1970.

Levine, Irving M., and Judith Herman. "The Life of White Ethnics." *Dissent* 19 (1972):286–294.

Levitan, Sar A., ed. *Blue Collar Workers: A Symposium on Middle America*. New York: McGraw-Hill, 1971.

Levitan, Sar A., and Robert Taggart III. "The Blue-Collar Worker Weathers the 'Ordeal of Change.'" In *Blue-Collar Workers*, edited by Sar Levitan. New York: McGraw-Hill, 1971.

Levitin, T. E., R. P. Quinn, and G. L. Staines. "A Woman is Fifty-eight Per Cent of a Man." *Psychology Today* 6 (1973):89–91.

Lewis, Hylan. "Culture, Class and Family Life Among Low-Income Urban Negroes." In *Employment, Race, and Poverty*, edited by Arthur N. Ross and Herbert Hill. New York: Harcourt, Brace and World, 1967.

Lewis, Oscar. *La Vida*. New York: Vintage Books, 1968.

Liebow, Elliot. *Tally's Corner*. Boston: Little, Brown, 1966.

Lifton, Robert Jay, ed. *The Woman in America*. Boston: Beacon Press, 1967.

Lipset, Seymour Martin. *Political Man: The Social Bases of Politics*. Garden City, N. Y.: Anchor Books, 1963.

Lipset, Seymour Martin, and Reinhard Bendix. *Social Mobility in Industrial Society*. Berkeley: University of California Press, 1964.

Lipsitz, Lewis. "Working Class Authoritarianism: A Reevaluation." *American Sociological Review* 30 (1965):103–109.

―――. "Work Life and Political Attitudes: A Study of Manual Workers." In *The White Majority*, edited by Louise Kapp Howe. New York: Vintage Books, 1970.

Lockwood, David. *The Blackcoated Worker*. London: George Allen and Unwin, 1958.

―――. "Sources of Variation in Working Class Images of Society." *Sociological Review* (1966):249–267.

Lopata, Helena Znaniecki. *Occupation Housewife*. New York: Oxford University Press, 1971.

―――. "The Effect of Schooling on Social Contacts of Urban Women." *American Journal of Sociology* 79 (1973):604–619.

Lopate, Carol. "Pay for Housework?" *Social Policy* 5 (1974):27–32.

Lui, William T., et al. "Conjugal Power and Decision Making: A Methodological Note on Cross-Cultural Study of the Family." *American Journal of Sociology* 79 (1973):84–98.

Lurie, Elinore E. "Sex and Stage Differences in Perception of Marital and Family Relationships." *Journal of Marriage and the Family* 36 (1974):260–269.

Lydon, Susan. "Understanding Orgasm." In *Intimacy, Family, and Society*, eds. Arlene Skolnick and Jerome Skolnick. Boston: Little, Brown, 1974.

Lynd, Robert, and Helen Lynd. *Middletown in Transition: A Study in Cultural Conflicts*. New York: Harcourt, Brace, 1937.

Mace, David R. "The Employed Mother in the U.S.S.R." In *The Family and the Sexual Revolution*, edited by Edwin M. Schur. Bloomington: Indiana University Press, 1964.

Mace, David, and Vera Mace, eds. *Marriage: East and West*. Garden City, N.Y.: Dolphin Books, 1959.

Mack, Delores E. "Where the Black-Matriarchy Theorists Went Wrong." *Psychology Today* 4 (1971):86–87.

Mackler, Bernard, and Morsley G. Giddings. "Cultural Deprivation: A Study in Mythology." In *The Urban R's*, edited by Robert A. Dentler. New York: Praeger, 1967.

Mainardi, Pat. "The Politics of Housework." In *Sisterhood Is Powerful*, edited by Robin Morgan. New York: Vintage Books, 1970.

Malinowski, Bronislaw. "Parenthood, the Basis of Social Structure." In *The Family: Its Structures and Functions*, edited by Rose Laub Coser. New York: St. Martin's Press, 1974.

Marine, Gene. *A Male Guide to Women's Liberation*. New York: Avon Books, 1972.

Marrett, Cora Bagley. "Social Class Values and the Balanced Community." *Social Problems* 21 (1973):251–268.

Massey, Garth. "Studying Social Class: The Case of *Embourgeoisement* and the Culture of Poverty." *Social Problems* 22 (1975):595–607.

Mayer, Kurt B. "The Changing Shape of the American Class Structure." *Social Research* 30 (1963):458–468.

———, and Sidney Goldstein. "Manual Workers as Small Businessmen." In *Blue-Collar World*, edited by Arthur Shostak and William Gomberg. Englewood Cliffs, N.J.: Prentice-Hall, 1964.

Meissner, Martin. "The Long Arm of the Job: A Study of Work and Leisure." *Industrial Relations* 10 (1971):239–260.

Meltzer, H. "Age and Sex Differences in Workers' Perceptions of Happiness in Self and Others." *Journal of Genetic Psychology* 105 (1964):1–11.

Miao, Greta. "Marital Instability and Unemployment Among Whites and Non-Whites: The Moynihan Report Revisited—Again." *Journal of Marriage and the Family* 36 (1974):77–86.

Miller, Herman P. "A Profile of the Blue-Collar American." In *Blue-Collar Workers*, edited by Sar Levitan. New York: McGraw Hill, 1971.

Miller, S. M. "Some Thoughts on Reform." In *Blue-Collar World*, edited by Arthur Shostak and William Gomberg. Englewood Cliffs, N.J.: Prentice-Hall, 1964*a*.

———. "The American Lower Classes: A Typological Approach." In *Blue-Collar World: Studies of the American Workers*, edited by Arthur B. Shostak and William Gomberg. Englewood Cliffs, N.J.: Prentice-Hall, 1964*b*.

———. "The 'New' Working Class." In *Blue-Collar World*, edited by Arthur Shostak and William Gomberg. Englewood Cliffs, N.J.: Prentice-Hall, 1964*c*.

Bibliography

———. "The Outlook of Working-Class Youth." In *Blue-Collar World*, edited by Arthur Shostak and William Gomberg. Englewood Cliffs, N.J.: Prentice-Hall, 1964d.

———. "Sharing the Burden of Change." In *The White Majority*, edited by Louise Kapp Howe. New York: Vintage Books, 1970.

———. "On Men: The Making of a Confused Middle-Class Husband." In *Intimacy, Family, and Society*, edited by Arlene Skolnick and Jerome Skolnick. Boston: Little, Brown, 1974.

Miller, S. M., and Frank Riessman. "Working-Class Authoritarianism: A Critique of Lipset." *British Journal of Sociology* (1961a):263–276.

———. "Are Workers Middle Class?" *Dissent* 8 (1961b):507–513.

———. "The Working-Class Subculture: A New View." In *Blue-Collar World*, eds. Arthur Shostak and William Gomberg. Englewood Cliffs, N.J.: Prentice-Hall, 1964.

———. *Social Class and Social Policy*. New York: Basic Books, 1968.

Miller, S. M., Frank Riessman, and Arthur Seagull. "Poverty and Self-Indulgence: A Critique of Non-Deferred Gratification Patterns." In *Poverty in America*, edited by Louis A. Ferman, et al. Ann Arbor: University of Michigan Press, 1965.

Miller, Walter B. "Lower Class Culture as a Generating Milieu of Gang Delinquency." *Journal of Social Issues* 14 (1958):5–19.

Miller, Warren B. "Sexuality, Contraception, and Pregnancy in a High School Population." *California Medicine* 119:14–21.

Millman, Marcia, and Rosabeth Moss Kanter, eds. *Another Voice*. Garden City, N.Y.: Anchor Books, 1975.

Mills, C. Wright. *White Collar*. New York: Oxford University Press, 1951.

Minuchin, Salvador, et al. *Families of the Slums*. New York: Basic Books, 1967.

Moers, Ellen. "Money, the Job and Little Women." In *The Family: Its Structures and Functions*, edited by Rose Laub Coser. New York: St. Martin's Press, 1974.

Moody, Kim. "Can the American Worker Be Radicalized?" In *The White Majority*, edited by Louise Kapp Howe. New York: Vintage Books, 1970.

Morgan, Robin, ed. *Sisterhood Is Powerful*. New York: Vintage Books, 1970.

Morland, J. Kenneth. "Kent Revisited: Blue-Collar Aspirations and Achievements." In *Blue-Collar World*, edited by Arthur Shostak and William Gomberg. Englewood Cliffs, N.J.: Prentice-Hall, 1964.

Morris, Naomi. "Correlates of Female Powerlessness: Parity, Methods of Birth Control, Pregnancy." *Journal of Marriage and the Family* 36 (1974):708–712.

Morse, Nancy C., and Robert S. Weiss. "The Function and Meaning of Work and the Job." *American Sociological Review* 20 (1955):191–198.

Moynihan, Daniel P. *The Negro Family: The Case for National Action*. Publication of the U.S. Department of Labor, Washington, D.C., 1968.

Myrdal, Alva, and Viola Klein. *Women's Two Roles: Home and Work*. London: Routledge and Kegan Paul, 1956.

Naffziger, Claudeen Clive, and Ken Naffziger. "Development of Sex Role Stereotypes." *The Family Coordinator* 23 (1974):251–260.

Nagasawa, Richard. "Social Class Differentials in Success Striving." *Pacific Sociological Review* 14 (1974):215–232.

Neal, Arthur G., and H. Theodore Great. "Social Class Correlates of Stability and Change in Levels of Alienation: A Longitudinal Study." *The Sociological Quarterly* 15 (1974):548–558.

New York City Commission on Human Rights. *Women's Role in Contemporary Society*. New York: Discus Books, 1972.

Nisbet, Robert A. "The Decline and Fall of Social Class." *Pacific Sociological Review* 2 (1959):11–17.

Nye, Ivan F. "Emerging and Declining Family Roles." *Journal of Marriage and the Family* 36 (1974):238–245.

Oakley, Ann. *Sex, Gender and Society*. New York: Harper Colophon, 1972.

Oakley, Ann. *The Sociology of Housework*. New York: Pantheon Books, 1974.

Olsen, Marvin E. "Social Classes in Contemporary Sweden." *The Sociological Quarterly* 15 (1974):323–341.

Olson, David H., and Carolyn Rabunsky. "Validity of Four Measures of Family Power." *Journal of Marriage and the Family* 34 (1972):224–234.

O'Neill, William L., ed. *Women at Work*. Chicago: Quadrangle Books, 1972.

Orden, Susan, and Norman Bradburn. "Dimensions of Marriage Happiness." *American Journal of Sociology* 73 (1968):715–731.

Palme, Olof. "Lesson from Sweden: The Emancipation of Man." In *The Future of the Family*, edited by Louise Kapp Howe. New York: Simon and Schuster, 1972.

Papanek, Hanna. "Men, Women, and Work: Reflections on the Two-Person Career." *American Journal of Sociology* 78 (1973):852–872.

Parenti, Michael. "Politics of the Classroom." *Social Policy* 4 (1973):67–70.

Parker, Richard. *The Myth of the Middle Class*. New York: Harper Colophon, 1972.

Patterson, James. "Marketing and the Working-Class Family." In *Blue-Collar World*, edited by Arthur Shostak and William Gomberg. Englewood Cliffs, N.J.: Prentice-Hall, 1964.

Pearlin, Leonard, and Melvin Kohn. "Social Class, Occupation, and Parental Values: A Cross-National Study." *American Sociological Review* 31 (1966):466–479.

Pease, John, William Form, and Joan Huber. "Ideological Currents in American Stratification Literature." *The American Sociologist* 5 (1970):127–137.

Perucci, Carolyn, and Dena B. Targ, eds. *Marriage and the Family: A Critical Analysis and Proposals for Change*. New York: David McKay, 1974.

Peterson, Esther. "Working Women." In *The Woman in America*, edited by Robert Jay Lifton. Boston: Beacon Press, 1967.

Plaut, Thomas F. *Alcohol Problems: A Report to the Nation*. New York: Oxford University Press, 1967.

Pleck, Joseph H. "Work and Family Roles: From Sex-Patterned Segregation to Integration." Delivered at the Seventieth Annual Meeting of the American Sociological Association, San Francisco, California, August 25–29, 1975.

Pleck, Joseph H., and Jack Sawyer, eds. *Men and Masculinity*. Englewood Cliffs, N.J.: Prentice-Hall, 1974.

Price, Charlton, and H. Levinson. "Work and Mental Health." In *Blue-Collar World*, eds. Arthur Shostak and William Gomberg. Englewood Cliffs: Prentice-Hall, 1964.

Rabb, Theodore K., and Robert I. Rotberg, eds. *The Family in History: Interdisciplinary Essays*. New York: Harper Torchbooks, 1973.

Rainwater, Lee. *And the Poor Get Children*. Chicago: Quadrangle Books, 1960.

Bibliography

———. "Crucible of Identity: The Negro Lower-Class Family." *Daedalus* 95 (1966):172–216.

———. *Behind Ghetto Walls*. Chicago: Aldine Publishing, 1970.

———. "Making the Good Life: Working-Class Family and Life-Styles." In *Blue-Collar Workers*, edited by Sar Levitan. New York: McGraw-Hill, 1971.

———. "Some Aspects of Lower Class Sexual Behavior." In *Readings on the Psychology of Women*, edited by Judith M. Bardwick. New York: Harper & Row, 1972.

Rainwater, Lee, Richard P. Coleman, and Gerald Handel. *Working-man's Wife*. New York: MacFadden Books, 1959.

Rainwater, Lee, and Gerald Handel. "Changing Family Roles in the Working Class." In *Blue-Collar World*, edited by Arthur Shostak and William Gomberg. Englewood Cliffs: Prentice-Hall, 1964.

Rainwater, Lee, and William L. Yancey. *The Moynihan Report and the Politics of Controversy*. Cambridge, Mass.: M.I.T. Press, 1967.

Ransford, H. Edward. "Blue Collar Anger: Reactions to Student and Black Protest." *American Sociological Review* 37 (1972):333–346.

Rapaport, Rona, and Robert Rapaport. "The Dual-Career Family: A Variant Pattern and Social Change." In *Intimacy, Family, and Society*, edited by Arlene Skolnick and Jerome Skolnick. Boston: Little, Brown, 1974.

Reiss, Ira L. *The Social Context of Premarital Sexual Permissiveness*. New York: Holt, Rinehart and Winston, 1967.

———. "Premarital Sexual Standards." In *The Individual, Sex, and Society*, edited by Carlfred B. Broderick and Jessie Bernard. Baltimore: Johns Hopkins Press, 1969.

Reiter, Howard L. "Blue-Collar Workers and the Future of American Politics." In *Blue-Collar Workers*, edited by Sar Levitan. New York: McGraw-Hill, 1971.

Rico-Velasco, Jesus, and Lizbeth Mynko. "Suicide and Marital Status: A Changing Relationship?" *Journal of Marriage and the Family* 35 (1973):239–244.

Ridley, Carl A. "Exploring the Impact of Work Satisfaction and Involvement on Marital Interaction When Both Partners are Employed." *Journal of Marriage and the Family* 35 (1973):229–237.

Riessman, Frank. *The Culturally Deprived Child*. New York: Harper and Brothers, 1962.

———. "In Defense of the Negro Family." *Dissent* 13 (1966):141–144.

Rinehart, James W. "Affluence and the *Embourgeoisement* of the Working Class: A Critical Look." *Social Problems* 19 (1971):149–162.

Rist, Ray C. "Student Social Class and Teacher Expectations: The Self-Fulfilling Prophecy in Ghetto Education." *Harvard Educational Review* 40 (1970): 411–451.

Rodman, Hyman. "Middle-Class Misconceptions About Lower-Class Families." In *Blue-Collar World*, edited by Arthur Shostak and William Gomberg. Englewood Cliffs, N. J.: Prentice-Hall, 1964.

———. "The Lower-Class Value Stretch." In *Poverty in America*, edited by Louis Ferman, et al. Ann Arbor: University of Michigan Press, 1965.

Rogoff, Natalie. *Recent Trends in Occupational Mobility*. Glencoe: Free Press, 1953.

Roiphe, Anne Richardson. "Occupation: Mother." In *The Future of the Family*, edited by Louise Kapp Howe. New York: Simon and Schuster, 1972.

Rollins, Boyd C., and Kenneth Cannon. "Marital Satisfaction Over the Family Life

Cycle: A Re-evaluation." *Journal of Marriage and the Family* 36 (1974):271–282.

The Roper Organization. *The Virginia Slims American Women's Opinion Poll,* Vol. 3. Publication of Virginia Slims, New York City, 1973.

Rosaldo, Michelle Zimbalist and Louise Lamphere, eds. *Woman, Culture & Society.* Stanford: Stanford University Press, 1974.

Rosenberg, Bernard, and Saul Weinman. "An Interview with Myra Wolfgang: 'Young Women Who Work.'" *Dissent* 19 (1972):29–36.

Rosenberg, George A., and Donald Anspach. "Sibling Solidarity in the Working Class." *Journal of Marriage and the Family* 35 (1973):108–113.

Rosenblatt, David, and Edward Suchman. "Blue-Collar Attitudes Toward Health and Illness." In *Blue-Collar World,* edited by Arthur Shostak and William Gomberg. Englewood Cliffs, N. J.: Prentice-Hall, 1964.

Rosenthal, Robert. "The Pygmalion Effect Lives." *Psychology Today* 7 (1973): 56–63.

Rosenthal, Robert, and Lenore Jacobson. *Pygmalion in the Classroom.* New York: Holt, Rinehart and Winston, 1968.

Rosow, Jerome M. "The Problems of Lower-Middle-Income Workers." In *Blue-Collar Workers,* edited by Sar Levitan. New York: McGraw-Hill, 1971.

Rossi, Alice S. "Transition to Parenthood." *Journal of Marriage and the Family* 30 (1968):361–376.

Rossi, Peter H., et al. "Measuring Household Social Standing." *Social Science Research* 3 (1974):169–190.

Roszak, Betty, and Theodore Roszak, eds. *Masculine/Feminine.* New York: Harper Colophon, 1969.

Rowbotham, Sheila. *Woman's Consciousness, Man's World.* Harmondsworth, England: Penguin Books, 1973.

Rubin, Lillian B. *Busing and Backlash: White Against White in an Urban School District.* Berkeley: University of California Press, 1972.

———. "White Against White: School Desegregation and the Revolt of Middle America." *School Review* 84 (1976):377–394.

Rubin, Zick. *Liking and Loving.* New York: Holt, Rinehart and Winston, 1970.

Ruitenbeck, Hendrik M., ed. *Sexuality and Identity.* New York: Delta Books, 1970.

Ryan, Joseph, ed. *White Ethnics: Life in Working-Class America.* Englewood Cliffs, N. J.: Prentice-Hall, 1973.

Saario, Terry N., Carol N. Jacklin, and Carol K. Tittle. "Sex Role Stereotyping in the Public Schools." *Harvard Educational Review* 43 (1973):386–416.

Safilios-Rothschild, Constantina. "Family Sociology or Wives' Family Sociology? A Cross-Cultural Examination of Decision-Making." *Journal of Marriage and the Family* 31 (1969):290–301.

———. "The Study of Family Power Structure: A Review 1960–1969." *Journal of Marriage and the Family* 32 (1970a):539–552.

———. "The Influence of the Wife's Degree of Work Commitment on Some Aspects of Family Organization and Dynamics." *Journal of Marriage and the Family* 32 (1970b): 681–691.

———. "Answer to Stephen J. Bahr's 'Comment on the Study of Family Power Structure: A Review 1960–1969.'" *Journal of Marriage and the Family* 34 (1972a): 245–246.

———. *Toward a Sociology of Women.* Lexington, Mass.: Xerox Publishing, 1972b.

Bibliography

Samuels, Victoria. "Nowhere To Be Found: A Literature Review and Annotated Bibliography on White Working Class Women." Publication of the Institute on Pluralism and Group Identity, New York, 1975.

Scanzoni, John H. *Sexual Bargaining: Power Politics in the American Marriage.* Englewood Cliffs, N. J.: Prentice-Hall, 1972.

———. *Sex Roles, Life Styles, and Childbearing: Changing Patterns in Marriage and the Family.* New York: Free Press, 1975.

Schafer, Walter E., et al. "Programmed for Social Class: Teaching in High School." *Trans-Action* 7 (1970):39–46.

Schatzman, Leonard, and Anselm L. Strauss. *Field Research: Strategies for a Natural Sociology.* Englewood Cliffs, N.J.: Prentice-Hall, 1973.

Schneider, Louis, and Sverre Lysgaard. "The Deferred Gratification Pattern: A Preliminary Study." *American Sociological Review* 18 (1953):142–149.

Schoen, Robert. "California Divorce Rates by Age at First Marriage and Duration of First Marriage." *Journal of Marriage and the Family* 37 (1975):548–555.

Schrag, Peter. *Village School Downtown.* Boston: Beacon Press, 1968.

Schrank, Robert, and Susan Stein. "Yearning, Learning, and Status." In *Blue-Collar Workers*, edited by Sar Levitan. New York: McGraw-Hill, 1971.

Schur, Edwin M., ed. *The Family and the Sexual Revolution.* Bloomington: Indiana University Press, 1964.

Seashore, Stanley E., and Thad J. Barnowe. "Demographic and Job Factors Associated with the 'Blue Collar Blues.'" Mimeo, 1972.

Seifer, Nancy. *Absent from the Majority: Working Class Women in America.* Publication of the National Project on Ethnic America, New York City, 1973.

Sellin, Thomas, and Marvin Wolfgang, eds. *Delinquency: Selected Studies.* New York: John Wiley, 1969.

Sennett, Richard. *Families Against the City.* Cambridge, Mass.: Harvard University Press, 1970.

Sennett, Richard, and Jonathan Cobb. *The Hidden Injuries of Class.* New York: Vintage Books, 1973.

Sewell, William, and Vimal Shah. "Social Class, Parental Encouragement, and Educational Aspirations." *American Journal of Sociology* 73 (1968):559–572.

Sexton, Brendan. "Workers and Liberals: Closing the Gap." In *The White Majority*, edited by Louise Kapp Howe. New York: Vintage Books, 1970.

Sexton, Patricia Cayo. "Wife of the 'Happy Worker.'" In *Blue-Collar World*, edited by Arthur Shostak and William Gomberg. Englewood Cliffs, N. J.: Prentice-Hall, 1964.

———. *Education and Income.* New York: Viking Press, 1964.

———. *The American School.* Englewood Cliffs, N. J.: Prentice-Hall, 1967.

Sexton, Patricia Cayo, and Brendan Sexton. 1971. *Blue Collars and Hard Hats.* New York: Vintage Books, 1971.

Shainess, Natalie. "Toward a New Feminine Psychology." *Notre Dame Journal of Education* 2 (1972):293–299.

———. "Sexual Problems of Women." *Journal of Sex & Marital Therapy* 1 (1974): 110–123.

Shepard, Jon M. "Functional Specialization, Alienation, and Job Satisfaction." *Industrial and Labor Relations Review* 23 (1970):207–219.

Sheppard, Harold L. "Discontented Blue Collar Workers—A Case Study." *Monthly Labor Review* 94 (1971):25–32.

Sheppard, Harold L., and Neal Herrick. *Where Have All the Robots Gone?* New York: Free Press, 1972.

Sherfey, Mary Jane. *The Nature and Evolution of Female Sexuality.* New York: Vintage Books, 1973.

Sherman, Julia A. *On the Psychology of Women.* Springfield, Ill.: Charles C. Thomas, 1971.

Shewbridge, Edythe A. *Portraits of Poverty.* New York: W. W. Norton, 1972.

Short, James, and Marvin Wolfgang, eds. *Collective Violence.* Chicago: Aldine-Atherton, 1972.

Shorter, Edward. *The Making of the Modern Family.* New York: Basic Books, 1975.

Shostak, Arthur B. *Blue-Collar Life.* New York: Random House, 1969.

———. "Working Class Americans at Home: Changing Expectations of Manhood." Delivered at the Conference on Problems, Programs, and Prospects of the American Working Class in the 1970's, Rutgers University, Rutgers, New Jersey, September, 1971.

———. "Ethnic Revivalism, Blue-Collarites, and Bunker's Last Stand." In *The Rediscovery of Ethnicity*, edited by Sallie TeSelle. New York: Harper Colophon, 1973.

Shostak, Arthur B., et al. 1973. *Privilege in America: An End to Inequality?* Englewood Cliffs, N. J.: Prentice-Hall, 1973.

Shostak, Arthur B., and William Gomberg, eds. *Blue-Collar World: Studies of the American Worker.* Englewood Cliffs, N. J.: Prentice-Hall, 1964.

Silk, Leonard. "Is There a Lower-Middle-Class 'Problem?'" In *Blue-Collar Worker*, edited by Sar Levitan. New York: McGraw-Hill, 1971.

Silverman, Bertram, and Murray Yanowitch. "Radical and Liberal Perspectives on the Working Class." *Social Policy* 4 (1974):40–50.

Simon, William, et al. "The White Working Class: Research Needs." Unpublished N.I.H. Study, 1971.

Simon, William, and John H. Gagnon. "On Psychosexual Development." In *Handbook of Socialization Theory and Research*, edited by David A. Goslin. Chicago: Rand McNally, 1969.

———. "Working-Class Youth: Alienation Without an Image." In *The White Majority*, edited by Louise Kapp Howe. New York: Vintage Books, 1970.

———. "Psychosexual Development." In *Intimacy, Family, and Society*, edited by Arlene Skolnick and Jerome Skolnick. Boston: Little, Brown, 1974.

Simon, William, John H. Gagnon, and Stephen Buff. "Son of Joe: Continuity and Change Among White Working Class Adolescents." *Journal of Youth and Adolescence* 1 (1972):13–34.

Skolnick, Arlene S., and Jerome H. Skolnick, eds. *Family in Transition.* Boston: Little, Brown, 1971.

———, eds. *Intimacy, Family, and Society.* Boston: Little, Brown, 1974.

Smith, David N. *Who Rules the Universities? An Essay in Class Analysis.* New York: Monthly Review Press, 1974.

Smuts, Robert W. *Women and Work in America.* New York: Schocken Books, 1971.

Sokoloff, Natalie J. "A Description and Analysis of the Economic Position of Women in American Society." Xerox, 1975.

Spanier, Graham B. "Romanticism and Marital Adjustment." *Journal of Marriage and the Family* 34 (1972):481–487.

Spiegel, John. *Transactions: The Interplay Between Individual, Family, and Society.* New York: Science House, 1971.

Spinrad, William. "Blue-Collar Workers as City and Suburban Residents—Effects on Union Membership." In *Blue-Collar World*, edited by Arthur Shostak and William Gomberg, Englewood Cliffs, N. J.: Prentice-Hall, 1964.

Sprey, Jetse. "Family Power Structure: A Critical Comment." *Journal of Marriage and the Family* 34 (1972):235–238.

Stack, Carol B. *All Our Kin*. New York: Harper & Row, 1974.

Stein, Annie. "Strategies of Failure." *Harvard Educational Review* 41 (1971): 158–204.

Steinitz, Victoria A., et al. "Ideological Development in Working-Class Youth." *Harvard Educational Review* 43 (1973):333–361.

Stockard, Jean, et al. "Sex Role Development and Sex Discrimination: A Theoretical Perspective." Delivered at the Seventieth Annual Meeting of the American Sociological Association, San Francisco, California, August 25–29, 1975.

Storr, Catherine. "Freud and the Concept of Parental Guilt." In *Intimacy, Family, and Society*, edited by Arlene Skolnick and Jerome Skolnick. Boston: Little, Brown, 1974.

Straus, Murray A. "Leveling, Civility, and Violence in the Family." *Journal of Marriage and the Family* 36 (1974):13–29.

Streib, Gordon F., ed. *The Changing Family: Adaptation and Diversity*. Menlo Park, Calif.: Addison-Wesley, 1973.

Sussman, Marvin. "Family Systems in the 1970's: Analysis, Policies, and Programs." In *Intimacy, Family and Society*, edited by Arlene Skolnick and Jerome Skolnick. Boston: Little, Brown, 1974.

Swerdloff, Peter M. "Hopes and Fears of Blue-Collar Youth: A Report from Akron." *Fortune* 79 (1969):148–152.

Tanner, Leslie B., ed. *Voices from Women's Liberation*. New York: New American Library, 1970.

Tausky, Curt. "Meanings of Work Among Blue Collar Men." *Pacific Sociological Review* 12 (1969):49–55.

Terkel, Studs. "A Steel Worker Speaks." *Dissent* 19 (1972):9–20.

———. *Working*. New York: Avon Books, 1974.

TeSelle, Sallie, ed. *The Rediscovery of Ethnicity*. New York: Harper Colophon, 1973.

Theobald, Robert, ed. *Dialogue on Technology*. Indianapolis: Bobbs-Merrill, 1967.

Thernstrom, Stephan. *Poverty and Progress: Social Mobility in a Nineteenth-Century City*. New York: Atheneum, 1972.

Thernstrom, Stephan, and Richard Sennett, eds. *Nineteenth-Century Cities: Essays in New History*. New Haven: Yale University Press, 1969.

Thorsell, Siv. "Employer Attitudes to Female Employees." In *The Changing Roles of Men and Women*, edited by Edmund Dahlström. Boston: Beacon Press, 1971.

Tiller, Per Olav. "Parental Role Division and the Child's Personality Development." In *The Changing Roles of Men and Women*, edited by Edmund Dahlström. Boston: Beacon Press, 1971.

Torbert, William R. *Being For the Most Part Puppets*. Cambridge, Mass.: Schenkman Publishing, 1973.

Turk, James L., and Norman W. Bell. "Measuring Power in Families." *Journal of Marriage and the Family* 34 (1972):215–223.

Tyler, Gus. "White Worker/Blue Mood." *Dissent* 19 (1972):190–196.

United States Bureau of the Census. *Statistical Abstract of the United States: 1974.* 95h ed. Washington, D. C.: U.S. Government Printing Office, 1974.

United States Commission on Civil Rights. *Racial Isolation in the Public Schools.* Washington, D. C.: U.S. Government Printing Office, 1967.

United States Department of Health, Education, and Welfare. *Alcohol and Health: First Special Report to the U.S. Congress.* Publication of the National Institute of Mental Health, Washington, D. C., 1971.

———. *Teenagers:* Marriages, Divorces, *Parenthood, and Mortality.* Washington, D. C.: U.S. Government Printing Office, 1973a.

———. *Work in America.* Cambridge, Mass.: M.I.T. Press, 1973b.

United States Department of Justice. *F.B.I. Uniform Crime Reports for the United States.* Washington, D. C.: U.S. Government Printing Office, 1973.

United States Department of Labor, Women's Bureau. "Working Wives—Their Contribution to Family Income." Publication of U.S. Department of Labor, Wage and Labor Standards Administration, Washington, D. C., 1968.

United States Department of Labor, Bureau of Labor Statistics. *Handbook of Labor Statistics—1975.* Washington, D.C.: U.S. Government Printing Office, 1975.

United States Senate Committee on Labor and Public Welfare. *Worker Alienation.* Hearings, Subcommittee on Employment, Manpower, and Poverty, July 25–26. Washington, D. C.: U.S. Government Printing Office, 1972.

United States White House Conference on Youth. *Profiles of Youth.* Washington, D.C.: U.S. Government Printing Office, 1971.

Valentine, Charles A. *Culture and Poverty: A Critique and Counter Proposals.* Chicago: University of Chicago Press, 1968.

———. "Deficit, Difference, and Bicultural Models of Afro-American Behavior." *Harvard Educational Review* 41 (1971):137–157.

Vernon, Glenn. "Religion and the Blue-Collarite." In *Blue-Collar World,* edited by Arthur Shostak and William Gomberg. Englewood Cliffs, N. J.: Prentice-Hall, 1964.

Veroff, Joseph, and Sheila Feld. *Marriage and Work in America.* New York: Van Nostrand Reinhold, 1970.

Walker, Kathryn E. "Time Spent in Household Work by Homemakers." *Family Economic Review* (1969):5–6.

———. "Time Spent by Husbands in Household Work." *Family Economic Review* (1970):8–11.

Wallin, Paul. "Cultural Contradictions and Sex Roles: A Repeat Study." *American Sociological Review* 15 (1950):288–293.

Walsh, Robert H., et al. "Premarital Sexual Permissiveness Attitudes, Behavior, and Reference Groups: A Study of Two Consecutive Panels (1967–1971; 1970–1974)." Delivered at the Seventieth Annual Meeting of the American Sociological Association, San Francisco, California, August 25–29, 1975.

Walster, Elaine. "Passionate Love." In *Intimacy, Family, and Society,* edited by Arlene Skolnick and Jerome Skolnick. Boston: Little, Brown, 1974.

Weisstein, Naomi. "Kinder, Kuche, Kirche: Psychology Constructs the Female." In *Sisterhood Is Powerful,* edited by Robin Morgan. New York: Vintage Books, 1970.

Weitzman, Lenore J., et al. "Sex-Role Socialization in Picture Books for Preschool Children." *American Journal of Sociology* 77 (1972):1125–1150.

259

Bibliography

White, Martha Sturm. "Social Class, Child Rearing Practices, and Child Behavior." In *Class and Personality in Society*, edited by Alan L. Grey. New York: Atherton Press, 1969.

Wilensky, Harold L. "Orderly Careers and Social Participation: The Impact of Work History on Social Integration in the Middle Mass." *American Sociological Review* 26 (1961):521–539.

———. "Mass Society and Mass Culture: Interdependence or Independence." *American Sociological Review* 29 (1964):173–197.

———. "Class, Class Consciousness, and American Workers." In *Labor in a Changing America*, edited by William Haber. New York: Basic Books, 1966.

Williams, Gurney, and Jerry Parker. "How They Get Away From It All." In *The White Majority*, edited by Louise Kapp Howe. New York: Vintage Books, 1970.

Williams, Raymond. *The Country and the City*. New York: Oxford University Press, 1973.

Wilson, Kenneth L., and Alejandro Portes. "The Educational Attainment Process: Results From a National Sample." *American Journal of Sociology* 81 (1975): 343–363.

Wohl, R. Richard. "The 'Rags to Riches Story': An Episode of Secular Idealism." In *Class, Status, and Power*, edited by Reinhard Bendix and Seymour Martin Lipset. New York: Free Press, 1953.

Wood, Myrna. "Working-Class Mothers May Not Have Much, But There's A Lot Of Us." In *The Future of the Family*, edited by Louise Kapp Howe. New York: Simon and Schuster, 1972.

Wortis, Helen and Rabinowitz, Clara, eds. *The Women's Movement: Social and Psychological Perspectives*. New York: John Wiley, 1972.

Wortis, Rochelle. "The Acceptance of the Concept of the Maternal Role by Behavioral Scientists: Its Effects on Women." In *Intimacy, Family, and Society*, edited by Arlene Skolnick and Jerome Skolnick. Boston: Little, Brown, 1974.

Wright, James D. "The Working Class, Authoritarianism, and the War in Vietnam." *Social Problems* 20 (1972):133–150.

Yankelovich, Daniel. *The New Morality: A Profile of American Youth in the 70's*. New York: McGraw-Hill, 1974.

Young, Michael, and Peter Willmott. *Family and Kinship in East London*. Baltimore: Penquin Books, 1962.

Zaretsky, Eli. "Capitalism, the Family, and Personal Life: Parts I and II." *Socialist Revolution* 3 (1973):69–126; 19–70.

Zellner, H. "Discrimination Against Women, Occupational Segregation, and the Relative Wage." *American Economic Review* 62 (1972):157–160.

Zunich, Michael. "A Study of Relationships Between Child Rearing Attitudes and Maternal Behavior." In *Class and Personality in Society*, edited by Alan L. Grey. New York: Atherton Press, 1969.

INDEX

Index

Index

Index

Index